OBSCURE BELIEVERS

OBSCURE BELIEVERS

The Mormon Schism of Alpheus Cutler

by Biloine Whiting Young

ISBN 1-880654-27-X
Library of Congress No. 2001-135315

Book design and typesetting by Percolator

Cover design by Mighty Media

Maps by Matt Kania

PHOTOGRAPHIC AND OTHER CREDITS

Danny L. Jorgensen for the photographs at pages 44, 119, 130, 163, and 194
The Reverend Johnson Loud for the painting at page 146
David S. Harris for the photograph at page 26
Kathleen Castillo for the photographs at pages 19 and 110
Minnesota Historical Society for the photographs at pages 70 and 111
Otter Tail County Historical Society for the photographs at pages 104 and 170
All other photographs from the author's collection.

CONTENTS

INTRODUCTION

History is not devotional writing. But it may be writing about the history of devotion. *Obscure Believers* is such a history.

I begin this introduction on a personal note. My grandmother was a Cutlerite. Lottie Gould Williams, my mother's mother, was born in 1882 at Battle Lake, Minnesota. Her parents had grown up as part of the Cutlerite colony at nearby Clitherall. Grandmother's mother was a granddaughter of the group's founder, Alpheus Cutler. Before her birth Lottie's parents had left the Cutlerite Church and joined the "Josephites," another sect of dissident Mormons. Throughout her life she claimed her Cutlerite descent, though, she would say, she rejected "the Cutlerite religion."

When Grandmother was six, her family departed from Minnesota in a covered wagon, bound for Independence, Missouri. Independence was the original Mormon "Center Place." It was, declared the Mormon Prophet Joseph Smith a half-century earlier, "Zion, The New Jerusalem." The doctrine that the "Saints" would one day in the Lord's Time be "gathered back to Zion" was a principal doctrine of the Cutlerites. It was also "Josephite" Church headquarters.

I knew Grandmother well. She and Granddad lived with my family on a farm when I was a child. I remember her humming tunelessly as she worked. "Hmmm, hmmm; [breath] hmmm, hmmm." In her head and in her heart, she was singing a hymn. Hymns were the only songs she knew. Once in awhile a phrase would break out: "beaut-ti-ful, *beaut*-ti-ful ZI-YUN!" Her belief in Zion never wavered. She remained in Independence, Missouri, save for brief periods away, until her death at age ninety-seven. She was forever a loyal member of The Reorganized Church of Jesus Christ of Latter Day Saints (since renamed Community of Christ), the "Josephites" that her parents had joined in Minnesota. But much of her distinctive religious disposition remained Cutlerite. She passed it on to my mother who did her best to pass it to me and even to my children.

1

The birth of Mormonism was something like the birth of the Universe. An initial efflorescence of energy was followed by a train of dynamic consequences flung out into time and space—consequences, seemingly, without end. *Obscure Believers* is the story of the Cutlerite Mormons, one of those consequences. The Cutlerites were a comparatively minor group if judged by their numbers. Biloine Young calls their story "a footnote to Mormon history." But their small number is not the only criterion of their significance.

The Cutlerites were followers of one Alpheus Cutler, a Mormon leader who in 1847 refused to follow Brigham Young and the main body of Mormons to Utah. That great trek, following the assassination of the Mormon Prophet Joseph Smith, Jr., in Illinois, is well known to American history. Less well known is the history of the Saints who did *not* go west. They became the many "ites" of Mormonism—Strangites, Hedrickites, Josephites, and Cutlerites, among others. The "ites" (a device of Mormon speech) were named after their principal leaders—James J. "King" Strang, Granville Hedrick, Joseph Smith III, Alpheus Cutler.

The "leader principal" was a characteristic of the Mormon religion definitely *not* analogous to the Big Bang of the Universe. Mormonism was powerfully centripetal in its government and social organization. Mormons looked up to and followed a single, all-powerful leader. The first such figure, the prototype for those who would succeed him, was the Prophet Joseph Smith, Jr. The Mormon Church was founded upon his oracular and prophetic powers. One of many Mormon reinterpretations of Scripture spoke to the issue. In Matthew 16:18, Jesus said, "Thou art Peter; and upon this rock I will build my church." The "rock," Mormons declared, referred not to Peter but to "revelation." They believed in "One True Prophet, Seer, and Revelator," who was to "lead them in All Things," and "reveal to them All Truth." Mormons sang, "A church without a Prophet is not the church for me!" At the outset, when Smith first opened the Windows of Heaven, others in the movement arose to declare that they too could draw down the Divine Word. Smith rebuked and successfully suppressed them. In so doing he established a central principle of Mormon government: sovereignty and legitimacy in matters both spiritual and secular, "both in Heaven and in Earth," reside solely in the Prophet-President of the Church.

Joseph Smith did not sufficiently contemplate his own mortality. He was young and healthy (only thirty-nine-years-old when he was killed), and seemed sincerely to believe that he would live to see the Second

Coming, which he urgently foretold. Fatefully, he did not establish a clear-cut method for succession in the prophetic office. When he died, a fierce political struggle for the leadership was inevitable. It was a Byzantine affair that concerns us only to reach the following conclusions: First, it divided Mormons into two groups—those who followed Brigham Young, and everyone else, no matter whom they followed (all were anti-Brigham). Second, as time passed and the world did not end as they had expected, Mormonism developed a somewhat new character around the legitimacy issue. The ultimate triumph of Brigham Young out West should not obscure the continuing schisms and "apostasies" directed against his rule. Only if one comprehends the Mormon obsession about legitimacy in the prophetic office can the religious history of the "ites" be comprehended—including the history of the Cutlerites.

Alpheus Cutler was an early convert to Mormonism. Born in Massachusetts in 1784, he was nearing sixty when Mormon Nauvoo, Illinois, was in the process of building. Cutler was Master Mason of the great limestone temple under construction there. The Nauvoo Temple was to be the city's grand monument. New secret rites would be performed there. Cutler was also a High Priest in the hierarchy of the Mormon lay priesthood. Just before Smith's death, he was initiated into the highly secret Council of Fifty, "the Living Constitution of the Kingdom." Cutler's later claim to ultimate prophetic authority grew out of his membership in that body, as well as from a special charge the Prophet gave him in the Council. Cutler was to proselytize among the Indians, or "Lamanites" in Mormon parlance.

Smith was killed in 1844. In 1846, the Saints were driven from Illinois. In 1847, Cutler quarreled with Brigham Young in western Iowa, and refused to continue the journey west. Young was having trouble solidifying his claim to the leadership—and not only with Cutler. Enough Mormons sided with Cutler, and were willing to remain with him, to form the nucleus of a small colony. Many of them were Cutler's kith and kin, including six plural wives.

Brigham Young was eager to make peace with Cutler in order to get him to Utah. As Temple Master Mason and member of The Council of Fifty, Cutler had been a man of some consequence in the leadership at Nauvoo. But Young was unwilling to accept Cutler's demands regarding the legitimacy issue. Cutler grew ever more bitter and angry and the break became irreparable. The dissidents remained in Iowa and in time became "the Cutlerites."

Though little is known of the details of Cutler's leadership in Iowa, a few salient facts are clear. Cutler, like all good Mormons, was a highly intentional man. He clung tenaciously to the Prophet Joseph's charge to go to the Lamanites; and in 1848 he took a kind of mission colony into Indian Territory, the present State of Kansas. It lasted an agonizing five years, and was a disaster. Not only were few if any Indians converted, but many members of the colony died of privation and disease. They retreated back to Iowa and established themselves in a quiet pastoral life southeast of Kanesville, modern Council Bluffs, at a place they called "Manti" (rhymes with "dry"). It was a name drawn from *The Book of Mormon*.

During the Manti years, Alpheus Cutler grew old and exceedingly infirm. But before he died at eighty in 1864, he finally drew from Heaven his own prophecy—an addendum, as it were, to the Prophet's commission. He saw in a vision "a land between two lakes," far to the north. The Cutlerites must go there and finally carry out the Indian mission. Cutler's Heaven-sent vision secured his power beyond death over succeeding generations of his followers.

The location of the "land between two lakes" was not specified; but it was surely in Minnesota Territory. More than 15,000 lakes were in Minnesota, a fact mercifully unknown to the Cutlerites at the time. Anyway, their going was the Will of God. The Holy Spirit would lead. And the world pressed them. The Civil War raged. The Iowa State military draft was ever closer. So they went north, two detachments in 1864, and a third the following year.

They went to "save" the Indians. But, as it turned out, the Indians "saved" the Cutlerites. Lewis Denna, a descendant of a New York Indian tribe and a convert to Mormonism, had remained with the Cutlerites at Manti. Denna knew Minnesota Indians—a fortuitous connection. Though the Cutlerites had to run a gauntlet of Indian politics in Minnesota, the danger and intrigue of which was almost beyond imagination, in the end Indians brought them to a particular place between two lakes. It seemed to them the right place.

The lakes were named Clitherall and Battle. The locale was in the new Otter Tail County, on the far-western Minnesota frontier devastated three years earlier by the bloody Sioux Uprising of 1862. The Cutlerites are remembered in county history as "the first permanent white settlers." The previous white settlers had fled. Like all New England Yankees-cum-Mormons, the Cutlerites settled in a village even though they were predominantly farmers. They named it Clitherall, after the lake on whose shore it was situated.

Who were the Cutlerites? What were they like? They totaled less than 100 family groups altogether. English surnames predominated— Whiting, Fletcher, Sherman, Murdock, Cutler. They were closely inter-related among themselves—not surprising, inasmuch as their marriages were typically endogamous. Some were related to high officials of the Church in Utah. For example, Alpheus Cutler was the father-in-law of Heber C. Kimball, Brigham Young's First Counselor.

Theirs was a typical Yankee demographic profile of the time. Sociologist Danny Jorgensen concludes that at least eighty percent were from the New England states plus New York, Pennsylvania, and the states of the Old Northwest Territory—Ohio, Indiana, Illinois, Michigan, and Wisconsin. Historian Catherine Cleveland wrote, in *The Expansion of New England, 1800–1850,* that by the mid-nineteenth century more New England Yankees lived in the states west of New England than remained at home. (My Gould ancestors were pioneers traveling west who wandered into Clitherall from Wisconsin.)

In culture the Cutlerites were, like most Mormons, New England Puritan Yankees. They were yeoman farmers and craftsmen including a mason, a chairmaker, a tinsmith, and carpenters. Most were surely carpenters, whatever else they did. Mormons were ever moving, ever building anew, perpetual pioneers all. The children, and the children's children, grew up pioneers.

Perhaps half of the Cutlerites, like Cutler himself, were among the earliest Mormon converts. Many had held high offices in the leadership. Many had received their "endowments," a special rite, in the Nauvoo Temple. As Biloine Young explains, Cutlerites wore the unique Mormon "Temple garment," a sacred article of underclothing which was never to be totally removed.

Young offers credible evidence that Alpheus Cutler was unable to write his own name. By contrast, Cutlerites typically had a primary school education. As Mormons, they were a people of words. They believed that "Light and Truth" included literacy and even literary skill. Clitherall soon had a school. Young's ancestor Zeruah Whiting taught in it, and thus became the first school teacher in Otter Tail County. The memoirs and reminiscent writings of the women are sources from which Young has crafted a rich account of the texture of their lives. The women wrote well; and they evidenced in their writing a refinement of taste and feeling.

Were the Cutlerites a "church" in the legal or institutional sense? Yes and no. Mormonism expressed a profound sense of order in its complex hierarchy of lay "priesthood," a sacred fraternity intended to include all males. "The Church" as an institution resided in this ordering. In this respect the Cutlerites were surely Mormon. Their particular situation lessened the need for legal formality. On the frontier, legal institutions were believed to be largely irrelevant. They were a face-to-face community and they made decisions as primary groups do. They valued consensus, and strove to obtain it. "Father" Cutler had apparently been the de facto government while he lived. His death before the northward migration raised the leader question. An orderly succession apparently took place then, as it did in succeeding years. However, after Cutler, no other charismatic leader arose. Carelessness concerning the legal status of the church caused a terrible problem in later years because of an issue relating to a land title. The result was an ecclesiological nightmare, an obscure but important event whose story Young has finally disentangled.

Obscure Believers is in a sense two histories. One is that of the Cutlerite movement, a history of one of the "ites" of midwest Mormonism in the last half of the nineteenth century. The other is that of the personal stories of Cutlerite pioneers, especially stories of women and children, on a difficult, far-north frontier. Both accounts are carefully objective, but also fully personal—no small feat for an historian to accomplish.

Biloine Whiting Young is a direct descendant of the Whitings and the Murdocks, two principal Cutlerite families. Chauncey Whiting was a Cutlerite Church president. Her family tree and mine were intertwined at Clitherall. Her forebears, like mine, joined "the Josephites." We both grew up in the RLDS Church. We grew up, and out. But something of the thrall of Cutlerism still shadows our memories, just as it once bound our families' roots in its silken steel bands of faith, loyalty, experience, and blood.

I began by saying my grandmother was a Cutlerite. That was true only in a certain sense. In much she was not Cutlerite. She never belonged to the Cutlerite Church. She was a town woman, a high school graduate, socially upwardly-mobile, and ambitious for her four daughters. She had executive qualities, and in a later generation would have been in business or the professions. In such ways she was far from the remote, communal quietism of Clitherall.

But Grandmother had a Cutlerite spirit, and many Cutlerite ways. She got them from her parents, who grew to adulthood in Clitherall. She passed them on to my mother who was in many ways much like her. My mother tried to pass them on to me and even to my children. Grandmother expressed her Cutlerite traits most vividly during her farm years. The Great Depression of the 1930s drove her and Granddad onto hard-scrabble farms provided successively by sons-in-law. No electricity, no running water, virtual shacks for houses, cooking on a wood stove, braving heat and cold, lacking all comforts, working until you dropped, anxiety, poverty, loss of middle class status—I believe she loved it. It was pioneering.

But it was not only glorying in the paucity of material things that revealed her Cutlerism. It was in her mixing of religious faith and superstition, in her folk healing practices, and in her proto-modern worldview. She believed in faith healing. Her grandfather George Gould had been a famous faith healer in Clitherall. She "doctored" the whole family with such specifics as kerosene, turpentine, sulfur, lard, salt, vinegar, and horse liniment (the high alcoholic content of the latter either was unknown to her or was ignored). She also used Granddad's "consecrated oil" as a remedy. It was olive oil "consecrated" (i.e., set apart with prayer) that Granddad used to anoint the heads of the sick and injured (me, as often as not) during "administration." Administration was the sacramental prayer of healing. An ample quantity of consecrated oil was a major item in Grandmother's cabinet of medicaments. The oil was ancient and rancid so it had an evil smell and taste that medicine was supposed to possess. She prescribed it for both external and internal use.

Though Grandmother had a firm belief in Satan, she had no faith in witches, spells, or curses—which the Cutlerites did, according to Biloine Young. But she would address warts, boils, "cankers," and similar maladies by winding string around the afflicted part, then burying the string in the full of the moon under a great oak tree while muttering special incantations—"prayers," my mother called them—known only to herself.

All of this was part and parcel of my grandmother's religious faith—and she was a very pious woman. Faith was practical. It worked. It saved you and yours in this world. The world to come was not unim-

portant; but if you did right, it would take care of itself. Hers was a Cutlerite faith.

History is a humane enterprise, enlightening and civilizing. Still, it
is an enterprise that can light only a few dim candles above the deep,
dark abyss of the past. *Obscure Believers* lights another candle.

Robert Flanders
Emeritus Professor of History
Southwest Missouri State University
September 24, 2001

PREFACE

I first visited the villages of Old and New Clitherall and the lake of the same name at the age of four. My parents drove to Minnesota from our home in Council Bluffs, Iowa, to visit friends and relatives in Otter Tail County. That initial visit introduced me to the surviving "old timers" of Clitherall and began a family routine that was to continue for several years.

Upon their arrival at the cabin my parents would extend an invitation to the local residents (many of whom were relatives) to come visit us at the lake. My father and I would then spend the next few days catching scores of bluegill, sunfish and rock bass to feed the crowd. The visitors would gather early in the evening and as they ate my mother's fried fish, potato salad, and baked beans would recount their parents' and grandparents' experiences as pioneers in Otter Tail County. These individuals were remarkable storytellers, having developed their talents before the days of television or even radio. In that northern latitude the sky would remain light until well after 10 P.M. For five hours, of an evening, while smudge-pots poured out smoke to repel mosquitoes, the storytellers of Clitherall would keep the group entertained with tales of their families' pioneering experiences.

Ellis Murdock, my father's double cousin and close friend, was one of the most accomplished of the raconteurs. His grandson, sociologist Danny Jorgensen, has since become a recognized expert on the Cutlerites, the Mormon Church offshoot that claimed the allegiance of that first band of settlers. A glance at the references, which list only some of Professor Jorgensen's scholarly papers, reveals but a small portion of my indebtedness to him. Danny and I both descend from two of the pioneer Cutlerite families, Francis Lewis and Ann Jeanette Whiting and Hirum and Rachel Murdock.

Frank and Norma Tucker, now in their eighties, steadfastly collected and preserved letters, correspondence and writings by the Minnesota Cutlerites and Josephites at a time when few others were interested in the history of this obscure group of Mormons. Others who collected and published memories of the early settlers were Hallie Gould and Alta Kimber, granddaughters of the original pioneers. Kimber was a granddaughter of Warren Whiting whose early photographs constitute the only pictorial record of Old Clitherall.

Several distinguished Mormon scholars provided generous and helpful advice. Mike Riggs emphasized the influence of magical thinking and the occult on Cutler's decision to break with Brigham Young. Dick Howard reminded me of the Latter Day Saints' brief sojourn in Clay County, Missouri. Professor Robert Bruce Flanders, a descendant of Alpheus Cutler, shared a deeply personal engagement with the topic as well as detailed editorial advice and comment that improved the book immeasurably. I am profoundly grateful for his gift of time, wisdom and historical expertise to this project. (He is, however, in no way responsible for the shortcomings that inevitably appear as soon as a work is frozen in print. For these I am solely responsible.)

Another whose assistance was invaluable was that of Ronald Stabnow, my friend since that initial visit in 1930. Ronald grew up in Clitherall on the site of one of the original Cutlerite homes and, except for time spent in the service in World War II and away at college, has lived in Otter Tail County all of his life. He served for 24 years as mayor of neighboring Battle Lake. On two occasions, when he tried to retire from office, the citizens wrote his name on the ballot and elected him anyway. In addition to serving as Battle Lake mayor, Ronald is Commander of the American Legion Post, Treasurer of the Clitherall Lake and Mt. Pleasant Cemetery Associations, past president of the Otter Tail County Historical Society, Secretary-Treasurer of the Reorganized Latter Day Saint (now Community of Christ) Church in Clitherall and, as if that were not enough, has 35 years of perfect attendance at the local Lion's Club. Anyone who wants to know the history of Clitherall or Battle Lake knows to ask Ronald Stabnow.

For many visitors, the area around Lake Clitherall and Old Town is full of spirits and memories. Fourth and fifth generation descendants of the pioneers find themselves inexorably drawn back, year after year, to walk the sandy paths trod by their ancestors, to spend an idle summer day under the scrub oaks, to marvel at the clarity of the water in spring-fed Clitherall Lake. Several of us have purchased cemetery plots on Mt. Pleasant and my husband, Dr. George Patrick Young, is buried there.

The Cutlerites and the community they founded in Otter Tail County are but a footnote to the story of Minnesota's settlement and America's religious history. Yet their sacrifices and struggles wove a piece of the fabric of the country. Enthralled by the stories that I heard of Clitherall and the Cutlerites from the time I was a four-year-old, it was perhaps inevitable that, more than half a century later, I should be the one to tell their story.

Biloine Whiting Young
St. Paul, Minnesota
October 24, 2001

THE SIGNIFICANCE
OF NAMES IN THE
CUTLERITE TRADITION

Any account of the Cutlerites must deal with the problem of many names. While this is a story of individuals, it is, as well, a story of names organized into extended family groups. The Cutlerite story is a story of families and of those families' loyalty, over generations, to faith and to community. As historian Robert Flanders has observed, "one of the powerful, wonderful and *most terrible* things about Mormonism is the tradition of familiarity and familiality that is evidenced in titling and naming—Brother, Sister, The Prophet Joseph, Brother Joseph, all the priesthood names. It binds their bearers with cords stronger than steel. Young Mormon missionaries, some not shaving yet, wear a little black badge titled 'Elder'. . . . Early Mormons often had little else, but they had names conferred by Heaven."[1]

When a later generation of Cutlerites questioned the beliefs of their parents, it was more than a generational shift in philosophy. It was a turning of their backs on the Family of Faith, on the sacrifices of those who had borne them, nurtured them, given them their sacred names. In a uniquely Mormon sense it was a rejection of their identity and a betrayal of a Celestial Family of which the Cutlerite community, to their way of thinking, was the earthly manifestation.

EARLY CUTLERITE FAMILIES

Alpheus Cutler (1784–1864) and
Lois (Lathrop) Cutler (1788–1878)
Children: Thaddeus, William, Franklin, Edwin, Louise, Lois (married Almon W. Sherman), Sallie Maria (married Buckley Anderson), Emily (married Franklin Pratt), Clarissa (married Calvin Fletcher), Phiness.

Elisha Whiting (1785–1846) and
Sallie (Hulett) Whiting (1786–1846)

Children: Charles (died as an infant), William (killed in Missouri), Edwin, Charles, Catherine Louisa, Harriett Amelia, Sallie Emeline (married F. Walter Cox), Chauncey, Almon, Jane Fidelia, Sylvester J., Francis Lewis.

Chauncey Whiting (1819–1902) and
Editha Ann (Morley) Whiting (1818–1893)

Children: Isaac Morley, Carmelia, Warren (married Zeruah Sherman), Alfred (died in Minnesota at age 21), Alonzo, Lurett, Chauncey, Jr., (called Chan), Theodore (died as a child in Iowa), Editha Ann, Louisa, Alfred, Lucy Emeline.

Almon Whiting (1821–1909) and
Lydia Marie (Garfield) Whiting (1837–1928)

Children: Emma, Charles H., Jennie Amelia, Almon, Jr., Edwin, Harra A., Josie, Bessie.

Sylvester Whiting (1827–1918) and
Rebecca Ann (Redfield) Whiting (1835–1908)

Children: Lucius Almon, Edwin Eugene, George Washington, William Walter, John Howard, Tryphenia Marie and Anna Eliza.

Francis Lewis Whiting (1830–1909) and
Ann Jeanette (Burdick) Whiting (1831–1917)

Children: Emma Lucine (married Edwin Anderson), Lucia Louise, Ella Jeanette (married Winfield Gould), Arthur Wellington (married Lois Murdock), Mary Belle, Sylvia Cordelia (married Orison Murdock), Francis Lester.

Hirum Murdock (1828–1896) and
Rachel (Kelsey) Murdock (1828–1889)

Children: Martha (died in Kansas), Charles, Caroline (died in Kansas), Alva, Emily (married Abner Tucker), Ellen, Didamia, Lois (married Arthur Whiting), Orison (married Sylvia Cordelia Whiting), Lyman E., Alman Lurette, Rachel, Sarah Emily.

Lyman Murdock (1833–1880) and
Sylvia (Kelsey) Murdock (1832–1860);
second wife Rebecca Elizabeth (Taylor) (1839–1928)

Children: Sarah Francis, Charles Emer, Olive Almira, Alma, Hirum James, Rosa Caroline, John, Lucy, Lyman, Cora.

Joseph Edmund Fletcher (1827–1906) and
Sarah Louisa Muir Fletcher (1842–1929)

Children: Louisa Amanda, James Andrew, Emery George, Elsie Armilla. Clyde Fletcher was a son of James. Rupert was Emery's son.

Isaac Whiting (1842–1922) and
Sarah Jane "Jennie" (Talcott) Whiting (1843–1929)

Children: Charles Llewellyn, Emily Augusta, Addie Belle, Nelson Francis, Rozelle, Ivan Erle, Julian Evenson, Roy Rockwood, Daisy Evangeline.

Warren Whiting (1847–1889) and
Zeruah (Sherman) Whiting (1844–1900)

Children: Birch, Delbert, Ora, Grace (married Ben Kimber), Fanny.

Abner Tucker (1850–1933) and
Sarah Emily (Murdock) Tucker (1855–1934)

Children: Orison (married Nina Gould), Frank (married Ethel Gould), Ellis, Nettie.

Winfield Gould (1852–1937) and
Ella (Whiting) Gould (1857–1947)

Children: Leon, Winfield, Maude, Hallie, Ethel (married Frank Tucker), Nina (married Orison Tucker), Iva, Gladys.

CHAPTER 1

The Departure

The frontier town of Manti, in west central Iowa's Fremont County, no longer exists. Established in 1853, five years after Iowa became a state, the village once boasted a school, a post office, three general stores, a harness shop, drug store, tavern, blacksmith shop, stage barn and J.R. Badham's music and candy shop. Fisher Creek, a tributary of the Nishnabotna River, flowed between the school and Myer's Store. The homes of Alpheus Cutler, Edmund Fisher, and the Pratt, Fletcher and Murdock families fronted on the stagecoach road that ran through the middle of Manti and on west to the ferry on the river. At the end of the street stood the Mormon Church and on the hill rising abruptly above the town in a grove of walnut trees was the cemetery. Manti was named for the "land of Manti" described in the *Book of Mormon,* the sacred scripture of the Latter Day Saints.

Manti had a sister village, the town of Clitherall in Otter Tail County, Minnesota. Old Clitherall also no longer exists. The two villages, though hundreds of miles apart, followed the same trajectory. Like many early American communities, they were founded by religious zealots whose ardor, though it blazed fiercely at the beginning, dimmed over time. Eventually the two towns, and the religion that founded them, faded into obscurity. The religious group that founded Manti in Iowa and Clitherall in Minnesota was one of more than one hundred sects that sprang from the teachings of the Mormon prophet, Joseph Smith.[2] The faction that pioneered in Utah developed the fastest growing religion in the western world. Most of the other groups, like the towns of Manti and Clitherall, disappeared. Though overshadowed and eventually eclipsed by their more dynamic religious cousins, these obscure bands of believers also explored new lands and left their mark on unsettled places.

The pioneer town of Manti was a station on the overland emigra-
tion route, called the South Tier, that ran west across Iowa, beginning at
the Mississippi River at Keokuk and passing through all of the county
seats of the southern tier of Iowa counties. The trail connected with the
South Platte Route on the Missouri River at Bennett's Ferry, across the
river in Nebraska. *The Wyoming Emigrant Guide* (1859) reported that
the South Tier route was the nearest way across Iowa "but not at present so much traveled." Immigrants were advised that the route "will be
found to abound in good grass, timber and water, with plenty of produce all along the roads and good accommodations at short intervals."[3]

In the winter of 1865 Manti had a population of about 300 people.
That number was about to decrease, however, for on January 16, six families and three men without their spouses and children were busily pack-
ing their possessions into covered wagons in preparation to leave Manti
for what they thought of as the far north—Minnesota. A pair of gray
horses, hitched to a covered wagon, stood before the door of Isaac Whiting's small home, built for him only the year before. Whiting, his wife
Sarah Jane (Jennie), and his sister Carmelia had started early that morning to load their household goods. In the front of the wagon was their
small No. 7 iron cook stove. Beside it was a dinner box and further back
in the wagon were stacked boxes of clothing, bedding, dishes and a few
valued books and pictures. In the rear of the wagon was a plow and piled
on top of the plow were two featherbeds, quilts and pillows.

By mid-afternoon the wagon had been packed and Isaac Whiting's
parents, Chauncey and Editha, came out to the road to say good-by.
Chauncey Whiting stood awkwardly by the horses' heads while his wife,
unable to hold back her tears, turned back into the house. Snow began
to fall and Isaac Whiting, embarrassed at his mother's grief and eager to
be off on his journey, gathered up the reins to his team. Chauncey Whiting raised his hat in farewell to his departing family while the horses
leaned into the harness and, overcoming the wagon's inertia, slowly
moved the load down the road.

Jennie leaned out of the wagon and around the canvas cover for a
last look at the home to which she had, so recently, come as a bride. A
sudden wave of sadness and regret swept over her. Seeing her sister-in-
law's sorrow, Carmelia began to cry and Jennie soon joined her. The
two women sobbed in each other's arms until one of them chanced to
glance up at the interior of the covered wagon and saw a hatbox Whiting had suspended on a rope overhead. The box was bobbing and sway-

Isaac Morley Whiting (1842–1922).   Sarah Jane Talcott Whiting (1843–1929), wife of Isaac Morley Whiting.

ing with the motion of the wagon and looked so comical to the women that their tears changed to hysterical laughter which Jennie, as she remembered and wrote in later years, claimed "did us a world of good."[4]

The falling snow soon obscured the rolling Iowa landscape and it was dark when the travelers reached their first night's campsite, barely four miles from Manti. They were not alone. Others had preceded them to the rendezvous. Campfires blazed in the field and lit up the smoky breaths of horses as they pawed at the frozen ground and of oxen that shifted uneasily on the periphery of the camp. Jennie could hear the muffled calls of men as they cared for their animals and the excited chatter of children. While Isaac Whiting went in search of wood to build a fire, Jennie and Carmelia rummaged through their box of provisions to prepare supper. Jennie's sadness was gone, replaced by the excitement of beginning a new adventure. On this first day with the softly falling snow mingling with the smoke of the campfires, the trip to Minnesota had begun to feel like a wonderful winter excursion.

The other families at the camp were Calvin and Mary Fletcher, with their five children, all under the age of ten; Jesse and Nancy Burdick with their baby boy; John and Mary Fletcher with their son Albert; Mary's twin sister Sarah with her husband Edmund Fletcher and daughter Louisa; and Edmund and Augusta Whiting with their three children: William, Florence and Nettie, the youngest, only twelve weeks old. That morning in Manti, Augusta had been so weak that she had almost fainted when the women came to help her get dressed so she rode lying down in the wagon with her infant. The three men traveling without their families were Erastus Cutler, Dewitt Sperry and James R. Badham.

What were these families, almost all with young children and infants, doing trekking north in covered wagons in midwinter? Why had they left prosperous Iowa farms, located on some of the most fertile land in the world, abandoned the thriving community of Manti with its close ties of kinship and religion to venture north through a country they knew nothing about and which only three years before had suffered the tragedy of the Sioux Indian Uprising?

If young Isaac Whiting had thought to answer those questions as he helped his wife spread out their featherbeds in the wagon he would have had to go back two generations to his grandparents, Elisha and Sallie Hulett Whiting, and the new religion they adopted in the 1830s. It was a controversial religion that had driven his grandfather and father on far more desperate journeys than his. To further understand why he and his family were camped this night in a snowy field instead of sleeping in their warm beds at home, Isaac Whiting would have had to unravel a tangled web of religious speculation and innovation, of persecution and flight, and analyze the thirty-five years of his family's devotion to and unswerving belief in the pronouncements and visions of the Mormon prophet, Joseph Smith.

Whiting would also have had to examine his faith in another man, recently deceased, a man he called by the honorific "Father Cutler."[5] Finally, he would have had to consider the "Cutlerites," a group of Mormons to whom he and his family had pledged their allegiance. The story behind Whiting's presence in a covered wagon heading north to Minnesota in midwinter involved all of this and one thing more—the disturbing fact of Mormon polygamy which Isaac Whiting and his relatives were now trying desperately to forget.

Barely six months earlier, Whiting, along with some 400 other followers of Alpheus Cutler, had laid the old man to rest in the hilltop cemetery at Manti. Though their leader Alpheus Cutler was dead, his influence was not. Before he died, Cutler had advised his followers to abandon their settlement at Manti and seek out a land to the north, in the new state of Minnesota, a place he had seen in a vision. Their land of promise, he told them, was covered with grass and lay between two lakes. They would know it because when they arrived the Lord would cause their hearts to burn within them giving them divine assurance that they, and their church, had found a home.

Thus the simple answer to why Isaac Whiting and his family were leaving Iowa in midwinter to migrate to Minnesota was that they were going as part of an advance scouting party in response to Father Cutler's vision. While the answer was accurate, as far as it went, the true reasons were far more complicated. The story began, not with Isaac Whiting's departure for Minnesota in 1865, but thirty-five years earlier, in 1830, with his grandparents, Elisha and Sallie Whiting, and with Joseph Smith, Jr., who founded a new religion on the American frontier known as the Latter Day Saints.

CHAPTER 2

Mormonism—
Conversion and Conflict

Elisha Whiting, Jr. was born in 1785, the son of a New England ship captain who died when Elisha was a young boy. His mother, not knowing what else to do, bound him out to a Quaker furniture-maker who was extremely cruel to the boy. Elisha never forgave his mother and other relatives for what they had done to him and after a few years he ran away from the Quaker to make his own way in the world. He married Sallie Hulett of Berkshire County, Massachusetts, and set himself up in business building wagons and furniture.

In a move that was to be fateful for future generations of his family, in the spring of 1815 Whiting moved to the village of Nelson in the Western Reserve region of northern Ohio. The Whitings' frontier dwelling consisted of one large room dominated by a fireplace extending across one wall. The fireplace was furnished with a large crane, which swung out into the room, and to which could be attached iron hooks of different lengths for kettles and other cooking containers. A large shallow kettle was called the "bake kettle." When bread was ready to be baked, Sallie would knead it into one large loaf, place it in the kettle, put the iron cover on and, setting the kettle on coals on the hearth, she would shovel more coals on the cover which baked the bread. Opposite the fireplace on the other side of the room were beds, chests, a table and chairs and an old-fashioned bureau made of black walnut. The boys in the family slept in the loft over the large room and the girls slept on trundle beds that were pulled out at night. In the absence of candles, blazing pine knots were used to light the room at night.[6]

The village of Nelson was only twenty-five miles from the town of Kirtland, where, in 1831, Joseph Smith moved the headquarters of his newly established church, the Latter Day Saints. It was not long after the church's move to Kirtland that a Latter Day Saint missionary, Thomas B. Marsh, visited the Whiting home and workshop.

Marsh recognized in Elisha Whiting a typical Yankee, one who reflected the values of the New England culture of the period. Whiting believed in a Christian/Protestant God. He practiced folk magic, accepted the political doctrine of Manifest Destiny, lived by Victorian sexual mores and supported democracy. In common with other Americans, he had moved to what was then the frontier in search of greater opportunity for his wagon and furniture-making business. In his daily life he was sober, moderate and upright. He and the members of his family stood apart from and looked down on the illiterate, hard drinking, culturally isolated, lower-class families they saw about them on the American frontier.

In a great many ways the beliefs of early Mormonism, as Marsh explained them to his hosts, meshed with values Elisha Whiting and his neighbors already held. They were occupying a new land that they believed divine destiny had offered them. By 1790 about forty percent of Americans were living in areas that had been settled by whites for less than thirty years. Many people uprooted themselves four or five times in a single lifetime and the father of the founder of Mormonism, Joseph Smith, Sr., moved his family seven times in fourteen years. Joseph Smith, Jr.'s intense identification with the Old Testament and the wanderings of the ancient Hebrews struck powerful chords with these roving New Englanders who saw themselves as modern-day pilgrims entering another Land of Canaan, a land "flowing with milk and honey."

Mormonism with its account of visions and spiritual visitations, was consonant with the prevailing folk beliefs. Elisha Whiting and his neighbors regularly used divining rods to find water, planted crops only during certain phases of the moon and believed in the existence of good and evil spirits. Residents on the frontier made few distinctions between science, religion and magic. Belief in the occult was commonplace. Villages supported folk healers with their potions, amulets and incantations and people regularly used occult methods to locate missing articles and ward off the possibility of being bewitched by hostile neighbors or unseen forces. Books on alchemy, astrology and the occult circulated widely. Fewer than 100 years had passed since Europe had experienced the Witch Craze, a collective hysteria in which individuals believed that they flew through the air at night to take part in Satanic rituals. In the frenzy of the Witch Craze thousands had been hanged or burned at the stake, suspected of practicing witchcraft. Though witches were no longer being hanged a belief in their existence continued.

Beliefs in the occult lingered below the surface of everyday life on the frontier like underground rivers. Joseph Smith, Jr., had spent his youth digging for buried treasure, supposedly located with the use of seer stones and hazel divining rods. Uncritical acceptance of the power of folk magic and good and evil spirits was so pervasive in early America that Smith's accounts of his experiences with visions and spiritual visitations did not seem, to Elisha Whiting and other Mormon converts, to be anything out of the ordinary.

The Whitings shared another belief with the early Mormons—a conviction that the end of the world was near. Like many of their neighbors, the Whitings believed that within their lifetimes, or most certainly those of their children, the old, corrupt world would be destroyed and Christ would come to rule for a thousand years. The Protestant gospel was linked with such themes as the Kingdom of God and a belief in the "Chosen People" who would bring about God's transformation of the world. Timothy Dwight, president of Yale University, spoke of America becoming "the principal seat of that new, that peculiar Kingdom which shall be given to the saints of the Most High."[7] John Adams looked on the settlement of the United States as part of God's plan to save humanity. Protestant preachers declared that Jesus would establish his glorious kingdom in America and that the two wars with Britain were preparing the way for the "last days" of the present corrupt order. The Millerites predicted the world would end in 1844. Responding to the Puritan dream of America as the Promised Land of God, New Englanders living on the frontier enlisted in religious crusades designed to bring about the perfection of mankind before the expected cataclysmic end of the world.

Joseph Smith's *Book of Mormon* provided a Biblical linkage between the Old World and the New and conveniently gave answers to some of the most vexing religious questions of the day—such as who may be baptized and at what age, ordination, the atonement, eternal damnation and the trinity. The Book even resolved one of the most puzzling issues of the time—the question of the origin of the Indians, and explained the special relationship the Mormons were to have with them.

The *Book of Mormon* identified the American Indians (called Lamanites) as Jews who migrated to the New World in ancient times. Their dark skin was the result of a curse placed on them by God for earlier disobedience. The "curse" of darker skin would be removed, according to the *Book of Mormon,* when the Indians learned of God's promises to them as descendants of Jews and took their place in an earthly Zion.

The miraculously revealed text of the *Book of Mormon* not only explained the origin of the Indians but also taught that the Indians must be brought to knowledge of their origins before the anticipated Millennium could come. As Mormon historian Lori Taylor points out, "the Mormons had to save the Indians to save themselves."[8] According to early Mormon belief, the Indians were to be the major players in this process leading to the Millennium with the Mormons acting as assistants to the Indians, not the other way around. Joseph Smith stood conventional wisdom on its head; he argued that American Indians were "God's chosen people," not the white conquerors from Europe. One of Mormonism's prime responsibilities was to reveal to the Indians who they really were.

The first Whiting family members to be converted to the Latter Day Saints were Sallie and her elder sons Edwin, Charles, and William Whiting and William's wife, Lydia Hurlbut. Elisha Whiting resisted baptism in the new religion until he became ill. According to his grandchildren Emma Anderson and Lester Whiting:

> "He became very sick, so sick in fact that all hope for his recovery was abandoned. Sallie begged him to allow the Latter Day Saint elders to administer to him, but he resolutely refused. His condition grew steadily worse until his jaws were set and he could no longer swallow. What were spoken of as the 'death hiccups' set in. By now everyone expected him to die. Sallie again pled with him to reconsider and allow the elders to come. He could barely move his head but she believed that he gave his consent so two elders came, anointed his head with oil and prayed that God would heal him of his sickness. Before the prayer was ended the hiccup ceased and as soon as they were finished praying Whiting called for a drink of water and was able to swallow. From that time on he began to recover and about four days later he was carried in his chair to the nearby creek where he received the ordinance of baptism by immersion."[9]

Elisha Whiting's conversion was complete. A few months later, he sold his land and moved his home and workshop to Kirtland where other converts to Mormonism were gathering.

While Elisha Whiting was undergoing his religious conversion a similar experience was happening to Alpheus Cutler. Cutler was born

February 29, 1784, in Plainfield, Sullivan County, New Hampshire, the son of a Revolutionary War veteran. Alpheus was a large heavy-set and powerful man, over six feet tall, who became a stone mason. In 1808 he married Lois Lathrop, the daughter of a prominent Lebanon, New Hampshire family. He later served in the War of 1812 at the battles of Chippewa Falls and Lunday Lane near Niagara Falls under the command of General Winfield Scott. Cutler, along with the Smiths, lived in an area where beliefs in the occult, divining rods, spirits and folk magic were common and accepted. Though it is likely that Cutler had some knowledge of Mormonism from living in the same area as the Smiths and their followers, he and his family did not join the church until 1832 when David W. Patton, a Mormon missionary, stopped by their home on his way to Kirtland.

The only known image of Alpheus Cutler, in a Daguerreotype photograph. Reproduced by permission of his great, great grandson, David Sherman Harris.

Patton, an imposing man over six feet tall, preached a sermon in the bedroom of Cutler's critically ill daughter, Lois, who was believed to be dying from tuberculosis. At the end of the sermon Lois cried out " I believe it," and asked for Patton to heal her through the rite of "administration," which was the Biblical "laying on of hands." When the prayer ended she rose from her bed, dressed, ate some food and declared that she was healed. The apparent miracle resulted in the conversion of Cutler and his entire family. Alpheus Cutler was baptized on January 20, 1833, and, as Elisha Whiting had done, he sold his farm and joined the Mormons gathering at Kirtland, Ohio, which many assumed was to be the site for the New Jerusalem.

Cutler was a forceful leader and rose rapidly in the church hierarchy. An accomplished stonemason, he helped build the Latter Day Saint Temple at Kirtland, attended the School of the Prophets, a study group organized by Joseph Smith for male leaders, and was a member of the committee that compiled the *Doctrine and Covenants,* a collection of the revelations given to Joseph Smith and the church. When the Kirtland organization began to splinter in disputes over Smith's policies, Cutler steadfastly supported him.

Though the Latter Day Saint community had been established in Kirtland for only a brief time, Smith, in 1831, presented a revelation to his followers that Zion was to be built, not in Ohio as many had supposed, but at Independence, Jackson County, in western Missouri.

> "Hearken, O ye elders of my church saith the Lord your God, who have assembled yourselves together, according to my commandments, in this land which is the land of Missouri, which is the land which I have appointed and consecrated for the gathering of the Saints: wherefore this is the land of promise, and the place for the city of Zion. . . . Behold, the place which is now called Independence is the Center Place, and the spot for the temple is lying westward upon a lot which is not far from the courthouse; wherefore it is wisdom that the land should be purchased by the Saints, and also every tract lying westward. . . ."[10]

At that date the Kansas border, a few miles west of Independence, was the frontier of the organized United States. Beyond was Indian Territory. The church was but six months old in October, 1830, when, responding to its Indian imperative, Smith sent four missionaries west to go to the

Indians he called "Lamanites" and preach the gospel to them. The elders were to build the city of Zion "on the borders by the Lamanites."

In June 1831, Joseph Smith and a group of associates, including Isaac Morley who would later become bound to the Elisha Whiting family through marriage and other ties, left for western Missouri to acquire land for the church. Thereafter, events moved very rapidly. Within two months, sixty Latter Day Saints from the Susquehanna area of New York had sold their land, moved to Missouri and established a settlement in Kaw Township, twelve miles west of Independence. Elisha Whiting's eldest son, William Whiting, and his family including his infant son, Edmund, were among the Mormon settlers in Missouri. That fall there were enough Latter Day Saints in Jackson and Clay counties in Missouri (perhaps as many as one thousand) for Smith to hold a church conference in the area. He dedicated the site for a new temple, similar to the temple in Kirtland, to be built on sixty-three acres of land just one-half mile west of the existing town square in Independence.

The temple site was central to Smith's town plan. Smith was not only a religious dreamer, but a social planner as well. He envisioned the city of Zion as a community one-mile square extending in all directions from the Jackson County courthouse. Streets were to be laid out at regular intervals and plots set aside for houses and gardens. The temple hilltop, almost as high as the hill on which the courthouse stood, was the place where, the Mormons believed, Christ would come in glory to his temple in the last days. From this Independence "center place," other cities would soon spring up (all one square mile in size) in an orderly progression across the American West until the shores of the Pacific Ocean were reached. The fact that the existing residents might have differing plans for this region was not of great significance to the Mormons intoxicated by Smith's vision.

The Missourians, southern sympathizers and sometime slave-owners, did not look with favor on this sudden invasion of the anti-slavery Yankees who, with their millenarian beliefs and conviction that the region was divinely set aside for them, appeared to be taking over the country. The Latter Day Saints, coming from the abolitionist New England states, abhorred slavery and W.W. Phelps, the editor of the church newspaper, editorialized their concerns. To the Missourians the Mormons were not just a radical religious movement but a burgeoning, subversive, nationalistic sect intent on reordering society and undermining American values. Before long fighting broke out, provoked, in the main, by unruly mobs of ruffians. In a skirmish with a mob (probably in 1833), William Whiting was fatally injured. The death of their eldest son may have been the event that brought Elisha and Sallie Whiting (and their remaining ten children) from Kirtland to Independence, Missouri.

In a letter to her family back in Ohio, Sallie wrote, "Elisha and I, with Elisha's mother and our boys, Edwin, Charlie, Chan (Chauncey), Lewis (Francis Lewis), Almon and Vet (Sylvester), have made our two-story log house quite comfortable—beds upstairs for the boys, two fireplaces in our main room downstairs calling for an abundance of firewood, a long dining table for our family and frequent wayfarers who stopped with us." Many of their visitors were fellow Latter Day Saints who entertained their hosts with stories of persecution, miraculous deliverance and hopeful prophecies of the future. Sallie wrote that they "enjoyed church services in a grove, in a log building reserved for the purpose on the Temple Lot and in various homes."[11]

Elisha and Sallie Whiting did not have long to enjoy church services on the Temple Lot or life in Independence. By July of 1833 tensions between Mormons and non-Mormons had reached a flash point and Mormon homes were attacked. On July 20 a mob broke into church member W.W. Phelps's house and print shop near the square in Independence, threw the press from the upstairs window, scattered the type in the street and, thrusting a log through the windows on the lower floor, wrenched the brick building from its foundation. Latter Day Saints Edward Partridge and Charles Allen were tarred and feathered on the Courthouse Square. In November, the doors of the Mormon-owned Gilbert and Whitney dry goods store were battered down and the contents thrown into the street.

By late 1833 the terrorist tactics of the Missouri mobs had become sufficiently violent that the Whitings, along with hundreds of other church members, abandoned their homes and shops and moved north across the Missouri River into nearby Clay County where they were, at first, welcomed by the residents. In the move north, Sallie lost a chest containing her best clothes and the cherished family Bible in which births and deaths through several generations had been recorded. As her son Chauncey Whiting explained, "Under false pretense the chest was seized upon and retained by a man heretofore professing to be a friend." The treasured Bible, which they had had in their Massachusetts home, carried in a covered wagon over the mountains to Ohio and then across the high prairies to Missouri, was lost in the panic of being driven from Independence.[12]

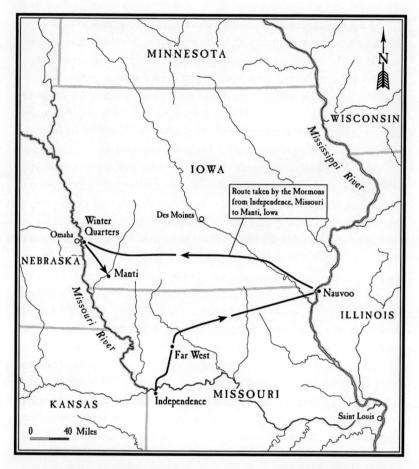

Mormon followers of Joseph Smith, and subsequently of Alpheus Cutler, fled from
Missouri in 1838 to Nauvoo, Illinois, where they remained until 1846. Their next journey took them to Winter Quarters and Manti, Iowa.

Church members in Ohio were outraged that fellow religionists
had been driven from Independence. In Kirtland, Joseph Smith organized a citizen army, called "Zion's Camp," to march to Missouri to restore the church members to their Jackson County homes—by
negotiation if possible and by force if necessary. Flying a banner em-
blazoned with the word "peace," about two hundred men led by Smith
(whom they called "General") marched almost one thousand miles
across Ohio, Indiana, Illinois and Missouri to bring support and supplies to their fellow religionists. When the marchers reached Clay
County they entered peacefully.

Smith had hoped to use the presence of Zion's Camp to negotiate a settlement with the militants of Jackson County. Unfortunately, he was unsuccessful. Within a few days of their arrival in western Missouri over one quarter of the Camp members became ill with cholera and several died. Negotiations with Missouri officials to regain or be compensated for lost homes and land went nowhere. After a brief stay in Clay County and following a revelation by Smith that the Camp should disband, members of Zion's Camp quietly drifted back to Ohio.

For almost three years the Mormons lived in relative peace with their neighbors in Clay County. Then their increasing numbers began to alarm the Clay County residents. In the early summer of 1836 the Mormons were again told they must move on. The final months of 1836 were spent negotiating with the Missouri legislature for land further north for Mormon settlement and in December Caldwell County was carved out of Ray County—specifically for Mormon use. There, in a place Smith declared had once been the home of Cain and Abel, they established the third Mormon community, called Far West. Here the Latter Day Saints believed they would at last find safety and a measure of peace in sparsely populated northern Missouri.

That was not to be. Within the next eighteen months Mormons moving into the area populated not only Caldwell County but spilled over into neighboring Davess, Clinton, Ray and Carroll counties. While Elisha Whiting was moving his family north to Far West in 1836 or 1837 Alpheus Cutler and his family were making their way to Far West from Kirtland. Joseph Smith and other church leaders moved to Far West in January of 1838. In the following summer the 700 remaining members of the church in Ohio abandoned Kirtland and the newly completed Latter Day Saint temple to join Smith in northern Missouri.

In Far West, Alpheus Cutler purchased land along the Crooked River, planted crops and helped build up the new Mormon community. On the Fourth of July, 1838, in a solemn public ceremony, Joseph Smith dedicated the site for yet another temple. The third Mormon temple was to be built at Far West in Caldwell County. Smith ordained Cutler to be the "chief architect and master workman of all God's holy houses."

Once settled in Far West, Elisha Whiting, too, planted crops and once again established his furniture-making business. For a few months all was peaceful, but soon raiders began attacking outlying Mormon settlements. The motivation for the attacks was not unlike that in Jackson County in 1833. The Mormons believed they lived on hallowed ground and made no secret of their plans to extend their dominion over the entire region. Non-Mormons were the enemy. As an answer to mob violence, the Mormons, if not encouraged, certainly allowed the formation of a secret band of avenging men, called Danites. Both the Danites and the Missourians provoked hostile incidents and by 1838 the region resembled an armed camp.

Pitched battles soon took place and in the fight at Crooked River on the night of October 25, 1838, David Patton, the missionary who had converted Cutler, was killed. Some of Elisha Whiting's sons may also have been involved in that struggle but none were injured. On October 27, Cutler lost his farm and crops to mob violence. This was followed by the attack by armed men on horseback on October 30 on Haun's Mill where about 30 Mormon families had gathered for safety. Having no means of defense, some saved themselves by running into the nearby woods. Nevertheless, seventeen men and boys were killed, one of them a nine-year-old boy who had hidden beneath some bellows. A dozen more were wounded.

Lester Whiting recalled his grandparents' experience when the raiders attacked their home near Far West. "Elisha Whiting was a wagon and chair maker when living in Far West, Missouri. He had purchased a lot of material and new lumber. One day when he was not at home, a mob came on horses and saw his wife, Sallie, sick in bed. The mob gave her children just twenty minutes to move her out of the house before they burned it. The children placed her on an old straw mattress and drug her from the house out into the cornfield. The mob came back and burned not only the house but all of the new material which Whiting had acquired for making wagons and chairs."[13]

Lester Whiting's father, Francis Lewis Whiting, was a boy of about eight when he saw settlements attacked, houses burned and the church leaders taken prisoner. He often told his children how terrible the howls of the mob sounded when they surrounded Far West.[14] On the same day as the Haun's Mill attack, the town of Far West was surrounded by 2,000 militiamen and terms negotiated for the town's surrender. The Mormons agreed to turn over church leaders to be tried. They would also give up their arms, and leave the state.

To the Mormons in northern Missouri the mob attacks were the designs of Satan, working to oppose the plans of the people of God. What the Mormons failed to understand was that their developing concept of the political Kingdom of God sounded to the ears of the Missourians like treason against the United States. The Mormons believed that the Second Coming of Christ was imminent and that when Jesus returned He would establish His Kingdom on earth. The Mormons were not to simply wait for that to occur, however. Their task was to establish a temporal kingdom of world government as preparation for the Second Coming. The first kingdom would be the militant kingdom, struggling against an evil and resistant world. The second, victorious kingdom, would come when Christ's enemies had been subdued.

While these ideas had not yet been institutionalized within the Mormon church, there was enough talk about them to frighten the Missourians who distorted the emerging concepts into a major threat to the established civil order. If the Mormons were not stopped, or exiled, the Missourians reasoned, they might become strong enough to overthrow the government, drive out the residents and take possession of the state of Missouri much as the Israelites had overrun the land of Canaan. There was another troubling issue. The fact that Joseph Smith insisted on controlling his followers in both their spiritual and temporal affairs appeared to the Missourians to violate the sacred constitutional principle of the separation of church and state.

When Governor Lilburn W. Boggs, who was from Jackson County, issued an order to exterminate or expel the Mormons in 1838, the Saints realized that they must flee the state to save their lives. For the fourth time in less than eight years Elisha and Sallie Whiting, along with the rest of the Mormons, packed up what possessions they could salvage, loaded their wagon and abandoned their home, workshop and land. Members of the church could be forgiven for identifying with the suffering of the ancient Israelites. Persecution, instead of weakening their faith, only confirmed for them the divine nature of their cause.

Smith arranged to purchase a tract of land in Illinois north of Quincy where he hoped to settle the impoverished members of his church. Much of the land was malarial, an insect-ridden marsh on limestone river flats along the Mississippi River. However, rising above the flat land along the river was a hill, a dramatic promontory that commanded a panoramic vista of the river and the surrounding countryside. Smith instinctively knew that this would be the ideal site for his fourth Mormon temple. Only the first temple, built at Kirtland, had ever been completed. Mob violence had prevented the temples at Independence and Far West from even being started. This new temple, at Nauvoo, Smith was certain would eventually be built.

The Latter Day Saints considered the building of temples to be a divine commission. Believing that Smith was commanded by God to begin the temple at Far West, the church leadership was deeply troubled that the cornerstone had not been laid before the Saints had been forced to flee. If they had laid the cornerstone, or even part of the foundation, they reasoned, it would have been evidence that they had acted in obedience to God's will. Once the cornerstone, a powerful symbol to the early Mormons, was in place God would certainly open the way for them to return in the future and complete the temple.

Smith's designation of Alpheus Cutler to be the "chief architect of God's holy houses" had had a profound influence on him. In April 1839, after having been driven from Missouri Cutler, along with other members of the Mormon leadership slipped back to Far West and, under cover of darkness, laid the foundation stone for the temple. The temple site was a field at the summit of a hill surrounded by outbuildings and the abandoned homes of the Mormons. In the middle of the night, leaving their horses tied to trees a distance away, Cutler and his associates crept onto the temple site cradling a large square-shaped rock in their arms. When they got their bearings and determined where the corner of the temple should be they knelt for whispered prayers. Then Cutler, being careful not to bang his tool against the rock, scooped away the soil and settled the chiseled stone into the earth. A dog barked but was calmed by an answering bark from another house. After a final prayer the men rose and slipped away in the dark to their waiting horses and the long ride back to Illinois. This daring and dramatic action, undertaken at considerable risk to their lives, accelerated Cutler's rise to prominence in the Mormon hierarchy.

Cutler was not the only Mormon to return to Far West. The older Whiting boys ventured back with a team to see if they could gather corn to use for bread and horse feed from a field they owned. As they were passing the house of one of the men who had participated in the burning down of their home and shop they noticed some sheep in a field that looked familiar. "Those look like our sheep," one of them said, and called out the name of a pet sheep they had raised by hand and who would come when called. One sheep left the others in the flock and bounded up to the fence where the boys stood. Because they were in hostile country they did not attempt to take back their sheep, but after dark they picked a load of their corn and drove with it back to Nauvoo.[10]

CHAPTER 3

Nauvoo—Doomed Kingdom on the Mississippi

O riginally a village of only a handful of people, Nauvoo quickly experienced explosive growth. A boomtown whose population doubled every year between 1839 and 1842, Nauvoo continued to grow until 1846. Within five years of its founding, Nauvoo grew from a community of a few hundred to a city that may have had as many as 20,000 people.[16] Nauvoo was the second largest city in Illinois, rivaling Chicago. Its city charter made Nauvoo virtually independent of the state government. The city was guarded by an all-Mormon Nauvoo Legion militia of more than 5,000 men.[17]

Alpheus Cutler and his family moved into the new town of Nauvoo where he would work as a stonemason and become one of the principal builders of the Nauvoo Temple. While Cutler was moving to Nauvoo, where he would become a confidant of Joseph Smith, Elisha Whiting and his family were settling at a place midway between Quincy and Nauvoo, originally called Lima. Initially, the settlement contained only sixteen people, all members of the Cox, Morley or Whiting families. Within a year, however, between three and four hundred Latter Day Saints moved into the community. Called Morley, or with the growing Mormon passion for secrecy, Yelrom (Morley spelled backwards), the village was a prototype for Manti in Iowa and Clitherall in Minnesota.

During the first winter in Illinois the settlers lived in tents. Isaac Morley's daughter, Cordelia, wrote in later years that:

> "Father pitched his tent in the back woods. This was our home and all the one we had. It was cold weather; the snow was falling fast. There was but little to eat and scant clothes to wear. The body of a log house had been put on the ground for a

claim. This father bought. He covered the house and the family moved into it without a door, window or floor. Father fixed the house as best he could. The next summer he built an addition, cleared the land and we were settled again."[18]

Elisha Whiting's household was a large one. In 1839, his son Chauncey was twenty, Almon eighteen, Sylvester twelve, and the youngest, Francis Lewis, was eight. A daughter, Jane, was fifteen. Also living with them were the children of his slain son William and William's widow Lydia. William's son, Edmund William Whiting, was fifty-three days older than his Uncle Francis Lewis. Edmund's sisters, twins, were two years younger.

With the help of his four unmarried sons, Elisha Whiting built a large furniture-making workshop and home at Morley. The lathes in the shop were powered by an old blind horse on a treadmill urged on by one or another of his grandchildren. The Whiting workshop turned out at least one of the wood beams for the Nauvoo temple. From contemporary accounts, the Morley settlement and surrounding area was a beehive of activity. It was as if the settlers were trying to make up for the time they had lost trying to establish themselves at Independence and Far West. A visitor recounted, "Hancock County, especially, was soon full of Mormons. Cabins and shops sprang up as if by magic. The quiet plains were soon humming with industry. The sod was soon turned into fields of corn; the groves were ringing with the music of axes. . . . From early morning until late at night they might be seen plying the daily tasks—the men in the fields, the groves, the shops; the women in the homes, cooking, weaving, making clothes, or washing and mending them." The farmers and craftspeople of Morley were a significant part of the society and economy of the burgeoning Mormon kingdom by the Mississippi.

The Morley community functioned much like a tribal society. The members became ever more tightly knit to each other through marriages among the three leading families. Elisha Whiting's son Chauncey married one of Isaac Morley's daughters, Editha, and in 1842 their son, Isaac Morley Whiting, was born. Chauncey Whiting's older sister, Sallie Emeline, married F. Walter Cox. In the Morley settlement, the Mormon Church and the civil government were the same institution, which, to the residents of Morley, seemed the proper ordering of society. At a church conference in June of 1843, Isaac Morley was named president of the local branch of the church with F. Walter Cox and Edwin Whiting his councilors. They could just as well have been called the mayor and his city councilmen.

The Mormons' previous experience with mob violence had created a crisis mentality among them that fostered an inward-looking group loyalty. Though their farms and factories appeared to an outsider to be functioning in an atmosphere of relative peace, in reality the residents of Nauvoo and surrounding communities were experiencing the artificial calm in the eye of a storm that was about to break around them. Their beliefs, which seemed so right and divinely ordered to them, were diametrically opposed to the tenets of personal freedom cherished by their neighbors. In many ways, Nauvoo Mormonism was a quest for security and for safety—both in this life and in the hereafter. The core of a millennialist belief is the desire for an end to change and social conflict and for the dawn of eternal peace.

Mormonism offered both refuge and certainty to those who were unsettled by the changes taking place in America, and who were disturbed by competition, secularism and the increasing pluralism of the country. In a world whose foundation felt like shifting sands, the church offered a utopia, a return to an imagined perfect society that had existed in the past when the religious, political and social orders were based on divine commands and governed by a priesthood which spoke with God. The legalisms of Mormonism provided freedom from doubt and a spiritual mechanism that implied a control of nature. If the rules were followed and prescribed duties performed, salvation was assured. It seemingly did not occur to the Nauvoo Mormons that the establishment of state religions in Europe had resulted in religious persecution. To the Mormons it was natural that "the one true church" should be at the center of all of their affairs, secular as well as religious.

Mormon beliefs alarmed their neighbors in Hancock County. They were fearful of what they perceived as Mormon despotism, terrified of the Nauvoo Legion and were sure that the Mormon theocracy, which governed every aspect of members' lives, threatened the foundation of American democracy. The first immigrants to the American shores were refugees from the religious wars of England. After centuries of such conflict in Europe the founders of the new nation sought an impenetrable barrier between religion and political life. To the non-Mormons in Hancock County, the control of Nauvoo's civil affairs by religious leaders violated the basic principle of the separation of church and state.

Their activities made a mockery of the Constitution and appeared to violate non-Mormon individual rights. When Smith encouraged his followers to vote as a block (as many immigrant groups did), it appeared to the people of Hancock County to threaten the integrity of elections.

While the Mormons were creating a theocratic oligarchy for themselves, the rest of the country was breaking away from a traditional, patriarchal structure of authority and moving toward a more individualistic social order. The country was becoming more egalitarian than it had ever been in the past. The Jacksonian era was the period that defined the basic elements of America's individualistic culture—a nation of free individuals pursuing their own happiness. Nowhere was that more evident than in Illinois where Andrew Jackson was idolized as the essence of freewheeling American individualism. The Mormon system of hierarchical, centralized, religious control could not easily co-exist with a citizenry inspired by the Jacksonian spirit of the independent, common man.[19]

The worst fears of the residents of Hancock County were confirmed when word circulated that on March 11, 1844, Joseph Smith had established a highly secret Council of Fifty, a semi-political body whose purpose was to establish the literal Kingdom of God on earth. The council was to be "The Municipal department of the Kingdom of God set up on the Earth, and from which all Law emanates, for the rule, government and control of all Nations, Kingdoms & . . . People under the whole Heavens."[20] One of the council's first actions was to nominate Smith for president of the United States. In other frenzied planning the Council of Fifty proposed huge colonizing projects in Texas and the western regions of the continent. Nauvoo, they theorized, could secede from Illinois and become an independent state.

Except for the chairman Joseph Smith (and later Brigham Young) members of the Council of Fifty were assigned rank by virtue of their age. This placed Alpheus Cutler as the fourth ranking member of the Fifty. This high level of authority in the Council later became significant to his followers. (On the city plat of Nauvoo, Cutler Street was located almost in the center of town, parallel and adjacent to Young Street.)[21] Each member of the Council chaired a committee. Cutler's committee responsibility was to "restore the Ancients [Lamanites] to the knowledge of the truth." In a ceremony meaningful to Cutler, Smith ordained him to serve a special mission to the Indians. All of the members of the Council of Fifty were given privileged information about polygamy and the emerging temple theology.

To the citizens of Hancock County, the establishment of the Council of Fifty was a call to arms. They saw it as a Mormon denial of the ideal of a pluralistic society, guaranteed by the constitution, where religious freedom was enshrined. Strangely, the Mormons in Nauvoo failed to grasp the fury their expanding political program and quest for empire was arousing in their neighbors. While the countryside smoldered, about to burst into flames, the Mormons appeared to be largely unaware of the intensifying feelings all about them. As a result they continued on a collision course with their neighbors, confident that God would protect them and lead them to victory.

Adding to the already considerable tensions between Mormons and their Gentile neighbors in Nauvoo were disturbing rumors of a new marriage practice instigated by Joseph Smith. A major theme of the *Book of Mormon* had been sexual sin, the evils of "fornication and lasciviousness" and family disorganization. The rituals begun in the temple at Kirtland reflected the themes of the ancient Old Testament patriarchs, Abraham, Isaac and Jacob, whose marriage practices were polygamous. Joseph Smith may have considered introducing polygamy to the church as early as 1831 while he was still in Kirtland, but the concept did not become developed, or even revealed, until the Nauvoo period.[22] Here, in a time of great community stress when Smith required absolute loyalty from his followers, the acceptance of polygamy became a supreme test of his followers' faithfulness to him.

Some of the impetus for plural marriage may have come about because a high percentage of church leaders defected following the exodus from Kirtland and the problems in Missouri, according to Kathryn Daynes, assistant professor of history at Brigham Young University and a researcher on Mormon plural marriage. Half of the top leadership left the church before the expulsion from Missouri in 1839. In response to that crisis, Daynes suggests that Smith may have looked for a higher level of moral obligation and ritual to tie his people to the church and to him. Because the apostasy of so many in leadership made loyalty questionable, the developing rituals featured oaths, implied penalties, and bound families to Smith and to each other in an ever tighter embrace. Plural marriages created unique ties among church leaders with all of the moral responsibilities that go with family relationships.

The acceptance of Joseph Smith's new doctrine, wrapped as it was in the cloak of temple rituals, required enormous sacrifice from its followers. When Smith told his Apostle Heber C. Kimball that Kimball was to take a second wife, he "shed bushels of tears over this order."[23] He had been asked to choose between loyalty to his wife and obedience to the prophet. Kimball made his decision and demonstrated that his primary loyalty was to the prophet. Whether or not this was Smith's intention when he instituted polygamy, the result was to tie the leadership to him with even tighter bonds.

Loyalty to Joseph Smith was the crucial element in the acceptance of polygamy by these essentially puritanical and monogamous people. As Daynes has noted, according to the accounts of those directly involved, plural marriage during Joseph Smith's lifetime was a product not so much of lust or romantic love but of loyalty—loyalty cemented by sacrifice and sacred covenants that bound families together under solemn moral obligations.[24] Many of Smith's followers had already lost family members in the Missouri struggles, suffered huge monetary losses and experienced untold suffering. Their psychic investment in the Mormon movement was enormous which was an additional reason for continuing to accept Smith's leadership, even as he led them onto the shoals of polygamy.

In altering the marriage practices among the Mormons, Joseph Smith changed the traditional New England view of marriage as a civil contract to the pre-Reformation belief that marriage was a sacrament. In Nauvoo Smith taught that there was another divine or "celestial" form of marriage that "sealed" couples together for eternity. In Smith's interpretation of the Old Testament, Biblical patriarchs had been directed by God in the daily routine of their lives, including marriage relationships. Believing himself to be a continuation of the ancient line of prophets it was not lost on Smith that men favored of God, such as Abraham, Isaac, Rehoboam, and David, had many wives. Solomon not only had seven hundred wives, he had more than 300 concubines! Convinced that he was to bring about "the restitution of all things," and with his strong identification with Old Testament patriarchs, it was but a small step for Smith to move from his ideas of celestial marriage to the introduction of polygamy.

Smith explained to his followers that earthly holders of church priesthood offices held the power given to St. Peter to define relationships in heaven as well as on earth. He redefined marriage to consist of two steps. Earthly secular marriage, the first, was for time only. This marriage was inferior, as it dissolved upon the death of one of the partners. A second, superior form of marriage was the "celestial" type. This marriage, when properly performed by the priesthood, would endure "for time and eternity," during an after-life in heaven as well as on earth.

Joseph Smith taught that it was only through such a celestial marriage that men and women could achieve the highest status and glory in heaven. Furthermore, neither men nor women could be saved if they were not part of a sacred marriage covenant. Polygamy was introduced as a form of eternal or celestial marriage. In Smith's explanation to his followers, the Old Testament precedents of Abraham, Isaac, David and Solomon, who had numerous wives, validated the practice. As he developed his concept of plural marriage, Smith reasoned that if celestial marriage with one wife would bring godly status for men in heaven, then multiple wives in this life and the next would accelerate the process. Women guaranteed their own salvation in heaven by becoming plural wives.

Smith produced an entire theological rationale for the introduction of polygamy, though for many it came down to one basic question: if they believed that Joseph Smith was a prophet of God they had to accept plural marriage. Though some Mormon scholars are convinced that polygamy was a secret practice in Kirtland in the 1830s, and rumors continually circulated to that effect, it was not until the period between 1839 and 1844 that Smith systematically taught polygamy to his inner circle at Nauvoo.

Smith was not alone in his speculation about relationships between men and women. Millennial sects always involved sex. Nearly all of the new religious groups in the Western New York area were involved in unorthodox marriage practices. The Oneida Perfectionists, who developed a communal society and practiced group marriage, were one of the many organizations that experimented with radically different sex roles and family relationships.[25] Believers looked to the imminent end of the old corrupt world and desired to live in a way of holiness in preparation for the Second Coming of the Savior.

Initially, only a small select group was initiated into the secret practice of polygamy and the resulting marriage ceremonies were performed in private. Smith's first officially recorded plural marriage was to a woman named Louisa Beaman.[26] She was married, disguised in a man's hat and coat, in a ceremony performed beside the Mississippi River by her brother-in-law, Joseph Noble, using a form dictated by Smith.

Members of the Morley community were among those to whom Smith revealed his doctrine. The idea was discussed in both private and public meetings. One day a messenger came from Joseph Smith himself, asking that Cordelia Morley, one of Isaac Morley's unmarried daughters, become one of his plural wives. As she recounted the experience, "In the spring of forty-four plural marriage was introduced to me by my parents from Joseph Smith asking their consent and a request to me to be his wife. Imagine, if you can, my feelings to be a plural wife! Something I never thought I could be. I knew nothing of such a religion and could not accept it, neither did I."[27]

Her attitude toward polygamy quickly changed, however. Within a year Cordelia Morley had become the second wife of F. Walter Cox, becoming a sister-wife to her friend Sallie Emeline Whiting Cox; and after Joseph Smith's death, she was sealed to Smith for eternity. As she later explained to her children, "I thought if one principle taught by Joseph was true, all he taught must be true."[28] On January 3, 1845, Elisha Whiting's son Edwin Whiting took Almira Mechitable Meacham to be his second wife.

Joseph Smith concentrated more and more power into his own hands as internal as well as external tensions grew within Nauvoo. Besides being the prophet and president of the church, he was mayor of Nauvoo, Lieutenant General of the Nauvoo Legion, a merchant, innkeeper and, in 1844, a candidate for president of the United States. As his organization spun out of control Smith attempted to manage every aspect of his followers' lives and became obsessed with teaching his ideas to his close associates. Smith's belief in his prophetic mission was so strong that he may have convinced himself that his speculations were divine in origin and must be given to his church as heavenly commandments. His doctrines came cloaked in an elaborate, magical, intellectual-doctrinal framework, complete with temple ceremonies, which had great power and appeal to his followers.

The rumors of polygamy found their way to hostile newspapers in nearby communities as Smith's ideas became more widely known around Nauvoo. Some of his closest associates within the church also were appalled at his new marriage doctrine and believed that he was a fallen prophet who must be removed to save the church. This group published one issue of an opposition newspaper, the *Nauvoo Expositor*, before the city marshal of Nauvoo, on Smith's orders, destroyed the press. The destruction of the press was the spark that inflamed a countryside already about to take fire. Joseph Smith and his brother Hyrum were arrested on charges of riot and treason and taken to the jail in Carthage. On June 27, 1844, both were assassinated by a mob that stormed the jail. Smith's death was a direct result of internal dissent among the Mormons over the issue of polygamy. Two years after Smith's death the Mormons, once again, were expelled from their homes.

There was relative peace for a few months following the deaths of Joseph and Hyrum Smith. Then mobs began in earnest to attack the outlying settlements, including Morley. On September 10, 1845, a neighbor ran to Emeline Whiting Cox's home to tell her that a mob of eighteen men was coming. Emeline's husband, F. Walter Cox, along with the other men, had been lured away from the village. A member of the mob pounded on the door and told the pregnant Emeline to hurry and take what she wanted out of the house. Her nine-year-old son was ill so she helped him leave the house and lie down on a blanket under a tree. Six-year-old Louisa held the hand of her two-year-old sister Eliza and little William, not yet five, followed his mother.

While Emeline struggled to save some of her household goods, other houses in Morley had already been set afire. Emeline especially wanted to save a cabinet but found herself unable to drag it out of the house. Desperate, she appealed to one of the men in the mob to help her and, after a moment's hesitation, the man went in the house and carried the cupboard out into the yard. Then he grabbed a pile of straw, threw it inside the house and set it afire. Others carried burning sticks that they used to torch haystacks and piles of unthreshed grain.

When the mob came to burn Chauncey and Editha Whiting's home, Whiting, too, was away and Editha asked the men's help to move her cook stove out of the house. The men obliged, moving many of her possessions to the garden where they would not be damaged by the burning house. One-year-old Isaac sat on the grass and watched his home burn. When Chauncey Whiting arrived home that evening he found his wife sitting in a rocking chair in the garden holding the infant Isaac and guarding their possessions. Nearby were the smoking embers of what had been their home. Since Whiting now did not have a wagon, he tied up a bundle of their clothes, put it on his wife's back, put her on his horse with the baby and led the horse to Isaac Morley's home which had not been burned.

At Elisha Whiting's home, one of his sons was gravely ill with a fever. For some reason, the mob showed compassion and did not burn the house or workshop. Later, after the mob had departed, the sick and homeless were moved into the Whiting home. When F. Walter Cox arrived back in Morley that evening to find his home burned to the ground, he helped Emeline cook dinner over the coals of his house. The next morning Cox loaded his remaining possessions, including the rescued cabinet, into his wagon and, in a heavy rainstorm, drove his family to

Chauncey Whiting (1819–1902).

Nauvoo. When church authorities learned of the attack on Morley, the Church Council sent 134 men with teams to bring the survivors of the torched community to Nauvoo where they moved in with friends and relatives. During the fall of 1845, over 200 Mormon homes and farm buildings located outside the city limits of Nauvoo were burned.

The interrelated group of Whitings, Morleys and Coxes were now living together in Nauvoo during that city's frantic final months. Alpheus Cutler, master stonemason of the Nauvoo Temple, was working feverishly to complete the building, which was essentially finished on May 24, 1845. As Captain of Smith's personal bodyguard, Cutler had been called to the Nauvoo High Council, the city's chief governing body, in 1839, as well as to the secretive Council of Fifty and an even more arcane group, the "Anointed Quorum."

Alpheus Cutler and his wife Lois were among the earliest, secret initiates to Temple Mormonism. On January 14, 1846, in the Nauvoo Temple, Alpheus and Lois Cutler were sealed to each other for time and eternity. With Lois's consent, Cutler on that same day married Luana Hart Beebe Rockwell for time and eternity. Luana's children were also sealed to Cutler. On February 3, 1846, Cutler took five more wives in Temple ceremonies: Margaret Carr and her sister Abigail, Sally Cox, Daisey Caroline McCall and Henrietta Clarinda Miller.[29]

Luana Hart Beebe Rockwell was 32 years old when she became Cutler's second wife in the Nauvoo Temple.[30] Luana was previously married to Orrin Porter Rockwell, a second cousin of Joseph Smith, and bore Rockwell five or six children. Rockwell was notorious for his spirited defense of Smith and was suspected of attempting to assassinate Missouri's Governor Boggs. Rockwell and Luana separated sometime before 1842 and, although there is no record of an official divorce, she apparently felt free to remarry. Following her marriage to Cutler, Luana had three more children, two of whom, Jacob and Olive, survived. However, the paternity of the children was kept a secret, even from them. Jacob was told that his father had died as a scout for the Mormon Pioneer Company so he used the surname of Boyd (Cutler's mother's maiden name). Olive, at different times, used the surnames of Baldwin and Perry, reflecting Luana's subsequent marriages to Wheeler Baldwin and Isaac Perry.

Other members of Cutler's family, like many who eventually became Cutlerites, also participated in plural marriages. Clarissa Cutler, Alpheus's 21-year-old daughter and her younger sister, 16-year-old Emily, both married Mormon Apostle Heber C. Kimball in the Temple, becoming two of the sixteen plural wives he had taken by the end of 1845. (Kimball had 38 plural wives by the time he left Nauvoo.) A son, Abraham Alpheus, was later born to Clarissa and Heber and another son, Isaac Alpheus, was born to Emily and Heber. As their father Alpheus was involved in temple construction and their husband was a confidant of Joseph Smith, the two young women made their own contribution by sewing the cotton curtains and veils for the "endowment rooms" in the attic of the temple.

In January 1846 the State of Illinois revoked the charters of the City of Nauvoo and the Nauvoo Legion, taking away what legal protection the Mormons had. The Nauvoo city charter was a device of dubious constitutionality that had been designed by the Mormons themselves to create a sovereign state within the state of Illinois. It had been granted originally because both the Democrats and Whigs wanted the Mormon vote. Its repeal was a signal that the leading political figures in Illinois no longer needed the Mormons and, instead, were turning against them. An Anti-Mormon Convention at Carthage decreed that the Latter Day Saints must leave Illinois as soon as weather permitted in the spring of 1846.

Activity in the temple became frenetic as it became ever more clear that the Mormons would be forced to abandon Nauvoo. Temple activities, to the Mormons, were profound religious obligations, essential parts of their contract with the divine. Only in the temple could certain religious ordinances essential to their salvation be conducted. The Nauvoo temple, built of grey limestone and measuring 88 x 128 feet, stood 165 feet high on a bluff overlooking the city. The famous sunstone image (seen on the cover of this book) served as capitals on the 30 temple pilasters. Mormons had worked on the building for five years and it dominated the city. The temple cost over $1 million to build, an enormous sum of money for the period.[31]

Baptisms for the dead, marriages and sealings were performed all-day and late into the night as the time for the evacuation of Nauvoo neared. Isaac Morley took seven wives; Edwin Whiting took his third wife as did F. Walter Cox, and Chauncey Whiting was sealed to his father-in-law Isaac Morley in a ceremony joining the two men in a father-son relationship for eternity. Isaac Morley's youngest daughter, Theresa, became yet another wife of Heber C. Kimball while Chauncey Whiting's sister Jane, along with his widowed sister-in-law Martha, both married the Mormon scout Return Jackson Redding. The interrelationships became ever more complicated. Calvin Beebe, the brother of Cutler's plural wife Luana, performed celestial and plural marriages in the Nauvoo Temple and his brother, as well as his father, may have taken plural wives there. Between 1841 and 1846 when Nauvoo was abandoned, at least 119 men entered into polygamous relationships with 437 women producing 612 children for a total of 1,168 individuals involved in the new marriage relationships.[32]

Throughout the winter of 1845–46 Mormons prepared their wagons to evacuate Nauvoo and move west under the leadership of Brigham Young. In February, only nine months after the completion of the temple, the first group, including Cutler who captained a company, crossed into Iowa on the thin ice of the frozen Mississippi. The Whiting, Morley, and Cox families, who were traveling as a group, waited until March when they could make the crossing on flatboats. Among the groups traveling together were Elisha and Sallie Whiting with their unmarried sons Sylvester, Almon and Francis Lewis; Elisha's two widowed daughters-in-law (the wives of William and Charles) and their children including Edmund; Chauncey and Editha Morley Whiting with their children including four-year-old Isaac; F. Walter Cox and Emeline Whiting Cox with five small children and Edwin Whiting, who had temporarily left his three wives and children in Nauvoo. Interrelated through marriages and sealings, they moved together more as a tribe than as independent families. Once across the river in Iowa, they camped at one of the first staging areas on Sugar Creek, about seven miles from the Mississippi.

Cutler's daughters, Clarissa and Emily, both seven months pregnant, were left behind in Nauvoo with most of Kimball's other wives. Kimball took only some of his wives (perhaps twelve to fourteen) and some children with him, leaving the rest of his family, including four pregnant wives, behind in Nauvoo until he could make a home for them further west. Either because Kimball was slow in sending for them, or the women preferred to travel with their parents, Cutler's daughters eventually traveled west with Alpheus and Lois Cutler rather than with their husband. When they reached the Missouri river they continued living with their parents—first at Cutler's Park, the initial Mormon settlement west of the Missouri in Indian Territory, and then at Winter Quarters (now Florence, Nebraska), three miles west of Cutler's Park and closer to the river. Somehow the Cutler-Kimball infants survived the hard winter of 1846–47 in Winter Quarters. In the spring of 1847, 143 men, three women and two children left with Brigham Young for the Great Basin in Utah. Heber C. Kimball, a member of Young's party, took only one wife with him on the trip, leaving Clarissa, Emily, and his other wives behind in Winter Quarters.

CHAPTER 4

The Break with Brigham
Young and the Mission
to the Indians

The trek across southern Iowa between the Mississippi and Missouri rivers in the cold, wet spring of 1846 was a more arduous journey for most of the fleeing Mormons than the far longer journey across the prairies and mountains to Utah would be. Wagons sank in the mud, food was scarce, people sickened and died. Progress was measured in a few miles a day. Small camps were established every few miles with a larger one located at Garden Grove, where Brigham Young made his head-quarters for a time. Another, more permanent, settlement was made in south-central Iowa at a place selected by Parley P. Pratt. He called it "Mt. Pisgah" because of its lovely park-like setting.

It was April when the Whiting-Morley-Cox group reached Mt. Pisgah so they immediately decided to stop, plant crops and stay for the season. With the astonishing speed with which communities were established on the frontier, the group fenced the land, planted crops, and built temporary log homes. The Whitings constructed yet another chair shop and F. Walter Cox cut down trees, split the trunks and made benches for a little school that was held in a grove. The Whiting chair shop became the site for dances and socials. Several of the men, including the Whiting brothers, could play violins for entertainment and dances. Edwin Whiting and others now headed back to Nauvoo to pick up the wives they had left behind and bring them on to Mt. Pisgah.

Residents in the settlement at Mt. Pisgah were able to survive on their stored supplies and from hunting game until their gardens began to produce food. Except for a shortage of bread, they ate well and most were healthy. That changed in late August when the community was stricken by a fatal illness—possibly cholera. Emeline and F. Walter Cox lost two little girls, as did Edwin Whiting, and Emeline herself almost died. Death claimed Sallie and Elisha Whiting along with a hundred others. All were buried in what are now unmarked graves. The widows of William and Charles Whiting also died at Mt. Pisgah or during the Iowa crossing. In the fall, after the crops had been harvested, many families, including F. Walter Cox with his three wives and surviving children, left Mt. Pisgah for Winter Quarters, the final departure point for the journey west to Utah.

Elisha and Sallie Whiting's sons—Edwin, Chauncey, Sylvester and Francis Lewis—stayed through the winter in Mt. Pisgah, making chairs and taking them in loads pulled by a team of oxen into Missouri to sell. They even took chairs as far east as Quincy, Illinois. Edwin and Sylvester Whiting and Orville Cox were returning from one such trip with their team of oxen when they were stopped by a fierce Iowa blizzard. Though they knew that they were near Mt. Pisgah, the swirling winds and snow confused them and as the cold intensified, they were forced to stop, make camp and build a fire. They unyoked their oxen to allow the animals to seek shelter on their own and, with the three matches they had between them, attempted to build a fire. The first match sputtered out—then the second. Carefully, because without a fire they would soon freeze to death, they hunted for dry leaves and twigs under the snow, put them in a wooden bucket they used to feed grain to the oxen, inverted another bucket over that, and gingerly struck the last match. The tiny flame caught the tinder in the bucket and from that, despite the howling wind and snow, they were able to build a fire. When the storm ended and dawn broke they found they were only a short distance from their own fences at Mt. Pisgah. The only damage was to the oxen's noses, which had frozen in the cold and split open.

When spring came the immigrants again packed their wagons, abandoned their cabins and the chair factory, and moved on west to the Nebraska border. Thousands of Latter Day Saints were now scattered in dozens of camps and settlements across hundreds of square miles of southwest Iowa territory. Evidence of Young's extraordinary organizational and leadership skills was his ability to maintain contact with these scattered settlements, infuse his followers with optimism and keep the goal of westward movement continually before them. The largest settlement was Winter Quarters, the encampment on the Nebraska territory side of the Missouri River. Here was the headquarters of the church and the staging area for the trek to Utah. Alpheus Cutler helped select the site of Winter Quarters and in August 1846, he was sustained as President of the Municipal High Council (in effect, mayor of Winter Quarters), solidifying Cutler's position as one of Brigham Young's and the movement's most trusted leaders.

When Young returned from the Great Basin on October 31, 1847, he faced the daunting task of getting his thousands of mostly destitute followers equipped, organized and motivated to make the difficult journey across the high plains and mountains to Utah. Hundreds were ill, exhausted, poverty-stricken and psychologically devastated by the conflict with their neighbors in Missouri and Illinois. The Missouri River marked the border of the United States and while some were prepared to cross it and leave behind a country they believed had failed to protect them, others feared unknown hazards that lay ahead. Young understood that the longer the Saints remained on the lush farmland of western Iowa, the harder it would be to convince them to leave for the long, hazardous journey across the plains.

Adding to Young's difficulties were conflicts over leadership of the Latter Day Saints. Joseph Smith had left no firm succession plans and after his death several men claimed authority to lead the Latter Day Saints. J.J. Strang took a group to Beaver Island, Michigan, while Lyman Wight convinced others to follow him to Texas. Even the slain prophet's brother William tried to gather followers around him. Though the vast majority of the church chose to accept the authority and leadership of Brigham Young, president of the Quorum of Twelve Apostles, the activities of dissidents presented a continuing problem. Young's solution was to move as quickly as he could to organize his followers for the trip across the plains. Immigrants were organized into companies. On January 27, 1848, Cutler was named president of Heber C. Kimball's company, which was to leave in the spring for the Great Basin.

Though Kimball's company departed on schedule, Alpheus Cutler did not make the trip. The reason he did not go west hearkens back to the Latter Day Saints's beliefs about their mission to the Indians. In the last years of his life, Joseph Smith had given Cutler the commission to take the message of the gospel to the Indians. Before his death, in an action weighty with significance for Cutler, Smith had committed to Cutler "the keys to open the gospel to every Lamanite nation." Coming from the mouth of the prophet himself, this was a powerful and authoritative assignment. Cutler, along with others who had received commissions from Smith, believed their primary responsibility was to obey these commands. Brigham Young also sensed the lingering authority of Smith's orders.

Upon returning to Winter Quarters in the fall of 1847, Brigham Young met with Lewis Denna, a chief of the Oneida Tribe and the most prominent Indian to join the Mormons during the lifetime of Joseph Smith.[33] The meeting had long-term consequences for the Cutlerites. Denna's father, John Denna, had been an interpreter during the negotiation of the removal treaty of the Oneidas of Wisconsin in 1836 and Lewis, himself, was an interpreter for five or six Indian tribes.

In 1840 Denna was acting as an agent for a band of Oneidas who wanted to move from the Green Bay area to a site west of the Missouri River. Denna, his wife, and two children were traveling down the Mississippi by canoe when they chanced to land for the night on the bank of the river just below Nauvoo. There they met Allen Dimmick, a young Mormon, who invited the Indian family to his parents' home. A friendship developed, the Dennas stayed in Nauvoo for several weeks, and were converted to the Latter Day Saint faith. Church records list Denna as the first Indian to have been given the priesthood and "the first Lamanite who has been admitted a member of any Quorum of the Church."[34]

The conversion of Denna resulted in a wave of optimism about Lamanites in Nauvoo. Phebe W. Woodruff wrote to her husband Wilford in England on May 4, 1840, "There was an Indian, his wife and daughter baptized in Commerce a few days since; they came some hundreds of miles to become acquainted with the work; they believed and embraced joyfully. They said every word of the *Book of Mormon* was true. He was an interpreter to six tribes and he said every one of his brethren would receive it, he knew it would be so." Woodruff published his wife's letter in the *Millennial Star,* a Mormon publication in Liverpool.[35] Soon Denna was honored by being named to the secret Council of Fifty. Denna's wife and one child, a daughter, later died and he married a white woman named Mary Gont.[36] Denna was short and stocky with high cheek-bones, a long nose and wide mouth. He did not wear a beard and his hair was long, becoming tinged with gray toward the end of his life. Denna read and wrote English, did not use tobacco but smoked the bark of a certain kind of willow.[37]

Denna told Brigham Young, when the two met at Winter Quarters, that the United Tribes in Indian Territory, in particular the Delaware tribe living west of Jackson County, Missouri, on the Grasshopper (now Delaware) River in Kansas, were requesting help from the Latter Day Saints. Denna was working to settle a group of Oneidas from Wisconsin on Kansas land. He told Young that the Indians wanted schools, mills, teachers, a blacksmith, a carpenter and farmers. The Delaware chief implied that his people, given assistance, would be receptive to the message of the Mormon missionaries. Besides the Delawares in the area, there were Missouris, Iowas, Sauks, Kickapoos, Kansas, Shawnees, Chippewas, Peorias, Kaskaskias, Pottawatomies, Cherokees and Osages as well as a few remaining members of nine eastern tribes that the federal government had moved to Kansas and Nebraska from New York in 1838.

Brigham Young was well aware that before his death Smith had committed to Cutler "the keys to open the gospel to every Lamanite nation," and he may have felt some compunction to follow Smith's directive. In November 1847 Young sent Cutler and Denna to visit the Kansas Indians and to report back to him. "Let Father Cutler be the man to preside there," he said.[38] Cutler and a few associates visited the Delawares, southwest of Fort Leavenworth. Six weeks later they brought back to Winter Quarters a favorable report and a plan to secure government contracts to build mills and schools in Indian Territory in Nebraska.

While this would give the Mormons an opportunity to preach to the Indians and seek converts, conversion was not Cutler's only goal. He had another more elaborate idea. Cutler urged Young to organize the Indians to be Mormon allies in an attack on Missouri to regain Independence—the New Jerusalem from which the Mormons had been forcibly ejected. Cutler reminded Young that the "House of Israel" was to be built with the assistance of the Lamanites. If Young rejected the idea of an Indian attack on Independence, the Indians could still be organized to defend the Mormons in Nebraska in case the United States militia moved against them.

Cutler's idea was not an especially radical one. Both the Indians and the Mormons had major grievances against the government of the United States. Many Indians sympathized with the Mormons and Chief Oshkosh had wept at the story of the Latter Day Saints's persecution, saying the Mormons "had been treated almost as badly as Indians."

Young was interested in the economic advantages of Cutler's project, but, publicly, he rejected the idea of organizing any Indian military activity. Young clearly understood that a major purpose of the mission to Kansas was not so much to help the Indians, as to get help *from* them. Thousands of destitute Mormons, who had few friends among the officials of the United States, desperately needed support. Alliances with the Indians held the promise of both security and assistance. Though the expedition to the Indians in Kansas was supposedly to build a mill and school, one of its major purposes was to gain Indian allies who would come to the assistance of the Mormons if the need should arise.

Brigham Young realized the wisdom of not putting too much of these plans in writing. "Cutler has been there," Young told the Council. "He has got his verbal order what to do. I don't like to put out a piece of writing."[39] Whatever the specific details of their understanding, it was clearly agreed among Young, Cutler and Denna that they were to undertake an officially-sanctioned mission to the Delaware Indians in Kansas. Both Brigham Young and Cutler knew the dual purpose of the mission to Kansas. With Cutler now assigned to the Indian mission, Young prepared to evacuate Winter Quarters in the spring of 1848. The final move to the Salt Lake Valley was about to get underway. Though he had officially approved of Cutler's mission to the Indians, Young provided no further support for the enterprise, understanding that it was imperative that he remain focused on his primary task of moving the Latter Day Saints to Salt Lake City. Young also may have been unwilling to divert additional scarce resources to the Indian project.

With most of the Mormons on their way to Utah in May of 1848, the community of Winter Quarters was abandoned. The regional headquarters of the church moved out of Omaha Indian Territory back across the river to Kanesville, Iowa (later to be named Council Bluffs). Cutler's position as president of the High Council was dissolved in the move. Rather than staying in Kanesville, where Orson Hyde had assumed the presidency of the High Council, Cutler moved to a nearby Mormon encampment, about 25 miles from Kanesville, called the Big Grove on Silver Creek, in Mills County, Iowa. There he organized his mission to the Indians. Also at Silver Creek were the Whitings, Coxs and others who had moved west from Mt. Pisgah. Alpheus Cutler was named president of the church community with Chauncey Whiting and F. Walter Cox as his counselors.

Cutler was a powerfully-built man with strong opinions and a forceful manner of speaking. His ideas were cloaked in an allegorical, symbolic framework that reflected his magical world view—a world view that reflected the beliefs of many of the people around him. While Cutler was secretive about the real purpose of his Indian mission, others, such as his close associate Bishop Luman Calkins, were not. Calkins said openly that the Kansas mission was a cover for organizing the Indians to attack Missouri and reclaim Independence for the Mormons. According to Calkins, Young's only purpose in leading the Mormons to the west, was to keep them out of harm's way while the Indians and Missourians clashed over the retaking of Jackson County.[40]

The Cutlerites' loose talk of attacking Missouri with an army of Indians did not sit well with Hyde, Young and the leadership still left in Iowa. Young was exerting all of his efforts to get the Mormons safely across the mountains to Utah and he became concerned that the charismatic Cutler was influencing the remaining Mormons to stay in Iowa. Brigham Young wrote Cutler a letter on April 21, 1848, urging him to come west. Cutler replied that he would start for the Great Basin as soon as "circumstances will permit" and signed his letter "your brother in the new and everlasting covenant" which was Mormon code reminding Young that Cutler, too, had been a member of Smith's inner circle, was a high-ranking member of the Council of Fifty, and had demonstrated his loyalty by taking plural wives.

Instead of moving west, however, Cutler was busy fulfilling the commission he believed he had been given by both Smith and Young, which was to gain the support of the Indians for the Mormons while simultaneously proselytizing and running a mission. Cutler was a man who did not like to take orders. He believed that his membership in the Council of Fifty and the secret Anointed Quorum gave him authority over the church nearly equal to that of Young. Alone, acting on his mystical beliefs and remembering his charge to be the builder of temples, Cutler is said to have made the long trip back to Missouri and, as he had done years before in Far West, surreptitiously laid a symbolic cornerstone for the Missouri temple on the Independence Temple Lot.[41]

In performing this lonely task (if, indeed, he did) Alpheus Cutler fulfilled what he believed to be his divine commission to be the builder of God's temples. Cutler had worked as a stonemason on both the Kirtland and Nauvoo temples. At risk to his life, he had laid the cornerstone for the temple in Far West. He could now claim credit for the Independence temple which, he was convinced, would soon be built. The prophet Joseph Smith had said that the Kingdom would be built in Missouri, not in the Great Basin of the West, so Cutler's actions in secretly laying the cornerstone of the temple were to fulfill the prophecy that the "Saints of the Most High" would return to build their kingdom in Independence. In Cutler's view, the trek to the Great Salt Lake was but a detour on the road to their Missouri kingdom. He was certain that Zion was about to be built, if not in the next few years, almost certainly in his lifetime.

Orson Hyde, president of the Church High Council in Kanesville and a college-educated man, was not pleased with Cutler's dramatic and unilateral actions. Where Hyde was rational and logical, Cutler spoke in the esoteric, otherworldly and mystical terms that had been prevalent in the early years of the church. During the lifetime of Joseph Smith this magical world-view was understood and accepted. With the ascendancy of Brigham Young, a more rational and pragmatic approach gradually displaced the reliance on prophecy, mysticism and intuitive, spiritual hunches and feelings. Hyde saw Cutler's work among the Indians as a dangerous diversion from the goal of moving the people west. Young, who saw his control of the Kansas mission slipping away, was able to deny responsibility.

As tensions grew, the Mormons at the Big Grove on Silver Creek, now called "Cutlerites" after their leader, were summoned to appear before the High Council where their differing ideas and conflicts over authority were brought out into the open. Meetings were held and accusations flew back and forth. The result, in 1850, was the "disfellowship" of Cutler and some of his associates. The disfellowshipping of Cutler was sobering, but not as drastic as excommunication would have been as it left the door open for Cutler and his followers to return to the church in good standing.

Unwilling to see a man of Cutler's prominence depart, in October Brigham Young again wrote from Salt Lake City offering Cutler assistance in moving west, a house in Salt Lake City, and the hand of peace and fellowship. Young's offer, however, was dependent on Cutler and his followers moving to Utah. Cutler replied, asking for yet more time that he said he needed to complete his mission to the Indians. Then, he wrote Young, he would go wherever Young asked to him to go. Cutler, in thrall to a mystical view of the world and his role in it, agreed in writing with his leader but subsequently followed his own course.

Assisted by Lewis Denna and other Cutlerites, Cutler continued his mission to the Indians living in Kansas despite the cordial letter from Young, and his disfellowship by Hyde and the High Council at Kanesville. Taking his daughters, Clarissa, who in June 1849 had married Calvin Fletcher, and Emily, who had married Hiram Pratt, Cutler established a mill on the Grasshopper River, about ten miles from the present city of Lawrence, Kansas, near the community of Thompsonville. (Since the law did not recognize plural marriage, there was no need for the women to get divorces.) Other families who accompanied

Cutler included Murdocks, Pattons, Calkins, Taylors and Dennas. As many as twenty adults and thirty children were probably involved in the Indian mission at one time or another.[42] They built four or five cabins and a mill, farmed fifteen acres of land, and gave copies of the *Book of Mormon* to the Delaware Indians. For five long years Cutler, Denna and others traveled back and forth between the Kansas mission and Silver Creek, Iowa. After half a decade of unremitting effort Cutler had to accept the fact that his mission was unsuccessful. He had been unable to purchase land, as it belonged to the Indians; the government Indian agents (many of them missionaries themselves) were uncooperative and hostile; he had gained only a handful of possible converts to the church; and the majority of the Indians, while friendly, showed little interest in taking up the cause of the Latter Day Saints.

In 1852 or early 1853, discouraged and saddened, Cutler abandoned the project. A number of his followers had died in Kansas from cholera, including his two daughters Clarissa and Emily, and one of his plural wives, Harriet Clarinda Miller and her infant child. When he abandoned the mission, Alpheus brought his grandsons, Abraham and Isaac, along with a daughter born to Emily, back with him to his home in Silver Creek. In the opinion of Mormon historian Lori Taylor, although it failed as a mission, Cutler's work in Kansas stands as one of the great efforts to create lasting alliances between Mormons and Indians.[43]

Cutler still showed no signs of making preparations to leave Iowa for Utah, though he had not definitely refused to move to the Salt Lake Valley. Edwin Whiting, Isaac Morley and F. Walter Cox, with their families, already had gone west, but the four younger Whiting brothers and their nephew Edmund Whiting stayed behind. Orson Hyde was becoming more and more concerned. Cutler was a respected church leader and it looked to Hyde as if Cutler's followers were increasing in number. In 1850 he wrote to Brigham Young, "Everything is precarious with us here. Indian Cutlerism in 500 forms would rage like wild fire through this country if the strong arm of power were not upon it all the time."[44] Hyde ordered Cutler to appear before the Mormon High Council in Kanesville to explain why he continued with the Indian mission instead of moving to Utah as instructed. Cutler ignored the order. Accusations flew back and forth between Cutler's supporters at the Big Grove on Silver Creek and the church leadership at Kanesville. Finally, to Hyde's relief, Young eventually agreed with him and exercising his "strong arm of power" on April 20, 1851, he excommunicated (expelled) Alpheus Cutler from the Church of the Latter Day Saints.[45]

Cutler by now had other problems as well. Iowa had become a state and polygamy was against the law. The Iowa officials were so vigorous in prosecuting polygamists that F. Walter Cox was forced to hide two of his wives in an isolated barn (one of whom gave birth to a baby there) until he could spirit them away to Salt Lake City.[46] Unlike Cox, Cutler had no plans to leave Iowa. If he were to avoid prosecution, he would have to do something about his plural wives.

Cutler had entered polygamy because of his unquestioning belief in Joseph Smith. His status as a ranking Mormon leader, as a member of both Smith's inner circle and the Council of Fifty, required conforming to Smith's dictates. Now, however, Smith was dead. Cutler's leadership of the Cutlerites did not depend on his participation in polygamy. Instead, there was a growing sentiment that polygamy had been a mistake and, instead of conferring status, the practice was now arousing concern.

Cutler, under pressure from the civil authorities and, perhaps even with a sense of relief, "put aside" his plural wives. How the surviving five women—Luana Hart Beebe Rockwell, Margaret and Abigail Carr, Sally Cox and Daisey McCall—supported themselves or how they felt about the abrupt termination of their marriages is not known. Although every individual of that generation of Cutlerites had to have been acquainted with Cutler's plural wives, not one recorded their names and fates. Like Abraham sending Hagar into the wilderness, Cutler, with a single pronouncement, cast off the five women he had pledged to support and protect. There is no mention of where the five found the basic necessities of food and shelter, who befriended them or how they managed to survive. Four of Cutler's five plural wives simply disappear from Cutlerite history as if they had never existed. The fate of only one plural wife, Luana Hart Beebe Rockwell, who later married Wheeler Baldwin and then Isaac Perry, is known—though years of her later life are shrouded in secrecy.

Alpheus Cutler, now no longer a member of the Utah faction of the Latter Day Saint Church, told his followers that he, not Brigham Young, was the one destined to lead the institution founded by Joseph Smith. Having Lewis Denna, the most widely known and celebrated Mormon Indian among the Cutlerites, gave Cutler's claims to authority increased credibility. In 1853 with approximately 400 followers scattered over southern Iowa, Cutler founded his own schismatic Mormon movement, calling it "The Church of Jesus Christ." Basing his authority on his membership in the Council of Fifty and through tortured reasoning, Cutler claimed to be the legitimate successor to Joseph Smith.

Cutler explained to his followers that he and six others had been ordained at Nauvoo by Joseph Smith to a special, secret "Anointed Quorum" entrusted with all the "keys" and authority of the Priesthood and
Kingdom.[47] Members of this Quorum were taken through a private endowment ceremony of washings and anointings by Smith which, they believed, bestowed on them the "fullness of the Holy Priesthood which
order constituted the Kingdom."[48] Cutler's claims were impressive to his
followers. Cutler was the seventeenth man to be given his endowments
directly by Joseph Smith on October 12, 1843. Only four of the Twelve
Apostles obtained their endowments before Cutler. Just one month after
receiving his first endowments, Cutler was given his "Second Anointing."
In addition, Cutler had been given the exclusive mission to the Indians.

The murder of Joseph Smith was evidence, Cutler claimed, that the
Gentiles (non-Mormons) had rejected the gospel and that God was therefore repudiating them for "this dispensation of time." Only the "kingdom" remained. Attempts to proselytize among the Gentiles were to
cease. The only people not repudiated by God (and thus eligible for
conversion) were the Jews and the Indians—whom the Mormons considered to be Jews. Cutler was the last of the chosen seven who was still
alive, or had not gone into apostasy, lending legitimacy to his claim to be
the rightful leader of the Mormons.

The most persuasive arguments for Cutler and his followers, in sharp
contrast to the reasoning of the more logical Hyde, were those which encompassed mystical and visionary experiences. As his conclusive argument for claiming leadership of the Latter Day Saint movement Cutler
told his followers that Joseph Smith had advised him that he would have a
vision of "back-to-back-half-moons" as a sign that he was to reorganize
the church.[49] That magical event, Cutler told his people, took place in
1853. Throughout their history the Cutlerites would rely on similar magical and legalistic claims to establish their religious authority.

When Cutler assumed the leadership and prophetic role that had
been Joseph Smith's in Nauvoo, the Cutlerites began to identify the content of their own theology. They believed that the Bible, the *Book of
Mormon,* the *Doctrine and Covenants* (the book containing Smith's revelations) and the Constitution of the United States were divinely inspired
documents. They believed in the approaching end of the world and the
return of Jesus Christ to Zion. In their daily life they professed a belief
in a communal ideal in which their personal possessions would be held
in common through an early Mormon system they called the "Order of

Enoch." Though the Cutlerites now had grave doubts about polygamy, they accepted the rest of Nauvoo temple theology and ordinances such as the "sealing" of individuals and families to each other, baptism for the dead, and the secret rituals that had been performed in the Nauvoo temple. Early Mormons, regardless of the faction to which they gave their allegiance, considered themselves to be a "peculiar people." The followers of Alpheus Cutler took pride in this description and thought of themselves as being *in* the world, but certainly not *of* it.

In 1852 Cutlerite Edmund Fisher purchased a tract of land on Walnut Creek, a branch of the Nishnabotna River, renamed the creek for himself, and moved there. Cutler and about 40 families followed and the town of Manti was founded. It is probable that the Big Grove at Silver Creek did not have enough agricultural land for the growing community. By 1858 the Cutlerites had established three settlements in southern Iowa: the largest at Manti, another at Farm Creek and a third on the Platte River, in Taylor County.

The Cutlerite communities were thriving villages, and, as had been the case in Nauvoo, the church provided both religious ideology and civil government. The Mormon scriptures were the law of the settlements, the High Priests' Quorum acted as the executive and judicial branches of government, administering the law, conducting trials and meting out punishment. Manti, in particular, through its stores and services to the surrounding farmers, developed into a regional farming and commercial center. Located on rich Iowa farmland, the three settlements offered their residents the prospect of future prosperity. Life in the Cutlerite towns was peaceful and relatively untroubled until the summer of 1859 when, from the Cutlerites' point of view, disaster struck.

CHAPTER 5

Invasion of
the Josephites

Disaster arrived at Farm Creek, Iowa, in the persons of elders William W. Blair and Edmund C. Briggs who represented yet another faction of Mormons. These Mormons were Latter Day Saints who had never left the Midwest, who did not accept the authority or the leadership of Brigham Young, and who coalesced around the eldest son of Joseph Smith, Joseph Smith III. They were initially known as the "Josephites," after Joseph the third, and later as the "Reorganization."[50] Blair and Briggs were welcomed by the Farm Creek Cutlerites as religious cousins and when the visiting elders asked for an opportunity to preach and explain the Josephite beliefs, their request was granted. Meetings were held in homes and barns. The visitors were persuasive and by September 1859, Blair and Briggs had succeeded in converting almost all the Farm Creek Cutlerites to the Josephite organization. Among their converts were William H. Kelley and his brother Edmund L. Kelley who later became prominent leaders of the Reorganized Church.

Encouraged by their success at Farm Creek, the elders moved on to Manti where again they were greeted with wary courtesy. Here the former brothers in the faith preached in the Cutlerite church and by 1863 succeeded in converting twenty-two, including not only Alpheus Cutler's son and First Counselor Thaddeus and his wife, but Cutler's second wife, Luana Hart Beebe Rockwell Cutler, and her daughter Olive. In October, Joseph Smith III, who remembered Cutler from Smith's boyhood days in Nauvoo, came to Manti to visit with the old man. Joseph Smith III was looking forward to his visit with a man whom he had known and admired as a boy, but the meeting went badly.

As Smith wrote about the visit:

"He [Cutler] was a man of large and very powerful frame, more than six feet in height and broad in proportion. He had become partially paralyzed, had fleshened up a great deal, and was weighing something like three hundred pounds. Dressed in a garment made of common shirting, with a turned-down collar, he sat in a large chair firmly fixed on a raised platform, a blanket thrown over his knees. His hands, face, beard and the whole front of his shirt were covered with tobacco stains, and close beside the chair was a common milk pan filled with old tobacco quids and spittle, a very unpleasant sight. . . . He could not speak intelligibly. He would try and then would stop, get very red in the face, tears would well up in his eyes, and he would simply blubber like a crying child. I sat with him for about an hour, trying to converse with him, but with sorry results, and the whole experience was very distressing and painful for me."[51]

There is a possibility that Alpheus Cutler may have been illiterate or semi-literate. In 1998 Frank and Norma Tucker, in an attempt to authenticate a signature in a bible believed to be Cutler's, visited the county seat in Iowa where the deeds to Cutler's land at Manti were recorded. To their surprise, they found that the deeds had been signed, not with Cutler's signature, but with an "X." Iris Harris, whose husband is a descendant of Cutler, also looked up deeds and records and found an "X" between the words "Alpheus" and "Cutler." Above the "X" someone had written "His mark."[52] According to archivist Barbara Bernauer, the Community of Christ church archive contains only one letter from Cutler, written to Zenos H. Gurley on January 29, 1856. At the bottom of the letter is the word "copy," the initials "CD" and the signature "Alpheus Cutler." The signature is in the same handwriting as the body of the letter.[53]

Because the Cutlerites, as a group, were highly literate, wrote well and at considerable length, and all were people devoted to "The Word," it is hard to believe that their founder was illiterate. Cutler's sketches guided the construction of the Nauvoo Temple and he corresponded with Indian Agent Thomas H. Harvey while president of the Mormon High Council at Winter Quarters—though it is not known who actually wrote the letters. The only known picture believed to be of Cutler, a daguerreotype taken as a young man, shows him holding a book.[54] It is possible that Cutler's illness in later life (possibly kidney failure or "dropsy") made it difficult for him to write or sign his name.

At the end of his life Alpheus Cutler may have regretted his break with Brigham Young. In the early 1860s Abraham Kimball, Cutler's teenage grandson by his daughter Clarissa, left Manti to seek out his father, Heber C. Kimball, in Utah. After staying with Kimball for several months, Abraham returned to Manti to visit with his grandfather. He recorded the visit in his journal:

> "He asked me if I had seen my father, Heber C. Kimball. I told him I had. He replied that he was glad of it. He also asked if I had been baptized and I told him I had. He again replied that he was glad of it. He next asked me if I had received my endowments, and when I informed him that I had he seemed pleased. He then said, 'I have suffered you to be prejudiced to the extent that you were, and it is now my duty to remove the same. . . . I know that Joseph Smith was a prophet of God, and I know that Brigham Young is his legal successor, and I always did know it. But the trouble with me was I wanted to lead, and I could not be led. I have run my race and sealed my doom, and I know what I have got to meet. . . . One favor I ask of you, namely that you will not divulge this confession to those whom I lead while I live.'"[55]

Alpheus Cutler's deteriorating physical condition undoubtedly was a help to the Josephite elders in their attempts to gain converts. Another factor leading to the Josephite success may have been the Cutlerites' repeated attempts to form a communal society in which members were expected to turn over their personal property and real estate to the church. By 1857 many of the Cutlerites had deeded their homes to the church, though the fact that some families participated in what they called " the Oneness or the Order of Enoch" while others did not, caused continued friction in the community. In 1863, in an effort to encourage the donation of property, an entire week was set aside for church meetings. The days were to be filled with preaching, praying and manifesting "the gifts"—during which time individuals would speak in tongues and utter prophesies.

The climax of the week was to be the dedication and donation of their private property to the church. Women were told to prepare enough food for a week of feasting, men were to cut wood for fires and reduce their daily chores to a minimum. The week of church services went off as planned but at the conclusion few followed through with the desired contributions. As Isaac Whiting later remarked of the occasion, "They met in Manti, had a little feast and dedicated all things to the Lord; then they didn't put it in and we had to come to this cold country."[56]

Isaac Whiting's statement is revealing and touches on one of the basic appeals of Mormonism, the prospect of receiving an "inheritance in Zion." An "inheritance" was understood to be land and property, essential components of a literal Kingdom of God on earth. "Inheritances" were promised to faithful believers and were to be provided by the church through a system of property redistribution. To the landless poor, this was a powerful incentive to remain faithful to the church.

Within a short time of the founding of Manti, the fertile land around the town was occupied and there was little more available for the expanding Cutlerite population. Non-Mormons solved this perennial land shortage problem by moving further west. Mormons, however, looked to a Mormon solution—the provision of "inheritances" through the communal pooling of land and property. As Isaac Whiting indicates, few of the Cutlerite property owners actually followed through on the requirement that they dedicate their property to the Lord and he implies that this failure to hand over land and buildings to the church precipitated the departure of the members to Minnesota. The Josephites made no communal property requirements of their members, and instead "spiritualized" the concept of an inheritance in Zion, which, for many, was a powerful inducement to shift allegiances.

Another factor that aided Josephite conversions was the issue of polygamy, a source of increasing concern to the Cutlerites. That memories of polygamy had become a source of shame among the Cutlerites is revealed by the taunts the Cutlerite children flung at young Abraham and Isaac, the sons of Cutler's daughters, Clarissa and Emily, and Heber C. Kimball. Abraham wrote of his childhood experience in Manti, "Uncle Thaddeus (Cutler's son) neglected to provide us suitable clothing and food and the church assisted in our care. My brother and I were repeatedly ill-treated and were continually persecuted and called names for being polygamist children. In order to tantalize us, they would call us 'bastards' and 'Brigham Heber.' No children were worse frightened by stories about the Mormons . . . and we grew up with the most bitter prejudice and intense hatred in our hearts toward all who bore that name."[57]

Joseph Smith III insisted, despite overwhelming evidence to the contrary, that his father had not been involved in polygamy and, instead, that it was Brigham Young who instigated the practice in Utah. The issue of Smith's polygamy was to haunt Joseph Smith III for all of his life and he continually approached it from a spiritual or emotional viewpoint, refusing to give credence to the testimony of those who knew his father in Nauvoo. Joseph Smith III's position may have been a misguided effort to protect his parents or a desperate attempt to salvage the organization his father had established. In his steadfast denials Smith was acting on a common Victorian premise that a firm and unwavering declaration would somehow alter the facts. Whatever his reasoning, Joseph Smith III insisted that his father had not been involved in nor was he the instigator of Mormon polygamy. By accepting young Smith's position on polygamy (though the Cutlerites certainly knew differently) and joining the Josephites, the Cutlerites were able to erase an enormous embarrassment from their past.

The defection of so many to the Josephites had a devastating effect on the Cutlerites. Many of the converts were relatives and close friends, people with whom they had shared the suffering of the journey across Iowa and the disastrous failure of the mission to the Indians in Kansas. Now, to their sorrow, they saw these friends abandoning the faith. The issues dividing the two groups were "what is true" and "who has the priesthood authority and keys?" As recriminations and rumors flew from house to house and from neighbor to neighbor in the wake of the conversions to the Josephites, some of the Cutlerites lapsed into old patterns of belief and began accusing the others of witchcraft. The conversions to the Josephites, they said, did not take place because of differences in interpretation of religious authority, but because evil spells had been cast over the unsuspecting.

When a young Cutlerite woman fell ill and failed to respond to her family's faith, prayers and home doctoring, the suspicion grew that she had fallen under a spell, cast by a former Cutlerite who had joined the Josephites. A ritual was chosen to send the illness back to the individual who was supposed to have cast the spell. In the night following the magic incantations, the fever of the sick woman broke, she began to recover, and another woman, a former Cutlerite who had converted to the Josephites, suddenly became ill. To the believers in witchcraft, this was powerful confirmation of the identity of the troublesome witch.

By reverting in a time of crisis to old superstitions the Cutlerites were resurrecting a body of esoteric, magical beliefs that still claimed their allegiance. However, not everyone looked to witchcraft for an explanation of events. Francis Lewis Whiting was critical of the rumors and explained to his daughter Emma that the beliefs in witchcraft "had been handed down in some families from generation to generation, ever since the early settling of the colonies when they used to burn the witches at Salem."[58]

Alpheus Cutler died on June 10, 1864,[59] and his death cast his remaining followers into turmoil. As had been the case with Joseph Smith, no one had been designated to assume leadership of the church. Cutler's son, Thaddeus Cutler, the First Counselor and presumed heir to the mantle of leadership, had defected to the Josephites. At the last High Council meeting called by Cutler in Manti, the ailing leader had named twelve men who would be "the stem that would hold the priesthood." In descending order the twelve men were Almon Whiting, Frank Pratt, Wheeler Baldwin, Squire Eggleston, Calvin Beebe, Elisha Whiting (he may have been a grandson of the Elisha who had died at Mt. Pisgah), Amos Cox, Marcus Shaw, William Topham, Nicholas Taylor, L.D. Sperry and S. J. Whiting.[60]

In the ensuing struggle to select a leader, Cutler's list was apparently disregarded. After lengthy and prayerful discussion the leader's place was awarded "in a temporary capacity only" to the elderly Charles Sperry.[61] As Second Counselor the Council named Chauncey Whiting, a quiet, unassuming man who seemed the opposite of the assertive and dynamic Cutler. Unable to reach a definitive decision on leadership, by choosing Sperry and Whiting the Cutlerites postponed the selection of a permanent leader. Past decisions had been made for them by a charismatic leader who based his actions on the magical, otherworldly premises of Mormonism. Without the leadership of a dynamic individual like Cutler, it was difficult for them to make binding decisions.

Near the end of his life, after seeing his flock decimated by the Josephites, Alpheus Cutler had urged his followers to once again abandon their villages and seek out a place of safety for the church in a more remote region of America where they could practice their religion undisturbed and unchallenged. To the Cutlerites, the modern world was perceived to be evil, threatening and dangerous. Rather than seek an understanding and accommodation to secular society, it was better that the church should flee. The Cutlerites feared change and longed to recreate an Eden they believed existed in the past. Before his death Cutler told his followers that they would find the location for the church in a grassy area between two lakes in the new state of Minnesota. That would be their new Eden.

Other Cutlerite leaders supported Cutler's prophecy. Sylvester Whiting reported that "Father [Pliny] Fisher told us in the gift of tongues that the time would soon come that we could live on wheels and to take care of our wagon covers for we would need them, and also we would go to a place of many waters. Mrs. Sherman, by the gift of tongues, said the Lord always led his people out of danger and when we see danger on all sides but one, we should flee out."[62] As they debated what to do after Cutler's death, this prediction seemed to offer an escape. The solution it offered was migration, flight from all the uncertainty that threatened them, especially from the evangelizing Josephites. America, with its limitless supply of land, would again provide a refuge for God's Chosen People as they awaited the call to return to Zion for Christ's Second Coming.

Though their previous wanderings had taken them to northern Missouri, Illinois and now western Iowa, these millennialists—staunch believers in the coming end of the world—maintained a firm belief in Smith's prophecy that Zion would soon be built in Independence, Missouri. As a result, few of them planned to make permanent homes in Iowa. This belief was one of the reasons they had been reluctant to travel to the inter-mountain West, which would have put them hundreds of miles farther away from Independence, Missouri. When he visited Manti Joseph Smith III observed, with some astonishment, that the Cutlerites "had become imbued with the idea that God would soon command them to gather to Zion. So strong was this belief among them that they had made ready wagons, tents and other appurtenances of nomadic life and were ready, at a moment's notice, to throw their household goods into the vehicles and start for Independence."[63] The earliest belief of Mormonism, the belief that had sustained them through the violence of mobs, loss of their homes and flight from state to state was their conviction that the end of the world was near and, if they were faithful, they would witness the return of their Lord and Savior to the land of Zion in Independence, Jackson County, Missouri.

Events on the national scene, in particular the Civil War, were also disturbing to the Cutlerites. From time to time raiders from Missouri and Kansas ventured into Iowa destroying property and attacking those who opposed them. On one such raid a party of soldiers cut down the handmade "peace" flag that flew for several years at Manti.

Soldiers passing through their community were disturbing to the adults but the young people found the visits exciting. Emma Whiting

Anderson remembered that her teacher at the Manti School, James R. Badham, would dismiss classes when a company of soldiers marched down the main street. "He knew we could never keep our eyes on our studies when a regiment of soldiers were tramping by—or a company of cavalry with their fifes and drums sounding so musically and their flags waving so beautifully through the air."[64] Though the Cutlerites were abolitionists and a few of the men fought with the Union armies or enlisted in the Iowa Border Guard, most felt little obligation to the government that, in former years, had failed to protect them.

News of the war was filtered through the Cutlerites' unwavering belief in the prophecies of Joseph Smith. Smith had issued a "revelation" about the coming conflict between the states that the Cutlerites interpreted to mean that the South, rather than the North, would prevail. Following a southern victory, according to the Cutlerites' reasoning, the Indians would overrun the western states in a wild rampage killing all the whites in fulfillment of a passage from the *Book of Mormon* to the effect that the "Lamanites (Indians) shall be among them as a lion among a flock of sheep." In the Cutlerite interpretation, the flock of sheep represented the American people.

The Cutlerites often engaged in tortured theological reasoning. To explain the reason for their move to Minnesota, one of the pioneers enumerated the complicated mental steps that led to their decision. "This we verily believed was at hand, but that we, as the Church of Jesus Christ, could find deliverance with the remnant. Add to this another Scripture, 'Enter ye into thy chamber and shut the doors about thee until the indignation of the Lord be overpast.' Among the Indians would be the 'chamber.' Remembering the words, 'In Zion and in Jerusalem and in the remnant shall be places of deliverance,' it was for that purpose we went to the North, to the Chippewa Indians."[65]

In ways that seem excruciatingly painful, the Cutlerites searched the scriptures for guidance, reading into obscure passages the messages they wanted to hear. As a group, they yearned for refuge, for security, for a place to which they could flee from the modern world and all of its strangeness and temptations. The years of persecution had made the Cutlerites fearful, certain that dark clouds of calamity were about to descend upon them like summer storms. Based upon their past and these reasons the Cutlerites made their crucial decision to flee to the north for safety.

Not all of the Cutlerites thought leaving Manti was a good idea. At an August 1864 meeting of the High Council in Manti, Edmund Fisher, a wealthy member who had purchased the land for the town, opposed the move. Chauncey Whiting and his brothers favored it. It is probable that those who sought to practice "the Oneness" were in favor of going while those who had a larger economic stake in Manti wanted to stay where they were. The discussions ranged over themes of religious mysticism and church leadership, family relationships, the threats of war and the Cutlerites' mission to the Indians. Despite the tragic failure of their mission to the Indians in Kansas, they still believed that one of their primary religious duties was to convert the Lamanites. "The main reason for our people going north into Minnesota," Chauncey Whiting later wrote to an Indian friend, "was to share with your people what we consider the most precious thing in our lives, our religion. Our people felt that the time had come to take the gospel to the House of Israel, of which the Indians are a part. Also, our people wanted to worship their religion unmolested and be further removed from the war and bloodshed going on in Missouri."[66]

In the back of the Cutlerites' minds was the unspoken realization that if they stayed in Manti they risked further encounters with the Josephites, encounters that threatened the existence of their church. Already almost half of the four to five hundred members of Cutler's church had joined the Josephites. Moving away from their enemies had become the habitual Mormon response to trouble of any kind. After more than three decades, it had become automatic. To many Cutlerites it was apparent that drastic action was called for once again if the church were to survive.

The conflict over who should be Cutler's successor as leader of the Cutlerites also divided the church between those who wanted to stay in Iowa, and those who believed security would be found by leaving. Eventually a compromise was reached. On September 17, 1864, the Cutlerite Church High Council voted unanimously to send a few young families to Minnesota to seek a new location "that we might have a place of safety for a season to flee unto, yet leaving the matter in shape that we could go elsewhere as the Lord should direct."[67] As sociologist of religion Danny Jorgensen noted, "Authorization of an expedition to explore Minnesota represented an implicit compromise, satisfying those that wanted to move and allowing others additional time to make a final decision."[68] Chauncey Whiting later explained, "Some divisions arose relative to the rights of authority; the church became measurably broken up, so much so that those who were still desirous of continuing the principles adopted and also keeping up the organization, deemed it advisable

to hunt a new location for the church. Also, receiving some manifestations and encouragements through the gifts of the spirit so to do . . . led
to our removal to this land."[69] Whiting repeatedly talked around problems. The "principles adopted" he referred to undoubtedly were the difficulties encountered in convincing members to deed their property over
to the church.

Lewis Denna, an Oneida chief, was a prominent member of the
Cutlerite High Council, and he had been a member of the Council of
Fifty in Nauvoo. As early as March 1845, while still in Nauvoo, the
Council of Fifty had talked of sending Denna with a company of men
to find a home in the West "where the Saints can dwell in peace and
health and where they can erect the ensign and standard of liberty for
the nations, and live by the laws of God without being oppressed and
mobbed under a tyrannical government without protection from the
laws."[70] Denna had long wanted to find land where the more accultur-
ated members of his Oneida tribe could settle. Denna was already planning to go north in search of land for his Indian people. Therefore he
was named to head the scouting party to search for the northern land between two lakes that Cutler saw in his vision.

The selection of Denna to head the scouting party was significant.
None of the Cutlerites had ever been to Minnesota and the state was a
large one with more than fifteen thousand lakes. How could they hope to
find the land between two lakes that Cutler had seen in his vision?
Though he was not one of the religious leaders of the Cutlerites Denna
was named to head the scouting party because he, alone of all the Cutlerites, had a plan for how they should proceed. Denna's plan was to go
northeast into Minnesota in search of a man he may have known personally but certainly knew by reputation. That man was the Rev. John
Johnson Enmegahbowh, an Odawa Indian who had been ordained a
Deacon in the Episcopal Church in 1859. (Enmegahbowh, whose name
meant "he who stands before his people," would later become the first
American Indian to be ordained an Episcopal priest.) Denna was originally from Wisconsin, had interpreted for Indian treaties in the region,
and Denna and Enmegahbowh had been in the Minnesota-Wisconsin
territory at the same time. Denna knew that Enmegahbowh was living
in Crow Wing, Minnesota, so when the scouting party left Manti, Denna
led it directly toward Crow Wing where he planned to ask Enmegahbowh's advice on where the Cutlerites should settle.

Enmegahbowh was first converted to Methodism in his early teens.
He had Ojibwe relatives and his family lived in an Ojibwe village in On-

Reverend John Johnson Enmegahbowh, 1872.
Photograph by Hoard and Tenney.

tario. The Methodists and Episcopalians employed Indian clergy who studied in the Methodist apprentice program, working first as interpreters at mission stations and eventually as missionaries. In 1834 Enmegahbowh agreed to serve as an interpreter at a mission in the United States. By 1837 he was in Red Wing assisting and interpreting for a Swiss Presbyterian missionary, Samuel Francis Delton. Like the Cutlerites, Delton believed he had a special calling to convert the Indians of North America and he and a companion went to the Indian community at Red Wing to begin the work. The mission was unsuccessful, as the Indians had little interest in being converted to the Swiss Presbyterian God. When Delton eventually departed, Enmegahbowh moved further north in Minnesota where he married Biwabikogijigokwe or Iron Sky Woman, the niece of two of the most influential Ojibwe leaders, Hole-in-the-Day the Elder and Strong Ground.

Ojibwe tribal governance was organized along two parallel lines. The acknowledged chiefs were the civil leaders, men like Enmegahbowh, who were respected, deliberative and experienced village elders. These men, in general, advocated accommodation with the invading Americans. Their rivals were the warriors, younger men generally under the age of 40, who urged armed resistance. The civil leaders were deeply respected and had the allegiance of the majority of the Ojibwe people. They epitomized the values and standards of behavior most Ojibwe sought to live by. In the crisis brought on by the loss of their land to the Americans the Ojibwe struggled to maintain the proper division of responsibilities between the age-based hierarchy of civil leadership and the appropriate role in their society for the warriors.[71]

The political appeal of the warriors grew in the mid-1830s with the arrival of the early missionaries and the first land cession treaty in 1837. Over the next two decades the civil leaders of the Ojibwe signed several treaties ceding away millions of acres of their land. After each treaty more Americans moved into Minnesota where their farming, mining and lumbering activities seriously disturbed the ecosystems on which the Ojibwe relied for their subsistence. Under the terms of the treaty of 1855 (which many Indians opposed), the Ojibwe in the central and western part of the state ceded the bulk of their remaining land base to the Americans. The result was an immediate collapse of the Ojibwe standard of living and a plunge of Indian people into poverty.

When the warriors argued that their survival depended on armed resistance to the Americans, many Ojibwe agreed with them. The situation was complicated. While the Ojibwe did not welcome or wish to accept the political dominance of the warriors they did recognize their legitimacy as warriors. The bitter political division between the Ojibwe civil leaders and the warriors came to a head in 1862 with the outbreak of hostilities between the Sioux and the American settlers in what became known as the Sioux Uprising. As many as 500 white settlers were reportedly killed or injured in coordinated Indian attacks.

While in charge of the Episcopal mission at Gull Lake, Enmegahbowh learned that the Ojibwe chief Hole-in-the-Day the Younger, a leader of the warrior faction, was secretly planning to join his traditional enemy, the Sioux chief Little Crow, in the Sioux Uprising. As a civil leader Enmegahbowh opposed Hole-in-the-Day's actions. As Enmegahbowh described those days:

> "In 1862, when the Sioux nation raised their arms against their friends, the whites, the massacre began in earnest, killing both women and children. I was watching my people how it would affect them. Sure enough, in a few days I heard that Hole-in-the-Day had received a secret message from the Sioux war chief, Little Crow, though between them deadly hatred and warfare had been carried on for ages past. I thought Hole-in-the-Day would not accept it. But he had secretly sent messen-

gers to the interior country telling his people to take up arms to aid the Sioux nation who were massacring hundreds upon hundreds of the whites."

Little Crow had chosen a propitious time to attack. Many of the soldiers who manned the forts had been sent east to aid the Union forces in the Civil War and some of the forts were nearly empty of defenders. Enmegahbowh knew a crisis had been reached when his village at Gull Lake filled with warriors and drumming went on day and night. Hole-in-the-Day the Younger invited Enmegahbowh into his wigwam and told him of his plan to attack the white settlements. "Come, my fellow warriors, let us go forth to war," Hole-in-the-Day entreated. "For we are a dying people anyhow. We might as well hasten the day of our sufferings and death."

Enmegahbowh advised against it. "If you knew as much as I know of the greatness and power of the whites against whom you are expected to fight, you would not entertain the idea to thus strike against heavy rocks. You may kill a few in the beginning, but in the end you will all be swept away from the face of the earth and annihilated forever. I love you all. I see and know just exactly how the war will terminate. As a friend who loves you, I would ask you all as wise men to think and well consider whether your present plan is to your salvation or death. Think ye well." Hole-in-the-Day the Younger agreed with Enmegahbowh's assessment of the Indians' fate but added, "The plan has already come into its maturity. I am not able to control it."[72]

The white missionaries and traders fled from Gull Lake. When Enmegahbowh heard that the Indians were about to attack the agency at Crow Wing, he yoked up his oxen, took his wife and children and left by night to warn the people at Crow Wing. He had traveled about half the distance to the village when he was overtaken by four of Little Crow's warriors. They made him turn around and return to Gull Lake. Though Enmegahbowh was now a prisoner in his own home, Hole-in-the-Day the Younger visited him and promised that no harm would come to him.

A few days later another Ojibwe chief, Crossing Sky of Rabbit Lake, came to Enmegahbowh's house in the middle of the night and advised him to flee. "Hole-in-the-Day is going to march with his warriors to the Agency in two days from today and massacre all the whites. When he returns he will be ugly and spare no one whom he knows has sympathy with the whites."

Enmegahbowh and his wife determined to warn the people at Crow Wing and at Fort Ripley. With William Superior, a white man, and both of their families, Enmegahbowh loaded two canoes and slipped down the Gull River under cover of night. They had to wade part of the way, towing their canoes, as the river was low. They walked all night, arriving at Fort Ripley around two in the afternoon. Two of Enmegahbowh's children later became ill and died from exposure after the night's flight. When Hole-in-the-Day later launched his attack against the fort, he found the whites prepared and no one was killed. As a result of his friendship with the white settlers, Enmegahbowh's own home at Gull Lake was burned down and his church destroyed.

Enmegahbowh had come to the conclusion that the only hope for the survival of Indian people was for them to become Christian and abandon their traditional hunting and gathering lifestyle for the plough farming practices urged on them by the missionaries and Indian agents. The missionaries had convinced many Indian leaders that their program of "Christ and the plough" was the only form of economic organization that could support genuinely "civilized" human life. The Ojibwe had always maintained small vegetable gardens but these had been kept by the women, linked conceptually to women's unique reproductive abilities. Agriculture, as such, was believed by the Indians to be women's work. Most Indian women planted crops of corn, beans, squash and—after they were introduced by the fur traders—potatoes and turnips. The gardens were given minimal attention during the summer. In the fall the women harvested their crops and stored them in earthen pits to be used during lean periods in the spring when food was scarce.[73]

A shift from hunting to large-scale plough agriculture represented a cultural change of enormous magnitude for the Indians. Nevertheless, Enmegahbowh believed it could be done. The village of his birth in Canada had been a pitiable collection of destitute, broken people, stricken with disease and addicted to alcohol. Conversion to Methodism had dramatically improved their lives. Social disintegration was halted. Men took responsibility for cultivation and animal husbandry and adopted aspects of the European agricultural tradition. The men learned such skills as carpentry and bricklaying, constructed their own homes and barns, and formed self-supporting, autonomous communities. The villages became so successful that they established a school that Enmegahbowh attended for part of his early life.[74]

Because of his youthful experience, Enmegahbowh had a clear un-

derstanding of the bleak future faced by native peoples when white settlers came into the country. After the 1862 Sioux Uprising he accepted
the fact that the Indians had no choice but to accede to the government's
demands that they move onto reservations, abandon the life they had
lived for untold centuries and become corn and wheat farmers. Whites
were encroaching on Indian land, selling whiskey, taking timber, and
disrupting their lifestyle. Under pressure from the U.S. government the
chiefs of several Ojibwe bands, including the one at Gull Lake, had
signed a treaty in 1855 giving up most of north central Minnesota. The
Indians were allowed to remain in their villages and were promised annual payments. Few of the payments were ever made and by the 1860s
the Indians had become desperate. Money owed to the Ojibwe was going
into the pockets of government agents and traders. Bounty hunters were
enlisting young Ojibwe men to fight in place of white soldiers in the
Civil War.

Enmegahbowh had firm friendships and cordial working relationships with the Ojibwe leaders, many of whom would eventually lead
their people to the White Earth Reservation. Because of his early experience with community revitalization he could speak compellingly about
Ojibwe problems and offer a solution that seemed possible. Because
there were few alternatives, many Ojibwe leaders supported Enmegahbowh's concept of agrarian, self-sufficient, Christian villages. In a letter
written to a clergyman friend in the East Enmegahbowh related a conversation he had with an Ojibwe chief and colleague, Nabunashkong.

"In the summer of 1861," he wrote, " I invited him to have a little
talk about his people and their condition generally. I ask him, 'Nabunashkong, tell me plainly, and tell me as a friend, what is your hope for
your people? You know as a nation we are fast sinking. Your country
and your hiding places tell you, sooner or later you will in one day be
swept away from the face of the earth. And besides, a strong pressure is
now upon our people. This great continent will be peopled by a higher
class of nation—far stronger and more powerful than our chiefs and
warriors were. And this great and mighty movement of the Palefaces
has already taken place and has gone forward like some great tidal wave,
sweeping through to our beloved land and country. Now, Nabunashkong, tell me plainly, what is your future hope for our people?'"

Nabunashkong's reply reflected Enmegahbowh's pessimism but
also a determination to die fighting for a losing cause. "I love and pity
my poor people," he told Enmegahbowh. "I seek their interest. I have

made no provision for them but this war-club and the scalping knife. I have defended them day and night. Why? Because I love them. I will follow the brave steps of my fathers and will seal my blood for my country and people."

This answer was not what Enmegahbowh wanted to hear and he replied, "But, my friend, there is a far better and more efficient way to defend your people, without your war-club and scalping knife. It is to have [a] Missionary to tell you about the Great Spirit, to teach you how to worship Him. . . ." Enmegahbowh's argument had a strong effect on Nabunashkong who eventually became convinced that moving to a reservation and adopting an agrarian life style was a more reasonable choice than fighting. "To resist their [the Indians] removal was like throwing a stone against a rock, it would bounce back," Enmegahbowh insisted. Nabunashkong's decision to lead his people to the recently established White Earth Reservation was a controversial one and could have led to violence. As Enmegahbowh related the event, Nabunashkong asked him one last time if he should move to the White Earth Reservation and Enmegahbowh replied, "Arise and go; that was the best thing his people can do."

Nabunashkong demonstrated remarkable courage in defying the warrior group in his band. As Enmegahbowh explained, "The day was named when his band and others should start and bid goodbye to their beloved land and country. Hole-in-the-Day and a few of his warriors got ready to stop the movement and made war dances before Chief Tuttle (Nabunashkong's English name) and threatened that the first man whoever moved one step toward the new country was a dead man. The day arrived when all should move. Tuttle had put on all his war costume, with feathers waving on his head, and led the moving caravan—four hundred in number. Hole-in-the-Day, with his warriors, had already posted on the road where Tuttle should pass. Tuttle, when he saw them, walked with firm steps before them and passed unmolested. And when this was over, his people almost kissed him and said, 'Our leader! Our leader!' and his people loved him more and more."[75]

This was the background and experience of the man Denna and his party were seeking out for advice on finding their land between two lakes. Denna had information that Enmegahbowh lived at Crow Wing, Minnesota, so it was there that he directed the Cutlerites.

CHAPTER 6

Flight to the Wilderness

Cutlerites called the group going north with Lewis Denna "the committee" or the "scouting party." Despite the arduous nature of the trip the party contained women and young children. Accompanying Denna were Francis Lewis and Ann Jeanette Whiting and their five children (Emma, eleven-years-old, Lucia, nine, Ella, seven, Arthur, four, and infant May); Francis Lewis's older brother Sylvester Whiting, his wife Rebecca and their three children (Almon, Eugene and George); Francis's brother-in-law Jesse Burdick, his wife Nan and small son Cary; Marcus and Sarah Shaw with their two children Arvilla and Clark. Isaac Whiting and the remaining members of the party would leave a few months later. The caravan of covered wagons left Manti on September 29, 1864. After a late start they reached Four Mile Creek, a familiar stopping point.

Eleven-year-old Emma happily observed that when they started out there was ample food because the women had been baking and preparing for the journey. Dinner that first evening was quickly prepared and when it was over the children ran to the nearby creek to play, certain that their nightly dishwashing chore would be suspended during the trip. The children had been washing dishes for weeks while their mother baked and sewed in preparation for the trip. However they had no sooner arrived at the stream when they were called back to do their chores, Emma to wash and Lucia to dry the dishes, while their mother arranged the family beds for the night.

The wagon had been fitted with boards projecting out from the top of the box over the wheels so that all seven members of the family could sleep lying cross ways over the wagon. The beds covered the entire length of the wagon while underneath were stored trunks, boxes, and bundles and, at the back, the family cook stove. During the day, half of

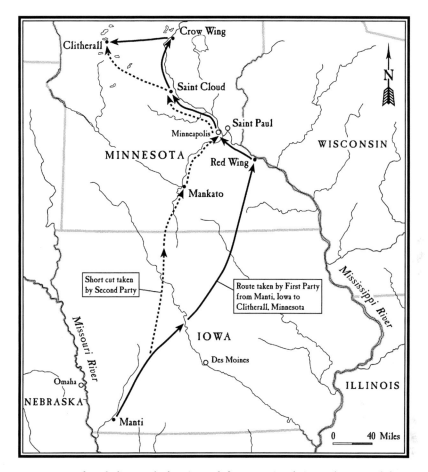

Two groups of Cutlerlites made the trip north from Manti to their new home at Clither-all, Minnesota. The first party left Iowa in September, 1864. The second group began their journey from Manti to Minnesota in January, 1865.

the slats had to be removed and the bedding piled on top of the other half to allow space in the front of the wagon for the spring seat and the dinner box.

After the dishes had been washed that first night on the road the children were sent to bed early in the rear of the wagon. As she was climbing into her bed Emma heard the sounds of other wagons arriving and realized that friends from Manti had come to hold a last service with their departing church members. She drifted off to sleep to the singing of hymns and the murmurs of prayers as the Cutlerites asked the blessings of heaven on the travelers.

Few of the travelers had any doubts that they would be directed by God in their journey. Just how that direction would be manifested worried Sylvester Whiting who confessed to having felt "somewhat tried in our feelings when we started." During the evening church service at the camp Francis Lewis Whiting was appointed president of the company, evidence that Denna's role was that of guide and not overall leader. Sylvester Whiting reported that "Mrs. Sherman spoke in tongues and gave us further instruction." These supernatural manifestations were accepted by the group as divine guidance and Whiting went to bed in his wagon that night content that "we proved the Lord to be with us at the very start of the move." Rational decision-making and a dependence on mystical feelings combined to form the unlikely road map that the Cutlerites would follow to Minnesota and their pioneering settlement in Otter Tail County.

The store of food the women had prepared before leaving Manti was soon exhausted. Before long they were eating a meager diet of bread and fried pork fat. Since they were traveling through settled country with frequent villages and farms where provisions could be purchased, it is apparent that the travelers were conserving what little money they had. One day Ann Jeanette told her husband, Francis Lewis Whiting, that she could not feed the children more pork fat and bread— they had to have beans. After she had picked over her store of dried beans she convinced Whiting to stop at a farmhouse for water in which to soak the beans in a milk can. The night was a stormy one and the travelers were late in finding a campground. Finally a fire was built and the beans put on to cook. Emma and her brother and sisters, tired and hungry, watched as the other members of the party finished their meals and prepared for bed. Ann Jeanette made up her children's beds on the projecting slats, and when it began to rain, ordered them into the wagon. "We dropped our shoes down in the front of the wagon and climbed to our places on the bed and there we sat, waiting for those precious beans. Finally they were cooked and tin plates with a tin basin of soup and bread were passed to each one of us. I have never forgotten how good that bean soup and bread tasted. We didn't have to do dishes that night but undressed and curled down on our pillows and went to sleep perfectly happy."[76]

Stormy weather, muddy roads and a constant shortage of food made travel difficult. One rainy Saturday the travelers were out of bread and other provisions and did not come to a town until after dark. Once in the village they were able to buy hay and oats for their animals and a piece of beef for their dinner. A man in the feed store took a lantern and guided the group to a vacant house on the edge of town where they could get out of the rain and stay for the night. The men quickly carried one of the cook stoves into the house, and, as the house was in some woods, they were able to find fuel for a fire. Emma long remembered the supper of fried steak, potatoes and biscuits they shared that night. The Whiting family slept on the floor of the vacant house, because of the rain, while the smaller families slept in their wagons. The next morning the women "set sponge" for bread while the children spent the day reading from their readers and primers.

On October 21st the travelers awoke from a night of camping near Red Wing, Minnesota, to find the ground covered with snow. They had traveled approximately 340 miles over muddy roads in nineteen days— taking Sundays off to observe the Sabbath. Iowa, which had a population in 1860 of 674,913, provided a choice of routes and frequent towns and farms from which to purchase supplies. Once they crossed into Minnesota, their choices were more limited as the population of the entire state was only 172,023 with most of it located in villages along the Mississippi River. Their route probably took them north of Des Moines, passing through Mason City, Iowa, and Austin, Minnesota, before reaching Red Wing. Though they had hoped to arrive in Crow Wing before the winter set in, the men decided they could go no further until spring, so they rented rooms for the winter. Red Wing had been established on land deeded by the Indians in 1853, only twelve years earlier, but it was already a thriving community with hotels, dry goods, furniture and drug stores, a saw mill and several hundred residents. The Cutlerites rented homes set back from the river. The children often took walks along the top of Barns' Bluff with its view of the Mississippi.

After they had settled their families in Red Wing, Lewis Denna, Sylvester and Francis Lewis Whiting left for Crow Wing in early November in search of the Rev. John Johnson Enmegahbowh. When they arrived at the village they found that Enmegahbowh had gone about 40 miles further north with his friends on a fishing expedition. The committee continued north looking for Enmegahbowh until the roads became impassable. While Denna continued the search the Whiting brothers went back to Crow Wing to await the two men's return. Several days later Denna and Enmegahbowh arrived in Crow Wing. When the Whitings finally met Enmegahbowh they found him to be a sophisticated man, generous with his advice and willing to help. At the conclusion of their visit, Denna and the Whiting brothers returned to spend the winter in Red Wing with their families.

All the Cutlerite children who were old enough attended the Christ Church Episcopal Sunday School in Red Wing, led by the Rev. Edward Randolph Welles who had come to Red Wing from western New York. Christ Church was barely six years old. It was the first church consecrated by Episcopal Bishop Henry B. Whipple after his ordination as Bishop. When Christmas arrived the leaders of the Sunday school arranged to have the children in the classes march from the church, on Broadway, to the courthouse and up two flights of steps into a large room where there was a Christmas tree. It was the first Christmas tree Emma Whiting, daughter of Francis Lewis and Jeanette Whiting, had ever seen. "As we were going up and came into sight of the immense tree all lit up with candles and ornaments, it seemed to me that we were marching right up into heaven." The enthralled children were each given treats of candies, nuts, popcorn and a small book. They returned home at about 9 P.M. just as their fathers, who had expected them home by dark, were leaving in search of them.

It was the end of January 1865 when the second party, led by Isaac Whiting, reached Red Wing to be greeted with relief and jubilation. The travelers arrived at mid-morning and were invited into the homes of those who had arrived earlier. Jennie Whiting fell into the arms of Ann Jeanette Whiting and later remembered how good it felt to eat dinner sitting around a table again. The trip in mid-winter had been difficult for all, but most especially for Mary Fletcher who had five children to cook for—the eldest ten-years-old, the youngest only eight months—and no cook stove. Mary cooked all of their meals over an open campfire in winter and somehow kept her children from freezing by covering them with quilts and featherbeds.

Jennie Whiting remembered that the trip consisted of "cold and often stormy days and evenings spent sitting around a roaring campfire visiting with our fellow travelers until bedtime, when all joined in singing a hymn and afterwards uniting in prayer before retiring to [our] several wagons to sleep. Oh! It was hard to get up early those bitter cold mornings, cook our breakfast shivering with cold while the menfolks fed the horses and greased the wagons."[77] With the arrival of Isaac Whiting and his company the band of Cutlerites now numbered 41 individuals.

In anticipation of their arrival Francis Lewis Whiting had rented rooms for the second party. Red Wing must have been crowded since the rooms he found for Isaac and Jennie Whiting were in a house already occupied by three other families. Whiting, Jennie and Carmelia had only a kitchen, a small pantry and a shed in which to store their things. Jennie was not discouraged. She wrote that "Isaac unloaded the stove, set it up and soon had a good fire going. Then he nailed up some bedsteads, filled some straw ticks and Carmelia and I made up the beds, swept the floor and arranged the few dishes we had brought on the pantry shelves and by supper time we had things in order and looking homelike." The newcomers found the people of Red Wing to be sociable and friendly and Jennie became so fond of the community that she began to wish that she and her husband could stay.

On February 14, 1865, Lewis Denna, with Sylvester Whiting and his family, left the main body of Cutlerites in Red Wing and went again to Crow Wing to confer a second time with John Johnson Enmegahbowh. By visiting with him the Cutlerites hoped not only to get advice, but to establish good relations with the Indians, convince them of their peaceful intent and learn from Enmegahbowh where they should go in their search for land on which to settle. For Enmegahbowh, their visit was further confirmation of his belief in the inevitability of white settlement in what had formerly been Indian Territory.

Enmegahbowh was deeply committed to the Ojibwe values of generosity and sharing. He had impoverished himself and his family during hard times and participated equally with the Ojibwe during good times. He lived his commitment to traditional Ojibwe values that called for the sharing of all their material goods with each other. The Ojibwe people fished together in the fall and hunted together in the winter. They purchased supplies jointly and for the benefit of the group. Decision-making in the Ojibwe community was rooted in mutuality, cooperation and consensus. In the Cutlerites' communal organization, mutuality and sharing, their religious devotion and desire to establish a self-sufficient agrarian village, Enmegahbowh recognized values similar to those held by the Ojibwe. He welcomed the return visit by Sylvester Whiting and Denna and housed them in Crow Wing until the main body of Cutlerites joined them six weeks later.

On April 6 (a day significant to all Latter Day Saints as it was the date on which Joseph Smith organized the church) the remaining Cutlerites in Red Wing loaded their wagons to continue north to Crow

Wing. Emma Whiting wrote, "We again took up our pilgrimage toward the north, hoping to find a refuge from the troubles that assailed us in Iowa and to be able to serve the Lord in peace and to carry the Gospel to the Lamanites as that had been Alpheus Cutler's mission and we who were left must needs carry out that work."[78] Emma's words have a ritual phrasing, as if from much repetition, a dream-like quality as if she were repeating a catechism. The experiences of the past had devolved into a formula, an explanation divorced from reality. To an objective observer, the Cutlerites had not had "troubles assailing" them in Iowa nor had they been persecuted or prevented from practicing their religion by their Iowa neighbors.

The night before their departure the Cutlerites were awakened by an uproar in the center of Red Wing. They could see flames rising in the night sky and thought a building must be on fire. Isaac Whiting went to investigate and learned that word had just arrived that the Civil War had ended. Men had piled barrels, crates and boxes into a huge pyramid in the center of town and then set it afire. Guns were fired and "there was much shouting and hurrahing going on."[79]

The travelers planned to get an early start, but it took a long time to load the wagons. Before they could get underway the men had to stop for "a season of prayer." As a result the caravan traveled only nine miles that first day before stopping for the night in a grove of poplars. As night fell it began to snow and by morning the falling snow had turned into a blizzard. When the men crawled out of their wagons the next morning, they took one look at the snow and told their families to stay bundled up in bed while they hitched up the teams and drove a short distance to a more sheltered space in a stand of trees. There the company stayed for four days while the spring blizzard raged around them. Some of the families were able to light fires in the cook stoves in their wagons to keep themselves warm. Emma remembered that her mother's stove was "too large for that so we had to tough it out the best we could though I remember crying bitterly with the cold."

Before long the snow reached a depth of twenty inches and the cold became intense, threatening not only the livestock but the travelers as well. Though the men prayed for deliverance from the storm, by the fourth day they could see that their situation was becoming desperate. Francis Lewis Whiting called the men into his tent and, after first asking them their opinion of what they should do—turn back or press on ahead—he stated his belief that "the Lord is able to open the way and that we should proceed on our journey." Seven men (a magic number) were named to spend that night in fervent prayer. During the night the temperature rose and a warm rain began to fall that melted enough of the snow so that they were able to continue on their journey. Though the weather again turned cold, forcing the men to break the trail for the animals by jumping on top of the frozen crust of snow, they were able to proceed.

The Cutlerites interpreted the experience of the blizzard in a religious manner. In their explanation God sent the storm to remind them of their dependence on Him, while the warm rain was proof that, "the Lord was with us in our trials and could bless us more than man could." The fact that several Indians in the area died from exposure during the storm was not reckoned with. The Cutlerites were adept at reading divine intentions into the events of their lives. When they reached St. Cloud they learned that President Lincoln had been assassinated. Sylvester Whiting said, "as all our men were strongly in favor of the course [Lincoln] had taken in the war, we were sorrowful to hear he had been murdered."

The road they followed to St. Cloud was a muddy track called the "government road" which ran along the Mississippi River past St. Paul to Little Falls where it branched west to the Winnebago Agency at Long Prairie. The road was the path of the "Big Squeak," the Red River ox carts that carried furs from Canada to St. Paul, the head of navigation on the Mississippi. The two-wheeled carts were held together with pegs and rawhide—no nails or metal were used in their construction. The wheels were solid discs of wood, five feet across and three inches thick, and the noise they made could be heard for miles across the prairie. St. Cloud was a stopping and transfer point for the ox carts. The volume of furs carried by the carts had been growing annually and the year the Cutlerites arrived in St. Cloud a train of two hundred Red River carts passed through the village carrying $80,000 worth of furs. The Hudson Bay Company fur trade brought a measure of prosperity to St. Cloud. In 1865 the town had 1,000 residents, mainly immigrants from Germany, fifty stores, mills and workshops.

From St. Cloud the Cutlerites traveled north, following the road along the Mississippi to Crow Wing. The village, populated by Indians, missionaries and traders, was located in a bend of the Mississippi that, with the Crow Wing River, curved about the village site like a protective arm. The main street of town faced the Mississippi and a boardwalk was

constructed to protect pedestrians from the mud of the road. Here the
Cutlerites reunited with Lewis Denna and Sylvester Whiting and his
family (Rebecca had given birth to a son, Will, in Crow Wing). In a
meeting at Enmegahbowh's home, Sylvester Whiting presented him
with a copy of the *Book of Mormon.*

The Cutlerites hoped to negotiate an agreement (which they referred to as a treaty) with the Indians and asked for Enmegahbowh's assistance in organizing a meeting with several of the chiefs. As Chauncey
Whiting explained, "We desire to enter into a treaty of peace with our
Red Brethren. We are aware that the Pale Face had often made treaties
with the Red Man and as often broken them, but we wish ours to be a
mutual and everlasting treaty." He added, "We believe great wars and
judgments are yet coming on the earth, or the Gentile Nations, because
they have rejected the Gospel, and we desire to find a place of safety with
our Red Brethren, and at the same time, be where we can do them much
good spirtually as well as to encourage them in the arts of civilization."[80]

A meeting with the chiefs was held at Enmegahbowh's home and all
agreed that the signing of a treaty would be an appropriate action. However, the chiefs wanted some time to think about the treaty and to consult among themselves. Enmegahbowh promised the Cutlerites that he
would write to them when they were settled and outline the particulars
for an agreement. In the meantime, the Indians assured the Cutlerites
that they could move into Western Minnesota without fear.

The Cutlerite peace treaty with the Indians was not signed until October 29, 1866, when Chauncey Whiting, Lewis Denna and Almon
Sherman met with Enmegahbowh and six chiefs at Enmegahbowh's tent
at Mille Lacs, Minnesota. The Mille Lacs meeting began at 8 P.M. with
seven chiefs in attendance. Chauncey opened with a prayer. With Enmegahbowh translating, he explained that the Cutlerites had three purposes for the meeting. The first was to sign a treaty of peace between the
Cutlerites and the Indians; the second was to "enlighten their minds in
regards to the principles of the Gospel of Salvation and of the promises
of the Lord to their forefathers;" and the third was "that we might teach
and instruct them in the arts and science of civilization." Following the
Cutlerites' statements, the Indians spoke at length, saying they wanted
to live in peace with all men "even the Sioux if they would come and
want to make peace." Chauncey wrote, "After many remarks and much
rejoicing, we all joined in shaking the friendly hand. The council was
closed by Brother Sherman singing 'Mt. Zion is My Home' and a prayer

by Chauncey Whiting." The meeting lasted until 11 P.M. "The time had passed quickly and joyfully away," Chauncey reported. The men slept in their wagons that night and left for Otter Tail County the next morning. The party arrived back with the main body of Cutlerites on November 4 and immediately called a meeting to announce their success. Chauncey Whiting reported that "the hearts of the brethren and sisters were cheered in hearing the glad tidings that reached their ears."

Enmegahbowh was key to the success of the Cutlerite negotiations both at Crow Wing and later, at Mille Lacs. He was the spokesperson for the Cutlerites in the negotiations, translating for the other chiefs who were present. Alta Kimber, in an early history of Otter Tail County, wrote that 17 chiefs signed the treaty that was eventually drawn up, including Enmegahbowh, Hole-in-the-Day, Tat-todge, and Poka-noga. It is doubtful that Hole-in-the-Day the Younger was a signer as he and Enmegahbowh were enemies.[81]

Regardless of which chiefs signed the treaty for the Indians, it was a source of great pride to the Cutlerites who regarded it as evidence of their special relationship with Native Americans. Chauncey Whiting remembered that "one chief remarked that if all the white people would follow our example and carry it out in actions, they never would have cause to fear or apprehend danger or trouble from the red man. Indeed, from that time forward, they used every endeavor to prevent trespass or acts of injustice being committed by their people upon the settlers, and whenever these bounds were over-reached and the chiefs informed, they would invariably come and order such offenders to desist or march on. They even offered to pay all damages where any losses were sustained."[82] Jennie Whiting asserted that "those who scoffed at our work among the Indians probably owed their lives to the signing of this very paper, as the treaty was never broken even though it was so short a time after the great massacre of 1862, and the red men were still filled with the war spirit."[83]

Enmegahbowh knew west central Minnesota well. It was almost certainly on his advice that the Cutlerites, after leaving Crow Wing, headed their wagons directly west into Otter Tail County. Evidence of that knowledge is contained in a letter he wrote about the events of 1869 and his journey to the White Earth Indian Reservation. In his letter to his friends in the East he wrote, "In about two weeks I was ready to bid my last farewell to the land and country I loved so well and started to follow the steps of Nabunashkong [the chief whom he had earlier con-

vinced to obey the government directive and move to the reservation]. I
started with my own caravan which consist of three ox-teams, and with
all my war implements always ready for any case of emergency."

Enmegahbowh continued, "When the chiefs heard I had started for
White Earth, Chiefs Nabunashkong, Washburn, Twing and a few of
their warriors started to meet me. As we were trudging along peacefully
on the beautiful prairie, between what is now called Palmer and Otter
Tail City—this was then a wild country, Otter Tail was only inhabited
by a few half-breeds—as we were walking on peacefully, all at once we
saw a half a dozen horses in full gallop, men on the horses, feathers waving on their heads, making toward us. Sure I said, as the Maineites would
say, 'goner!' My hairs all stood straight up and shook like the leaves for
my wife and children. We thought they were Sioux. Imagine how we
felt. The war-whoop and how to wield my implements of war of flesh,
I have not learned. As they approached near and nearer, we saw them,
they are our friends! Chief Nabunashkong took and grasped both of my
hands and said he was as glad as man can be to see me."[84]

Enmegahbowh had not immediately joined his friend Nabunashkong on the White Earth reservation because of his fears of what Hole-
in-the-Day the Younger might do. As he explained, "I had made up my
mind that I would not take a step toward White Earth while Hole-in-
the-Day was a living man for I knew he was a man of blood and that he
never would give a peace to Tuttle and his people until he carry out his
wicked project against them." Hole-in-the-Day was later assassinated by
his own people and after that, Enmegahbowh felt free to move to the
reservation.

That Enmegahbowh shared the Cutlerites' vision of religious-based
rural communities is evidenced in a letter he wrote to the Rev. Samuel
Hollingsworth of Greenfield, Massachusetts. Enmegahbowh wrote from
the reservation, "I do hope if the government do not again disturb us
from our present homes, in a few years my people will be self-supporting
and become citizens of the United States. Christian religion has made us
happy homes, made us industrious, sober and above all things, made us
to love God in our hearts."[85]

Faced with the inevitability of white settlement of the Indian lands,
Enmegahbowh may have felt that sending the Cutlerites to his beloved
Otter Tail region was the better choice of an otherwise poor bargain.
The Cutlerite values of community, of sharing, of holding property in
common, as well as their plans to form an agricultural community based

on the tenets of their religion were consonant with Enmegahbowh's own deeply held Ojibwe beliefs. Both he and the Cutlerites shared the Puritan and Jeffersonian ideal of the small agricultural community as the true source of moral purity. It is probable that the first permanent white settlement of Otter Tail County was made at the instigation of two Native Americans, Lewis Denna and John Johnson Enmegahbowh.

The Cutlerites were far more inclined to credit divine inspiration for their ultimate destination than the advice of any individual. However, if the travelers had west central Minnesota as their destination when they departed from Manti, they took a roundabout route to get there. From western Iowa they traveled northeast to the Mississippi and Minnesota's boundary with Wisconsin, adding hundreds of miles to their journey. It is clear that Lewis Denna had planned, from the time they left Manti, to find and consult with Enmegahbowh and that it was Enmegahbowh's advice that determined where they would settle.

The first challenge the settlers faced after leaving Crow Wing and heading west was crossing the Mississippi River. The ice had gone out and the river was too deep to ford. Some of the men said they would have to wait two weeks for the river to fall before they would be able to cross. Though it was already one o'clock in the afternoon, Sylvester Whiting spoke "with a feeling of assurance that if they would do as I would tell them, we would all be across the river and camped before sundown." The men searched the riverbank and found an old ferryboat that was very dry from having been out of the river for two years. Whiting "told the brethren to get some rags and a knife and we would all go to calking the boat." They did so, and with two men bailing they were able to keep the boat from sinking long enough to ferry eight teams and wagons across the river. They made the cattle swim the stream and by nightfall the whole party was camped on the western side of the river. It was here that Jennie Whiting had her first encounter with a strange Indian, a man wrapped in a green blanket who was standing on the bank of the river watching their crossing. As Jennie clambered up the bank the man greeted her with a friendly smile and a "How." Jennie, despite her Mormon belief in the centrality of the Indians to their religion, found the man disgusting and wondered if she "could endure life among such dirty, repulsive looking people."

When the caravan reached an area of pine forest, Jennie found the evergreens to be beautiful "with the road running like a silver ribbon through them." She was overjoyed to discover wintergreen, an herb she had not seen since living in Ohio. "I eagerly began gathering some of the leaves and munching them. They were not very good as they were the old leaves, which had grown the year before. June is the month when wintergreens are at their best. Then they are young and tender and of a delicious flavor."[86] The berries, she decided, tasted fine.

From Crow Wing to Otter Tail City much of the government trail was covered with logs that floated in high water and provided a jarring surface for the wagons. Emma Whiting found the condition of the road difficult to bear. "Our road lay through a rough country, no good roads, but long stretches of old corduroy that needed repairing badly, just the bare logs and poles, no dirt or hay covering. I shall never forget those awful corduroys for I had caught cold and been sick and was so sore . . . that every jolt was agony." The caravan of wagons passed through tamarack swamps and woods that were ablaze, endangering the wagon covers and bedding. In spite of the difficulties and—they were certain— with the aid of divine providence, in early May they reached the ruins of what had been Otter Tail City at the north end of Otter Tail Lake. Empty shells of the five log cabins that had constituted the village were all that remained. Most of the residents had fled due to the Sioux Uprising.

From 1858 to 1861 there had been a government land office at Otter Tail City, presided over by Major George Bush Burgwin Clitherall. Clitherall was the grandson of two well-to-do Southerners, one of them a Tory sympathizer. His paternal grandfather, Dr. John Clitherall, signed a letter of congratulations to British General Cornwallis following the British victory at Camden and served as a medical doctor for the British troops. George Clitherall's maternal grandfather, though a supporter of the Revolution, had strong business connections with Great Britain and, as a result, his home in Wilmington "the most considerable house in town" was commandeered by Cornwallis for his headquarters. Cornwallis stayed in the Burgwin home for about three weeks before his final defeat at Yorktown.[87]

George Clitherall entered the United States Military Academy at West Point on September 1, 1831, but lasted only four months before being discharged for being "deficient in mathematics." He was also criticized for having poor study habits and having little aptitude for the service. Clitherall's rank of "major" came about through his later involvement with the Mobile Rifle Company, an Alabama organization. In 1857 he received an appointment from President James Buchanan to serve as agent at the United States Land Office in Otter Tail City, an impressive name for the tiny cluster of log cabins on the shore of Otter Tail Lake. Clitherall, his wife Sallie Ann and daughter Elizabeth, first moved to St. Paul where the 1858–59 *City Directory* records them living at the American House Hotel on the corner of Third and Exchange streets.[88]

Clitherall was from Alabama and may have nurtured hopes of making Minnesota a stronghold of slavery. In the 1860 census he was listed as having real property valued at $50,000. His assistant, William Sawyer, had real property valued at $30,000. The Homestead Act had not yet been enacted. It is probable that Clitherall had a "preemption claim" on 40,000 acres of land directly from the federal government at a price of $1.25 per acre. Such claims were common practice by land speculators and the land was seldom paid for until it was developed or sold to others. Since Clitherall left Minnesota two months after the outbreak of the Civil War it is doubtful that he ever paid for the land. However the preemption prevented anyone else from claiming or buying it. The most real property credited to any other settler in the census was $2,500 and only two had property valued at more than $1,000.[89]

The empty houses made a strong impression on the travelers. Jennie Whiting, as she stood on the shores of Otter Tail Lake watching the waves, felt she had reached "the end of the world. At the north end of the lake I could see a dim mysterious-looking forest, back of me was a row of log houses and north of those was an Indian burying ground. The houses were . . . so filthy we could not even step inside. I suppose they had been built by white settlers before the raid and perhaps the savages had murdered them all. As I thought of their possible fate, I turned away shuddering."[90]

Otter Tail was their destination, undoubtedly suggested by Enmegahbowh. Jennie Whiting wrote, "We had been directed only this far on our journey and where to go next was the question." Though the cabins were abandoned, the land had obviously been claimed so the pioneers could not settle there. When in doubt about what to do, the Cutlerite practice was to gather together and ask the Lord for guidance. A prayer meeting was held that evening, "the direction was made known," as they later reported, and instead of looking north of Otter Tail Lake, as they had planned, Isaac, Sylvester and Francis Lewis Whiting went south to the outlet of West Battle Lake.

The outlet teemed with fish, offering a major distraction to avid fishermen Isaac and Francis Lewis Whiting. To Sylvester Whiting's annoyance, the two men stopped to fish before making their way around to the north shore of Battle Lake where a broad pasture appeared to offer a likely place for settlement. Late in the evening they returned to the group awaiting word at Otter Tail and the next day the entire party moved their wagons to the Battle Lake meadow. This location looked promising to many in the group who immediately began to stake out plots for gardens. They were farmers and knew they should not delay getting crops into the ground. One man cut down a large tree and hollowed it out to make a rude canoe.

Though most of the travelers were satisfied with the Battle Lake location, Sylvester Whiting was not. He had a dream during the night that he believed contained a message for the Cutlerites. As he told the company the next morning, "I saw in my dream an old woman and she came to where we were and seemed to be very angry with us. She had a broom in her hands and with her broom she swept or drove us all off." Concerned about the meaning of his dream and leaving the two fishermen behind, Whiting convinced Calvin Fletcher, Marcus Shaw and James Badham to explore the south shore of Battle Lake with him. Here they crossed a narrow strip of land and discovered, beyond it, Lake Clitherall. They walked along the north shore of Clitherall Lake, stopping in a grove of trees for prayers before continuing on to a broad plateau overlooking the lakeshore. As Whiting said, "When I first stepped on that spot of ground the load or burden that had been on my mind left me instantly and I felt a witness that this was the chosen place of the Lord for us to settle. I, for one, was satisfied but the Lord wanted more than one to be satisfied and instead of our uniting together there, as we had been directed, we went on east a mile and a half more."[91] It was now growing late and the men were tired. Marcus Shaw and James Badham agreed with Whiting that the site by the shore of Clitherall Lake was the location where they should settle. Fletcher did not, contending that the inspiration he had received favored the Battle Lake site. The men returned to the camp, as Whiting said, "squarely divided in our minds."

The disagreement was profoundly disturbing to the men as they were convinced that their favorable feelings about the Clitherall site were divinely inspired. If God had spoken to all four of the men, why had He revealed a different message to Fletcher? They continued to pray about the problem until Badham and Shaw recalled that when they previously prayed in the grove, Fletcher had knelt in a spot a distance apart from the other three men. This violated the commandment that they must act in unity, which they interpreted in this case, as meaning they must kneel in close proximity. As one of them explained it, "Brother Calvin Fletcher was by himself and the adversary [Satan] took advantage of him."

This explanation satisfied them. The next day Sylvester Whiting, Francis Lewis Whiting, Calvin Fletcher and James Badham drove their teams around the lake and, crossing the outlet at the east end, came onto the shore of Lake Clitherall. They followed the shore until they came to the bluff overlooking the lake. Here the four men again knelt in prayer, asking God to tell them if this was the land between two lakes that Alpheus Cutler had seen in his vision. As the men prayed, Francis Lewis Whiting received what they believed to be the definitive revelation that this was, indeed, the place. Sylvester Whiting remembers Francis Lewis Whiting saying, as he bowed in prayer, "This is the place which the Lord is pleased to have His people settle in and it will become a holy place in as much as my people will make it holy. For a further testimony your brethren shall manifest their entire satisfaction with your location when they see it."[92] The two fishermen were also rebuked, being told that "had they not stopped to fish instead of going on as they had been directed, they would have found the place [Clitherall Lake] the first day."[93]

Convinced that they had found the place where they were to remain until the Lord called them back to Zion in Independence, Missouri, the men returned to the Battle Lake camp, packed up their wagons, and on the morning of May 6, 1865, drove their families and their possessions onto their promised land on the shores of Clitherall Lake.

They later learned that the meadow where they had camped on the north shore of Battle Lake was owned by speculators and therefore would not have been open for settlement. To the Cutlerites this was further proof of God's guidance of the pioneers. Their method of choosing a home site was not done entirely by religious inspiration, however. As Chauncey Whiting later noted, the village site was "almost surrounded by water and properly adapted to the speedy growth and maturity of crops and well protected from late and early frosts by the warm breezes arising from the lakes on either side."

Jennie Whiting remembered that season as having been a "backward spring." The ice had gone out of the lake only the day before, the grass "showed no vestige of green" and much of the land was covered with hazel brush. Francis Lewis Whiting parked his wagon near where he would later build his home and stretched a piece of canvas between his wagon and Isaac Whiting's to form a shelter.

To an outside observer, the Cutlerites would appear to have been a destitute band of pilgrims, strangers in a strange land, facing daunting odds of survival—if not from Indians resentful at their intrusion, then from the brutal Minnesota winters. That was not how the Cutlerites saw themselves. Poor though they were in material goods, they believed themselves to be rich in spirit and in God's grace. Their trek to Minnesota was in response to what they believed was a divine commandment, transmitted to them through God's spokesman, Alpheus Cutler. They were convinced that in the mind of God lay a plan for their lives and their only task was to discern the day-to-day details of that plan.

This belief led to an obsession with legalisms and forms (Calvin Fletcher knelt too far from the other brethren when they were praying) and to a reliance on dreams, intuitions and hunches. They believed that God was continually communicating to them. Their duty was to receive and understand His messages. An unseen but real world of the supernatural existed at the outer limit of their senses. Believing their lives directed by heaven, and their names known to God, the Cutlerites did not see themselves as poverty-stricken pioneers, but as a chosen people placing their suffering as a willing sacrifice on the altar of the Most High.

CHAPTER 7

Founding Clitherall

Though the Cutlerites created the first permanent white settlement in Otter Tail County, the land had been inhabited by humans for more than twenty thousand years. Ivory tools made from mammoths, camp refuse from around the shores of the ancient Lake Agassiz and prehistoric Indian mounds complete with skeletons, pottery, flint and agate implements were scattered throughout the area. Both the Sioux (Dakota) and the Otter Tail Band of the Pillager Ojibwe were well-established residents. Although traditional enemies they had informally divided up the territory. However, battles between the two tribes were frequent. By 1837, treaties with the Ojibwe and Dakota had opened Minnesota to white settlement. In 1847 the Indians ceded parts of what became Otter Tail County to the government for the relocation of the Menominee tribe from Wisconsin.

The Menominee never occupied the territory so by 1854 the land reverted to the federal government. The Ojibwe believed that the land should have been returned to them and they continued to use it until white settlement pushed them out. By 1851 the United States government claimed most of Minnesota through a series of treaties. By the middle 1850s wild land speculation had begun, interrupted only by the Sioux Uprising of 1862. About a thousand white people lived in Minnesota when the territory was organized in 1849 but by the time the Cutlerites arrived in 1865, the state had nearly 200,000 residents.

Otter Tail County was created in 1858 and is one of the largest counties in Minnesota, encompassing 2,039 square miles of land and 197 square miles of fresh water, with more lakes (approximately 1000) than any other county in the state. A chain of lakes, including Otter Tail, East and West Battle, Crane, Deer, Silver and Clitherall, drains through the

Otter Tail River into the Red River of the North and eventually into Hudson's Bay. The United States census of 1860 recorded 240 residents of the county, most of whom fled during the Indian conflict of 1862.

When the Cutlerites pitched their tents for the first time on the shores of Clitherall Lake they were dangerously short of food. Starvation stared them in the face and they were forced to live on half or quarter rations of their remaining supplies until they could get crops into the ground and look for game. Their first action was to build a log and brush fence extending about a mile from Clitherall to Battle Lake to keep their livestock out of the gardens. The land the Cutlerites had settled and would later file claims on were four quarter sections or 640 acres, a strip of land about one mile wide and four miles long lying between the north shore of Clitherall Lake and the south shore of Battle Lake. The village was located directly on the Clitherall lakeshore. While breaking sixty acres of prairie and planting it to crops and vegetables, they slept in their wagons. With the crops finally planted, the men of the party turned to the building of shelter for their families.

Isaac Whiting built his first home by driving stakes into the sandy ground, laying poles across the tops of the stakes and spreading quilts on the poles for a roof. Quilts were also hung on the sides of the structure to block the wind. His little cook stove was moved into this shelter and though it frequently set the quilts on fire, no great harm was done. Seeking to improve the shelter, Whiting replaced the quilts with strips of bark. When he had finished, and was feeling pleased with the result of his efforts, he asked his wife for a bowl of bread and milk. Jennie reported that she set it before him on the table and Whiting "drew up a box to sit on and began eating with great satisfaction when, all at once, some of the poles he had laid across slipped off and down came his bark roof. One pole struck him on the head, bark fell all around him, upsetting his dish of bread and milk and making a wreck of things."[94]

As soon as the planting was done the men began cutting logs for houses, moving the heavy logs out of the woods on levers. The cabins were small and simple. The floors, doors and window casings all had to be hewn with a broad ax, a time-consuming and laborious process. Nevertheless, by fall, fourteen cabins, thickly plastered with mud and clay, were built. Only a strip of the floor was laid in Isaac Whiting's cabin when, eager to get settled, Jennie and Carmelia moved the cook stove in. "Isaac had put up a long shelf for us to arrange our dishes on and Carmelia and I began at once to carry things in. We had lived out-of-doors so long that our rude log cabin looked like a palace to us."

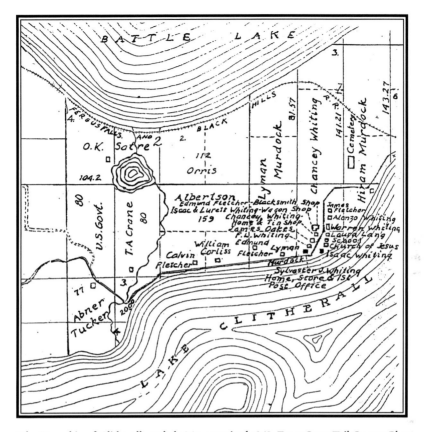

The Township of Clitherall, settled 1865, organized 1868. From Otter Tail County Plat Book of 1884.

Within a few days of their arrival at the lake Sylvester Whiting noticed that the bark had been cut and had then partially grown back from a spot on a tree. He pried off the new bark to find the word "Clitherall" carved into the wood. The Cutlerites decided to give that name to their community. It is possible they had heard of Major Clitherall earlier, because of his land office duties, but it is unlikely they would have named their village after him if they had known he was a southern sympathizer. Despite his connections to the south Major Clitherall retained fond feelings for Minnesota. The *St. Paul Pioneer Press* of March 11, 1890, records that he gave a chair that had allegedly belonged to George Washington and was once in the Mount Vernon library to the Minnesota Historical Society. The Society responded with a handsomely engraved resolution of thanks signed by Henry M. Rice and Charles E. Flandrau.[95]

While the exploring party of Cutlerites broke the prairie sod in Minnesota to plant their crops, the Cutlerites still living in Iowa debated what they should do. Mail had been received from the Minnesota scouting party and those in Manti now knew that a new home in Otter Tail County had been found for the Church of Jesus Christ. Members in Manti were divided over whether they should go north or stay where they were in Iowa. At a church meeting on April 9, 1865, Elder Squire Eggleston stated his ambivalent belief that "the Lord had a hand" in the members going north yet reaffirmed his belief that they would "eventually return to Zion." Local branch president Edmund Fisher said he did not approve of members moving north but added that they "could do as they pleased, go or stay."[96]

On April 6, 1865, the day the exploring party left Red Wing to trek north, the Cutlerites in Manti held their annual Church conference. They heatedly discussed two issues: the still unresolved question of who should succeed Alpheus Cutler as President of the High Priesthood (and thus, president of the church) and whether they should follow the scouting party and relocate the church in Minnesota. Despite the glowing reports from the north, many of the Iowa Cutlerites were reluctant to move. They were weary of travel and their Iowa farms and shops had become prosperous. Some believed they were too old to undertake an arduous journey to a new frontier and begin over again. Others had close ties to relatives who had joined with the Josephites and were reluctant to move so far from friends and family. Cutler's mission to the Indians was mentioned less and less after his death and the Civil War— a former concern and motivation for moving—had ended.

Those who favored the move north were, for the most part, younger families for whom pioneer life offered exciting new opportunities. They were also among the more zealous of Cutler's supporters. They were convinced of the correctness of Cutler's esoteric interpretations of Scripture and were guided in their own lives by personal religious experiences and "manifestations of the spirit." Aspiring leaders, such as Chauncey Whiting, may have welcomed the opportunity to take on a more prominent role in the church in Minnesota.

After much deliberation, on May 31, 1865, twenty-three families in thirty-five heavily loaded covered wagons left Manti and headed for Clitherall, Minnesota. Three yokes of oxen pulled the larger wagons. Among the travelers in this second party were Isaac Whiting's parents, Chauncey and Editha, with their ten children; the brothers Lyman and

Hirum Murdock, William Mason, Reuben Oakes, DeWitt Sperry, Uriah Eggleston, all with their families; Edmund and Augusta Whiting, Lois Cutler, the widow of Alpheus, her granddaughter Emily Pratt, Erastus and Martha Cutler, Tom Mason, William Cameron, Laura Lang, Almon Whiting, Lewis Denna's wife, Mary, and a woman identified only as Mrs. Shaw. Chauncey Whiting's son, Lurett, remembered "the terrible lonesomeness which came over me as we were about out of sight of the dear old home which had sheltered me in my happy childhood days."[97]

Lurett's sister, nine-year-old Ann, was heartsick at leaving Ring, the family dog, behind. "He had been our playmate so long that to see him sitting there wagging his tail and watching and listening for an invitation to go with us made the big lumps come up in our throats until we nearly choked. Father thought two dogs were too many to take along, and as we had another one which the boys called theirs, they won out and we had to leave Ring with our friends." Chauncey Whiting's decision was unfortunate for a few weeks later, at a campground, men hunting a badger cut down a tree to get at it and the tree fell on the boys' little black dog, injuring him so badly that he died. Ann recalled, "After that we longed for our little Ring more than ever but it was too late now. He was too far behind."[98]

The caravan went only four miles the first day, just as the two groups before them had done, before stopping at the familiar camping place for three days so everyone could assemble. When all were together and organized, they set off in a body, the older boys on horseback, the younger ones on foot, driving their herds of sheep and cattle before them. The roads were poor and often wet. Several wagons would get stuck in the mud at one time and teams of oxen would have to be unhitched from one wagon and put onto another to pull the wagons out of the mud. The caravan stopped every noon so the women could cook meals over campfires. At night the wagons were lined up like a small town, folding tables were untied from the sides of wagons, and families gathered to eat and later visit around blazing camp fires. The men shot wild game and bought provisions from the towns they passed through. Cows were milked daily and the milk that was not drunk was hung in cans under the wagons where the jolting churned it into butter. The wagon train and accompanying animals moved slowly, stopping on Saturdays and Sundays so the women could bake bread over open fires and do the week's wash.

Smaller streams had no bridges. Men waded into the streams leading their teams of oxen. Horses and cattle had few problems in shallow waters. To get sheep across the men waded into the water, holding hands until they formed a human chain all the way across. Then someone drove the sheep, one at a time, into the river, so that the men could push the animals from hand to hand until all were safely across.

The Hirum and Rachel Murdock family consisted of eight children: Charles the eldest at fifteen, Alva, Emily, Ellen, Lois, Didamia, Orson and Lyman. Hirum Murdock had hitched two yoke of oxen to his larger, heavier wagon while his wife, Rachel, with a five-month-old infant on her lap, drove a team of horses pulling the other covered wagon. When they forded a stream, Murdock would leave the oxen to take care of themselves while he came back to wade the stream at the head of his wife's team of horses. Young Charles walked the entire distance herding the family's sheep.

Both the prairie and the woods presented problems for the boys driving the livestock. As there were not enough horses for all to ride, many of the boys, such as Charles Murdock, made the entire journey on foot. Lurett Whiting remembered, "As we were all barefooted, the long walks often made our feet very sore. I can never forget how the sand would cut our faces when the wind was blowing hard across those long stretches of prairie, especially if one was on the side of the herd where the sand cut loose from the cattle's feet. The weather was intensely hot and sometimes our sufferings were quite severe." When they drove the livestock through woods "the cattle would hide away and it was very difficult to find them again. We were compelled to leave several head of the younger cattle behind as it was impossible to find them all."

The wisdom of making the trip was still not clearly apparent to everyone. After a few days' travel six of the twenty-three families that had started dropped out of the caravan and returned to Manti. Those who dropped out were considered, at the very least, to be weak in the faith. After the farewells as they watched the defectors' wagons turn around and head back south, "the remainder" as one of them later wrote, "being determined to set their feet upon the place which our committee and their comrades had waded through snow and endured privations, hardship and suffering, and even periled their lives to search out, continued their journey." Loyalty to the original scouting party and a desire to see the project through to the end kept the majority of the second party plodding north.

This second group of migrating Cutlerites followed a more direct route than had the initial party. Instead of traveling northeast to Red

Wing, they followed a route north through St. Paul and Alexandria on the ox cart track that ran from St. Paul north to Pembina. All three of the Red River ox cart trails ran through Otter Tail County. The "Woods Trail" went via Otter Tail City to Crow Wing, the "East Plains" or "Middle Trail"went via Dayton, six miles up the Otter Tail River from present-day Fergus Falls, and the "West Plains" trail went through Old Crossing, still further up the Otter Tail River. The "Woods Trail" was used by travelers fearful of traveling through Sioux Indian territory while government expeditions usually used the Plains Trail.

At St. Paul the Cutlerites bought provisions for the coming winter and marveled at the ox carts at the government trading post. Lurett Whiting observed that "These carts were never supplied with grease and every wheel was squeaking so hard one would think a hundred coyotes had turned loose." When they reached St. Cloud they found a message from the settlers at Clitherall giving them directions on how to find the village. "However we thought it expedient to rest our teams a day or two while we laid in a few stores by way of clothing and provisions." At Alexandria they saw the fort which was "thirteen or fourteen feet high with holes cut through the walls to shoot through in case the Indians should attack it," a store made of tamarack logs selling dry goods and a few log homes."

The transitional land the Cutlerites were traversing formed the border between the oak and maple savannas of the east and the prairies of the west. The land was flat with gentle rises and sparsely settled. The few settlers they passed warned them against going further north. Chauncey Whiting recalled that "many kind and feeling friends along the road, although entire strangers, most earnestly entreated us to abandon the idea of settling in Otter Tail County without an army to protect us. Otherwise, they said, the Indians would massacre the entire company of men, women and children. They cited to us the horrible scenes at New Ulm and elsewhere and, indeed, we could not blame them for being so dreadfully scared." Despite the warnings, the Cutlerites pressed on, convinced that, given an opportunity, they would be able to live in peace with the Indians.

At Chippewa (now the town of Brandon) the caravan turned off the ox cart track and headed east. Ahead on the skyline, barring their path, lay the broken ridges of the Leaf Mountains, one peak of which is the second highest point in Minnesota. The Leaf Mountains are a line of glacial drift deposits, the most massive moraine accumulation in Minnesota, running roughly west to northeast forming a line of jagged hills five miles across. The hills range from 1,300 to 1,700 feet above sea level and rise 350 feet above the surrounding terrain. Other than the ten miles of prairie beyond, the Leaf Mountains were the last obstacle the travelers had to confront before arriving at the village of Clitherall.

The settlers were aware of the imminent arrival of the second migration from Manti despite the fact that the nearest post office was 100 miles away in St. Cloud. Toward the end of July Jennie and Carmelia Whiting daily climbed to the top of Cowbar Hill, the highest piece of land, to scan the horizon for the sight of a train of covered wagons. On July 31 the watchers spotted the wagons. "They're coming. They're coming across the prairie around the east end of the lake." The first one to greet the caravan was Isaac Whiting who, upon hearing word the travelers were in sight, jumped on his horse and raced out to meet them. His younger sister remembered that "mother cried for joy when she recognized him. In a few hours we reached Clitherall and met our sister Carmelia, sister-in-law Jennie, uncles, aunts and cousins."

While the adults in the party were concerned with cutting grass for hay for their livestock and preparing for the coming winter, curiosity about the Indians consumed the children. Those who arrived earlier with the first party soon issued an invitation to the newcomers to visit the Indian camp. Emma Whiting wrote, "We were anxious to go and were led down by the lake shore where a lot of Indians were camped. But when we came in sight of them we were so frightened that Lide [Lucia Whiting] got behind me and hung to my waist so tight I could scarcely walk and my own teeth were chattering. But the girls declared they would not hurt us so we ventured close enough to the wigwams to get a peep at a papoose and this banished our fears, and it was not long until the Indian children were our playmates, though they were so rough we never enjoyed them much."[100]

The Indian camp the girls visited was on a point of land extending out into the lake across a marsh only a few hundred yards east of the settlement. The two groups lived in such close proximity that the Cutlerite men again sought an understanding with their Indian neighbors. Lurett Whiting remembered, "The Chippewa Indians were the only neighbors and we thought best to make a sort of treaty with them so we could understand one another and get along better. The chiefs were got together and a treaty arranged with the understanding that we should keep it and should expect them to do the same. I don't remember of its ever being broken and the Indians were always our best friends." Thus fortified with both Enmegahbowh's treaty and blessing and an agreement with the Indians on the point, the Cutlerites prepared for their first winter in Minnesota.

Not all of them would stay. Before the second winter arrived Squire and Uriah Eggleston, with their families; Erastus and Martha Cutler, Edmund and Augusta Whiting, James Badham, a Mr. Olmstead and a Mr. Oakes loaded their wagons and, before the first snow fell, headed back to Iowa. Approximately twenty-five households were left clinging to the lakeshore while their members made urgent preparations for winter.

The first winter the pioneers spent in Clitherall turned out to be severe. The log cabins they built, though the crevices between the logs had been "chinked" and plastered with clay, were inadequate for a Minnesota winter. The chimneys were made of sod and sticks and the fireplaces radiated little heat. They had no heating stoves, only cook stoves that had to be fed wood continually. Windows were covered with greased paper. Candles provided the only light. It became so cold at night that bread, placed next to the blazing fireplace, froze solid and had to be cut with an ax and steamed before it could be eaten. Twenty-one-year-old Zeruah Sherman, a granddaughter of Alpheus Cutler, sat for hours by the fireplace. By the light of a single candle she wove cloth for the settlers and knit socks, stockings and mittens for whoever needed them.

Isaac and Jennie Whiting grew twenty bushels of potatoes and dug a shallow cellar under their house to store them in—a method of preservation they had used in Iowa. The first cold spell in the fall froze the potatoes as hard as rocks, spoiling them for food. Their first child was also born that winter. Jennie was so weak after the birth of the child that she was unable to care for herself or the baby. On the night after the birth Carmelia, who was caring for the infant, made her bed on the floor in front of the fireplace and, cradling the infant in her arms, fell asleep. Whiting, also exhausted, lay down on the bed by Jennie to rest and fell sound asleep. Fortunately Jennie was too stressed to sleep and lay in bed watching the fire. Suddenly she noticed three trails of smoke arising from the pile of quilts where Carmelia and the baby were sleeping. The bedding had been set afire by exploding coals.

"I tried to call out and awake them," Jennie wrote, "but was so weak I could only whisper. Then I tried to reach Isaac to wake him but he was just beyond my reach. I expected every moment to see the bed clothing burst into flames and we all be burned alive."[101] Fortunately, at that moment the baby cried and awoke Carmelia who found that the fire had burned through every quilt and was about to catch her feather bed on fire.

By March three to four feet of snow remained on level ground and they had run out of hay for their stock. Since they would need strong animals to break the prairie sod in the spring, the men cut "browse" for their livestock. Browse consisted of small trees, bushes, shrubs, anything that could be cut down and put out for the animals to eat. The horses and cattle were able to survive on the browse but many of the sheep died, as they could not move about in the deep snow.

To make the provisions they had purchased in St. Paul last longer, the men killed game. "We had plenty of fish and venison and had no thought of starving," Lurett Whiting recalled. The woods were full of foxes, minks and muskrats, which they trapped and sold to an Indian trader from Crow Wing they called "Lying Jack." Lying Jack came through Clitherall with a sled (the snow was so deep he claimed not to have seen the top of his sled from Crow Wing to Clitherall) and bought the furs the men had trapped. "He gave us a good price for them," Whiting recalled, adding that Lying Jack "was a jolly fellow." Lying Jack paid five dollars for fox pelts, three for mink, ten to twelve cents for rats, and two to three dollars for wolves.

To get enough flour to last through the first winter, the Cutlerites sent Sylvester Whiting back to St. Paul by ox team. He had ten dollars of community funds to buy his supplies during his trip and pay for the flour. Along the way Sylvester hunted game for food and collected the pelts. A month later when he returned to Clitherall with a full load of flour, he still had the original ten dollars. The flour lasted the community until some buckwheat they had planted, ripened. They threshed the buckwheat by hand, ground it in their coffee mills and made cakes from it.

Emma Whiting remembered her mother making her a dress from unbleached muslin dyed with oak bark. A piece of birch bark covered with red calico was made into a sunshade. For shoes she had buckskin moccasins purchased from the Indians. Besides Lying Jack, the colony had occasional visits from soldiers stationed at Pomme de Terre and Abercrombie, about 35 miles from Clitherall. When the soldiers came, the Cutlerites somehow made room for them in their homes.

Indians were daily visitors, sometimes coming in groups of 20 or more. In the summer a party of Indians would gather in front of a dwelling and dance, singing, drumming and brandishing clubs and hatchets as they moved in a circle, around and around until a path was worn in the grass of the yard. Upon leaving, one would call at the door for "pe-quazh-i-gan" (bread or flour), "do-do-sah-bo" (butter), "skoot-i-sim-mi" (beans), "o-poin-nik" (potatoes) or "sin-zi-boh-quet" (sugar). In the winter the Indians did what the settlers called a "begging dance." The Indians would file into a cabin and stand in a circle, one behind the other, then dance around the room until the heavy post in the center, which held up the ridgepole, bounced up and down on the floor. Then they would file out and go to the next house. The Cutlerites understood the dances to be requests for food and they shared what game, flour, rutabagas or potatoes they could with the Indians. There was not much to share. Emma remembered that her father, her Uncle Sylvester Whiting and the children "were glad to make a meal of hardtack and water with a little sugar. If the water was warm we would soak the crackers awhile so we could eat them."

That first summer, Emma Whiting, though only twelve-years-old, gathered a few of the younger children under a tree and tried to teach school, following what she could remember of the methods of her old teacher, James Badham. The parents encouraged her and paid her $8 a month for her efforts. Emma said that she "tried to get the children to be good and try to learn. I guess they tried to mind for I don't remember any serious trouble." During the long first winter Marcus Shaw taught writing and arithmetic a few nights a week.

Not until the second winter of 1866–67 was a regular school organized. Zeruah Sherman, who had attended a year of college in Tabor, Iowa, was engaged by the parents for $16 a month to teach the children, thus becoming the first teacher in Otter Tail County. Classes were held in the cabin of Reuben Oakes. The building had a fireplace at one end, a roof of shakes and a floor of sawed planks. Three small windows let in feeble light. The books used by the teacher were the ones they had brought with them from Iowa: Wilson readers, McGuffey's spellers, arithmetics, grammars, geographies, slates, pencils and writing books. The children were starved for something more to read. Emma read the entire Bible by the time she was fourteen and remembered that "our old Wilson school readers were treasured as jewels rare."

Thirty pupils attended school that first year including George Johnson, the youngest son of Enmegahbowh, from Crow Wing. In a letter to Chauncey Whiting written a few months after the settlers' arrival in Clitherall, Enmegahbowh expressed interest in the settlement and in the

Zeruah Sherman Whiting (1844–1900), the
first school teacher in Otter Tail County.

school. "My wife has been long anxious to visit and see you people at
your new homes. . . . I feel more anxious about our children, especially
our boy, who is growing soon to be a man, to be educated among the
whites wheresoever there is an opening for us. If I cannot find a place
here, I must go down East among good friends. I find that Crow Wing,
or on these frontiers, are no place for children to be brought up. I prefer
it altogether that my children be educated among the Whites and . . . to
be associated among them."[102] Chauncey Whiting and Almon Sherman
had brought George Johnson with them to Clitherall when they returned from the treaty signing at Mille Lacs in late October 1866. The
boy boarded at the Sherman home.

Classes for the children were held every weekday except Monday
when the girls had to help their mothers do the family washing. When
the winter snow became too deep for the students to make their way to
the school, one of the men made a three cornered box, set it on runners
and hitched it to his team of horses. The driver stood on the box while
the horses pulled it from house to house and then to the schoolhouse,
plowing a deep path for the children to walk in to get to school.

Emma Whiting remembered that when she was fourteen two of the
women decided it was time to instruct the boys in their responsibility to

The school house and the log church in Clitherall, Minnesota, circa 1870.

see the girls safely home in the evening. After a social evening at a home, Alma Sherman's arm was firmly linked to Carmelia's and Emily was similarly joined to George. The boys were told to see the girls safely to their homes, which they did with suitable gravity. As all of the houses were only a few rods from each other, the trip was not a long one. Nevertheless Emma remembered George, her "first beau," for the rest of her life.

In the spring, beginning around the first of April, brothers Isaac, Warren, Alonzo, and Chauncey Whiting, Jr., operated a sugar camp in a grove of maples on the north shore of Battle Lake. During the winter they made 1,200 sap troughs out of basswood trees, charring the inside of the troughs to prevent them from checking and leaking. Larger trees were cut down and hollowed out to make storage troughs to hold the sap which, for a few days, would flow faster than they would be able to boil it down. Each storage trough held three or four barrels of sap.

In their first year using spiles made of basswood trees, the young men tapped up to a thousand maple trees making 300 pounds of maple sugar, one barrel of maple syrup and a barrel of vinegar. The sap was boiled in two sap-boilers, rectangular containers with a flat bottom of iron and sides of wood. The last sap from the trees was not suitable for making syrup so they turned it into vinegar. The men long remembered the nights they sat up boiling sap around the blazing fires while listening to owls hooting, wolves howling and, in the mornings, the partridges drumming. They often shot partridges for breakfast and dined on fried partridge, fish, roasted potatoes, fried cakes and sugar-sap gravy.

The men built a log hut to sleep in at the sugar camp with a roof made of sod laid over poles. To keep the dirt from falling down on them while they slept, they stretched a wagon cover over their sleeping area for a ceiling. The cover kept the dirt off the sleepers but it made a trampoline for the mice. As Lurett Whiting explained, "The mice got so blamed thick we could hardly sleep nights. They seemed to work in groups and would come out at night and dance over our heads on the wagon cover. So we got a long forked pole and when the mice got too plentiful we would give the wagon cover a good quick hoist and send the mice up against the roof a time or two, which would generally quiet them for a few hours."[103]

An Indian camp was located not far from the sugar camp. One evening an Indian woman approached the men and asked to borrow the large cast iron kettle the men used for cooking. They lent it to her and later, when one of the men went to a nearby stream for water, he saw their kettle suspended over a fire and filled with muskrats. The animals had been stuffed into the kettle headfirst with their tails left hanging over the edge providing a convenient way for the Indians to pull them out to eat when they were cooked. When the kettle was returned to the Cutlerites it reeked of muskrat and, despite numerous attempts at cleaning it, the odor remained.

When it came time to make maple sugar the next year, the men had discovered some improvements from the Indians. As Lurett Whiting explained, "We learned that our Indian friends used birch bark sap troughs, which were cleaner and much easier to handle than our wooden ones. So we secured all we could get of them. They were made of one piece of birch bark cut in such a way that when the edges were bent up and fastened at the top with basswood strings to hold them in shape, they made very good sap troughs holding about four quarts. But they had one fault: they were so light that when standing empty the wind would blow them away from the trees. To obviate this difficulty we weighed them down with sticks of wood." Nothing was wasted. Occasionally, when the sap boiled down and burned on the boiler, they scrapped it off and used the charred sap to make coffee.

In the first year, when they were not able to grow enough hay to carry their stock through the winter, the men cut wild hay for their sheep and cattle. On one of their searches for suitable grass to cut they came upon hollows covered with wild strawberries and marshes filled with cranberries near the present town of Battle Lake. Everyone shared in the bonanza of berries, which were an important addition to a meager diet. The peelings from potatoes were planted and, amazingly, many produced crops.

The settlers were better prepared for their second winter in Minnesota. They no longer depended on sod chimneys and fireplaces for heat and had acquired heating stoves purchased in St. Cloud with money they had made from trapping and the sales of agricultural products. They also dug deeper cellars that were filled with an assortment of vegetables. Almost every family owned a few sheep and the women spun the wool into yarn for cloth, making many of the garments worn by both men and women.

By the fall of 1867 Ann Jeanette Whiting had become concerned about her mother who was still living in Manti. According to her daughter Emma, "that fall my father and family returned to Iowa to get my Grandmother Burdick as mother could not rest easy in her mind until her mother was with her." The entire family made the trip back to Manti by covered wagon to spend the winter, returning to Clitherall the following spring. Four wagons made the return trip. Among the travelers headed back to Clitherall were Almon Whiting the chairmaker, Jesse Burdick and his family, and two youths, Edwin Anderson and Jacob Boyd. Though her name does not appear in the written record, it is probable that Jacob's mother, Luana Hart Beebe Rockwell Cutler, Cutler's first plural wife, also traveled with the party since, despite her conversion to the Josephites and being "put aside" by Cutler, she moved to Minnesota and lived for several years at Battle Lake, only three miles from Clitherall.

There is no indication from Emma's writings that she was aware Jacob Boyd was Cutler's son by his plural wife Luana, or that Boyd, himself, had knowledge of his paternity. A conspiracy of silence had fallen over the subject of polygamy. Though the Cutlerites rejected the proffered leadership of Joseph Smith III, they adopted one central element of his message—namely that they, and their leader Cutler, had never been involved in polygamy. By denying their participation they hoped to erase it from living memory. The Cutlerites' refusal to accept the reality of their past had become total and absolute.

Emma Whiting had reason to remember the trip because, for most of the journey, she and her younger sister, Lu, rode in a wagon with

Edwin Anderson and Jacob Boyd. As Emma explained, "Our wagon was heavily loaded, as there were now eight in our family. When the two young gentlemen of the party suggested that Lu and I ride with them in their wagon our parents consented as we were so crowded in our wagon. Lu and I thought we could sit together on the back seat and view the scenery from under the rolled-up wagon cover but we found that the young men had made a plan between themselves that one of them would sit in front and drive half the day and then take the back seat and let the other be the driver. So we girls had to make a bargain with each other that one of us could sit by Edwin half the day and the other one must sit by Jacob the rest of the day. Since we both liked Edwin better than Jacob that rule was strictly adhered to."[104]

The trip from Iowa to Minnesota took five weeks. On the last day, as the wagons were nearing Clitherall, the two girls put on new print dresses they had made for themselves. "With our light sewing aprons, white collars and a ribbon at the throat we felt ready for the day," Emma wrote. "We were excited when we could see the little village off across the lake and in my joy I unthinkingly swung the little poplar twig in my hand carelessly up and down, still glancing off toward home. To my surprise I saw that I was hitting Edwin's hand that held the lines. I glanced up at him embarrassed. He was smiling and said, 'I will dare you to do that again.' Of course I quickly swung the twig on purpose that time and as soon as it touched his hand I felt myself folded in his arms as he stole a kiss. Well, that was the first time but not the last." On April 5, 1870, the seventeen-year-old Emma became the bride of Edwin Anderson.

Though there were twenty Cutlerite households, they had filed claims on only four parcels of land, choosing the narrow strip lying between the north shore of Clitherall Lake and the south shore of Battle Lake. The Homestead Act, passed in 1862, allowed settlers to claim a quarter section or 160 acres of land. Those who filed claims on property for the church were the brothers Hirum and Lyman Murdock, John Fletcher and Chauncey Whiting. Their reasons for not claiming more land were, to the Cutlerites, entirely logical. They were in Minnesota to carry the gospel to the Indians. They had little intention of establishing permanent homes in Otter Tail County and expected to return to the "center place" [Independence, Missouri] as soon as conditions became favorable. Hirum Murdock was hauling logs for his barn when he remarked to a fellow worker that he hoped to be able to use those same log chains to haul rock for the foundation of the Independence temple.

In an 1867 letter to his sister Sallie Emeline Cox in Utah, Chauncey Whiting wrote "we know not how long we will stay in this land or as yet where we shall go when we leave here but we trust the good Lord will guide our footsteps to a place of safety where we may find a closet to enter in while the calamities are passing by and that at least we may land our souls in the paradise of God where sorrow will be no more. . . ." An escape from the wrath to come was a major element of Cutlerite belief. Whiting, in another letter written in 1888, wrote, "Indeed the times of the Gentiles is [sic] fulfilled, a day of calamity is at hand, the Lord's scourge shall pass over by day and by night, and the report thereof shall vex all nations, or people. This, as we understand, is the dispensation of the fullness of times. . . ."[105] Not only did the Cutlerites anticipate disaster, they appeared to welcome it—at least for the unbelieving Gentiles.

The Cutlerites were the only Mormon splinter group to practice the secret temple ceremonies initiated at Nauvoo and continued by the Utah-based Latter Day Saint Church. After erecting temporary homes, barns and a school, in 1866 the Cutlerites built a two-story log church, dedicating it on New Year's Day, 1867. The lower floor was for general meetings. To the right side of the door as they entered was an enclosed staircase with two low steps leading through a locked door to the upper story. Here the windows were covered with curtains and the space set aside for the secret temple ordinances they had learned in Nauvoo. In this upper chamber the blessings, sealings, baptisms for the dead, ordinations and other secret rituals of Nauvoo Mormonism were carried out by both men and women initiates. Cordelia Whiting, youngest daughter of Francis Lewis and Ann Jeanette, remembered as a child ironing her parent's "garments" or grave clothes, the ritual underwear worn by both men and women as a symbol of their religious convenants. Once put on, the garments were never to be completely removed. Ray Whiting remembered that his grandparents, Francis Lewis and Ann Jeanette Whiting, were buried in their garments.

The extreme hardship of the pioneer period at Clitherall is reflected in the experiences of Hirum and Rachel Murdock who arrived in Minnesota with few resources. At sixteen Rachel Kelsey had been working at a house in Carthage, Illinois, when she heard the shots that killed Joseph and Hyrum Smith. She later married Hirum Murdock, in a ceremony presided over by Brigham Young. Her sister, Sylvia Kelsey, married Hirum's brother Lyman Murdock. The two couples had barely begun housekeeping in Nauvoo before they were forced to flee, becoming part

The original Cutlerite log church, Clitherall, Minnesota, built in 1866.

of the Mormon exodus across Iowa to Winter Quarters, Nebraska. Deciding not to continue further west, they went to Manti and when Cutler began his mission on the Grasshopper River in Kansas, Hirum and Rachel Murdock, with their two children Charles and Martha, and Rachel's elderly mother, went to assist.

When the Indian Agents ordered Cutler's mission to leave the reservation, the Murdocks departed, leaving behind not only five years of work but also Rachel's aged mother and their daughter Martha buried in lonely graves. Another child, four-month-old Eliza, became chilled when her long dress was drenched as the wagons were crossing an icy river on their return to Iowa. Before the caravan could reach Manti, it stopped for the burial of the infant beside the trail. The child was buried with no casket and no headstone; a situation worse, to the grieving parents, than the way the Indians buried their dead.

Back in Manti, without a way to provide for their families, Hirum and Lyman Murdock went to the Cutlerite Platte River, Iowa, settlement to assist in the building and operation of a sawmill. After a time the mill failed and was sold, leaving the Murdock brothers again in a destitute condition. Emily Murdock's memory is that "among our neighbors and the school children, we children were always the poorest of them all."

Inside the Cutlerite log church at Clitherall, Minnesota, circa 1900.

Nevertheless, through extraordinary effort, Hirum Murdock had been able to acquire a herd of sheep, a few cattle, four or five oxen and a team of horses, all of which he moved to Minnesota.

Once in Clitherall, the family lived in a hastily built log cabin on the lake bank. The children spent the first three winters without shoes or stockings. Emily remembered one bright winter's day when the lake was covered with glare ice but no snow when a group of young people decided to walk across the lake to the woods on the opposite shore. Frustrated at being confined so long to the tiny cabin, Emily Murdock, her sister Ellen, her brother Alva and Will Oakes decided to join them. All four were barefoot. Every so often the girls would sit down on the ice and wrap their freezing feet in their petticoats to warm them.[106]

When Hirum Murdock filed the homestead claim on land one half-mile east of the community he built a new log home for his family on a high bank overlooking the lake. Now began what Emily remembered as "the hardest work we had ever known. It seems to me it was beyond human power to accomplish all that father did with only the help of his boys." There were now eleven children in the family, dependent on what their parents could plant and grow. They went months without income of any kind and still the children did not have shoes. On cold winter

Hirum Murdock, from a tintype perhaps taken by
Warren Whiting, circa 1880.

wash days, Rachel Murdock would take off her shoes and give them to
Emily so she could go outside and hang up the clothes to dry.

Calvin Fletcher, who had come with the scouting party, had managed to raise a crop of corn. Occasionally one of the Fletcher children
would give an ear of corn to one of the Murdocks. Emily remembered
that the ears of corn were "real treasures." One day Hirum Murdock
told his children that, instead of eating them, they should bring him all
the ears of corn they were given. If the corn grew in the spring, he
would pay them ten cents for each ear.

The semi-permanent Indian camp lay on the point of land extending out into the lake between the Murdock home and the Clitherall settlement. Inevitably the Indians' dogs began attacking and killing the
Murdock sheep. Hirum Murdock explained the problem to the Indians
who tried to control their dogs but the killing continued. After one mur-
derous attack, an enraged Charles, the barefoot boy who had shep-

herded their sheep all the way from Iowa, grabbed his gun and ran off to the Indian camp, vowing to shoot every Indian dog. Rachel tried to stop him but was too late. The Indians watched Charles' furious approach in silence although three men quietly picked up their guns, keeping their eyes on the boy. From the yard, Rachel looked on in terror, knowing that if Charles shot one dog, he would instantly be killed.

Fortunately, Charles regained his senses in time and no shots were fired. A few hours later the Murdocks looked out the frost-rimmed window of their log house to see a row of Indian women walking up the lake bank carrying huge pillows filled with the finest down of wild ducks and geese. When they were in front of the Murdock house, the women took out their hunting knives and slit the pillows wide open letting the feathers blow out over the icy lake and prairie. The Murdocks understood. The Indians, speaking in a universal language of suffering that could be understood across all cultural and racial barriers, had destroyed their own bedding to show they were sorry.[107]

CHAPTER 8

Self-Reliance
on the Frontier

Otter Tail County had been defined by an act of the Minnesota Legislature on March 18, 1858, but it was not formally organized until 1868 when officers were chosen. Otter Tail City was named the county seat, but since a majority of the legal voters lived in Clitherall, the first county meeting was held there on September 12, 1868. The governor appointed Marcus Shaw and Chauncey Whiting as county commissioners and Sylvester Whiting as auditor.

The new commissioners proceeded to organize the county, appointing Cutlerites Jesse Burdick as County Sheriff; Charles Sperry as Judge of Probate; and William Corliss (a recent convert) as clerk. The commissioners continued to meet in Clitherall until 1870. In 1868 a petition was presented to the commissioners to establish Clitherall Township, one of the first three in the county. The following March another petition asked for the establishment of District One school district, the first in the county. Signers of the school district petition were Marcus Shaw, Chauncey Whiting, Sylvester Whiting, Calvin G. Fletcher, Reuben Oakes, Francis Lewis Whiting, Hirum Murdock, Jesse Burdick, T. Mason and Charles Sperry. The millennial fervor that had given rise to the Cutlerites' ethic of separateness from society was diminishing over time.

Despite their organization of the county under the secular laws of the State of Minnesota, the Cutlerites attempted to run the county according to their religious beliefs. E.E. Corliss, an attorney and a brother of William Corliss, tried a criminal case before Jesse Burdick, who was then serving as Justice of the Peace of Clitherall. The case involved John Campbell, a non-Cutlerite who was accused by his wife of assault with intent to kill. Each time John Mason, the defense attorney, made a point, Justice Burdick would leave his seat, go out behind the barn and kneel in prayer. When Burdick had received what he believed to be an answer to his question, he would return to his judicial seat. In every instance, after engaging in prayer, Burdick ruled for the state. At the conclusion of the hearing Campbell was bound over for trial but the court allowed him to go north to get money to post bond. The man went to Canada and was never seen again in Otter Tail County.

Though the Cutlerite settlers had filed claims on four adjoining homesteads the town site on the lakeshore was located almost entirely on Chauncey Whiting's claim. With the population clustered on the southern end of the property along the lakeshore, the Cutlerites faced the problem of dividing the land into home sites and creating a town. Whiting received what was called a "land patent" on his homestead claim bearing the signature of President U.S. Grant on September 10, 1875. Following the receipt of that document, Whiting began a process of dividing the land into lots A through H, to reflect, legally, how the property had already been put to use. The lots were witnessed on August 28, 1882, but at least three deeds had been issued before the plat was witnessed. The lots varied widely in size and were measured out in "chains and links," a surveyor's method of measuring land—a chain being 66 feet long and a link 7.92 inches. One hundred links equaled four rods or 66 feet. (A rod is 16.5 feet.)

Beginning in the 1880s the land the founding Cutlerites had claimed as homesteads for the community began to pass into other hands. However every owner up until 1927 was a member of the Cutlerite church.[108] On March 25, 1882, Chauncey and Editha Whiting deeded lot G, about a 3 acre piece, to Sylvester Whiting for $30. On June 1, 1882, Hyram Oakes received the deed for lot F, about an acre and a half, for $20; Warren Whiting got lot C , almost 3 acres, for $20; and Isaac Whiting paid his parents $20 for the three and a half acre lot E. The parcels of land were later further subdivided when, for example, Sylvester and Rebecca Whiting deeded Joseph Edmund Fletcher the east three chains of lot G (one acre) and H.J. Oakes the west three chains of lot G. The land continually changed hands among the same small group as men died and their widows and children assumed ownership. The tract that Chauncey and Editha deeded to their son Chauncey, Junior, went next to Hirum Murdock who left it, after his death, to his nine surviving children who, one by one in 1898, signed it over to Abner Tucker.

The Otter Tail County Plat Book of 1884 identifies every principal building in the village of Clitherall. Coming into town from the north, the first house to be encountered was Hirum Murdock's, high above the lake on the bluff. From the Murdock house the road ran west for a short distance before swinging south around the marsh and dropping down the hill into the village. On the east side of the road, almost at the brow of the hill, stood the homes of James Fletcher and Alonzo Whiting. Next came Warren Whiting's house followed by Laura Lang's cottage, the school, the church and, at the shore of the lake where the road turned west, Isaac Whiting's home.

Across from Warren Whiting's home, on the west side of the road near the top of the hill, stood a log building that housed Joseph Edmund Fletcher's blacksmith shop and Isaac and Lurett Whiting's wagon shop. Beside it was Chauncey Whiting's home and tin shop followed by James Oakes' cabin and F. Lewis Whiting's home. On the corner, where the road turned west, stood Sylvester Whiting's home, store and the first post office in the county. These seventeen log buildings, with some sheds and barns, were the totality of Clitherall. Beyond the border of the village the road ran along the shore of the lake toward the outlet to Battle Lake, past the homes of Lyman Murdock, Joseph Edmund Fletcher, William Corliss and Calvin Fletcher.

In an early photograph, circa 1867–8, can be seen from left to right, Chauncey Whiting's house and his shop, the wagon shop of Isaac and Lurett Whiting, and Joseph Edmund Fletcher's blacksmith shop.

For the first few years the Cutlerites were dependent on outsiders for only a few services, such as milling their grain into flour. Until 1870, when a Scotsman named James Craigie built a mill at the outlet of Otter Tail Lake, the nearest gristmill was forty miles away in Alexandria, a long distance to travel with a load of grain. The nearest trading post was Sauk Center, sixty-five miles away. The Cutlerites' isolation forced them to draw on their own resources and they responded with Yankee ingenuity. Nothing was wasted. When one of Francis Lewis Whiting's oxen was killed, he took the skin from the animal's hind legs, sewed up the bottom ends, put straps on the top and, with the hair still on them, wore them for boots claiming that they were warm and durable.

Like pioneers elsewhere on the frontier, the Cutlerites had the requisite skills to sustain themselves. All of the men were farmers. In addition Joseph Edmund Fletcher was a blacksmith, Marcus Shaw was a stone mason and plasterer, Chauncey Whiting a mechanic and wagon-maker, Almon Whiting made chairs, and Sylvester Whiting was a storekeeper and postmaster. All were skilled hunters. Among them the men had the ability to make wagons, furniture, tools and farm machinery and build houses, sheds and barns. The women spun thread, wove cloth, made clothing, knit hats and mittens, kept gardens, cooked and preserved food. Those who did not have candle molds made candles for light by repeatedly pouring melted tallow over a string until it was the diameter of a candle.

The Cutlerites had not been able to bring many farm implements with them from Iowa and so had only a few plowshares, one breaking plowshare and a few blacksmith and carpenter tools. None of the tools had handles so their first task was to cut and shape wooden handles before they could begin their farm work. They mounted the breaking plowshare on a homemade wood frame, attached a wooden axle-tree, about four feet long, and hitched two oxen to the contraption. It worked and was used to break all the land initially used by the Cutlerites. The grass was as high as the men's waists. During the heat of summer, the men would begin breaking ground at three o'clock in the morning and work until eight. Then they would stop until evening when they would begin again, not stopping until eleven at night when it was too dark to see.[109]

A harrow (called a "drag") was made from a forked tree. They bored holes in the tree limbs about eight inches apart with a two-inch auger and inserted twenty-inch-long wooden teeth. They could smooth out about an acre a day with oxen pulling the harrow. Grain was all sown by hand, either carried in a wooden pail or in a sack containing a half-bushel of seed strapped over one shoulder. The sower walked along the prepared field, broadcasting the seed by throwing it out a hand full at a time. Corn, too, was planted by hand—each hill covered with soil with a garden hoe. Once the grain grew, it was cut with a scythe called a "cradle." A cradle consisted of a long curved scythe blade attached to a handle. Five or six cradle fingers made of ash or hickory were fastened about five inches apart to a frame that hung below and had the same curve as the blade. (This was called a "snath.") The fingers of the snath hung out below the blade to catch the falling grain as it was cut and laid it out in straight swaths. Another worker followed who raked the swaths and tied them into bundles. A good cutter could cut five or six acres of grain a day with a cradle.

When winter came the settlers discovered they needed sleds. They fashioned six-foot runners from trees and held them together with three cross beams. The tongue was a forked tree. When the snow was deep they discovered they could not turn the sled around without either breaking the tongue or tipping the sled over altogether. In the 1890s Francis Lewis Whiting began making regular bobsleds, calling them "McKinley Sleds," which left no doubt as to his politics.

Early beds were made from four round posts cut from trees with the bark still on. Bed rails were made from tree branches, driven into auger holes cut into the bedposts. A strong rope, called "bed-cord," was woven across each way with the mesh about eight inches square. A tick filled with straw or hay was placed on top of the ropes to sleep on. Since new ropes stretched easily, sleepers often found themselves closer to the floor when they woke up than when they went to bed. Milk, butter and cheese were kept cool in the summer by putting the items in a bucket and suspending the bucket from a rope in a well.

When Almon Whiting arrived in 1867 he set up the first horse-power lathe in the county to make his chairs. (Chauncey and Isaac Whiting previously had put together a small foot lathe.) Almon Whiting searched through the forest for the best wood for his furniture using oak and ash for the frames, basswood for solid seats and elm and maple for rails. His youngest daughter rode the horse as it walked in circles to turn the lathe. Whiting made his own glue from deer horns and hoofs and mixed his own paints. Woven seats were made from swamp ash he found about five miles from his home. He split the ash into one-inch square strips from eight to ten feet long. These pieces were steamed in a

Almon Whiting (1821–1908), the chairmaker.

vat and then pounded until the wood separated into splints. Using a tool called a "froe" that had a blade mounted at a right angle, he cut the splints apart and scraped them smooth, removing splinters with a piece of broken glass and a drawing knife. Most of Whiting's chairs were given a base coat of red paint with black painted over it, perhaps to imitate rosewood. Designs were often stenciled on the front rails of the chairs in different colors and the rungs were decorated with white, yellow and red striping.

The chairs were never carelessly made. Almost every family in the county soon had some of Almon Whiting's chairs. The incoming settlers needed rugged, inexpensive chairs and Whiting could undersell distant mass producers. None of his chairs resembled furniture made in the Michigan factories. He made splint-bottomed chairs, dining room chairs,

One of Almon Whiting's armless sewing rocking chairs.
From the collection of the author.

great roomy arm chairs, armless sewing rockers, children's chairs and high-chairs for babies. Whiting could have no inkling that, in the future, his chairs would be eagerly sought after by collectors and housed in museums. (One of his chairs was included in a 1989 exhibit of Minnesota folk art called "Circles of Tradition.")

The trip north from Iowa had been hard on the group's wagons and many of them were in disrepair. Chauncey Whiting's sons, Isaac and the twins Lurett and Alonzo, undertook to repair wagons. They chose the best oak they could find and cut, split and dried it around the stoves in their homes until it was suitable for use. Isaac Whiting turned wagon wheel spokes on the hand lathe. The hubs were made from blocks sawed out of large oak logs into the proper length, hewed round, with a two-inch auger hole bored in the center. Iron came from Janney, Semple

Company in Minneapolis in fourteen to fifteen foot lengths, two inches wide and one-half inch thick. Chauncey Whiting made his sons a contrivance to bend the iron into tires. As his son Lurett Whiting explained, "He took a piece of oak plank about three inches thick, three feet long and 10 inches wide and rounded one edge about the right curve for a wagon wheel. Then this plank, having the upper edge circular, was bolted solid to a big oak tree near the shop and a big iron clamp [was placed] at one end of the circle. All we had to do was to stick the end of the tire bar through the clamp, pull down on the long end, thus bending the bar around the curved plank, and as it became bent properly we could slide it on around through the clamp and bend another section until we had the bar in a complete circle."

Lurett Whiting finished the wagons by decorating them with brightly colored stripes. He was painting a wagon when a group of Ojibwe Indians stopped to watch him work, fascinated by the way he handled his brushes. The Indians asked if they could have some paint. Whiting went to his paint cupboard, showed them the different colors and invited them to select what they wanted. "They took some vermilion red, Persian blue, lamp black and green. They mixed it with water and painted red rings around their eyes, put blue on their noses, green and black on their cheeks and with their finger tips they spotted their faces, hands and arms. After that they came often for paint." Over time the Whiting boys manufactured farm wagons as well as smaller wagons, two-wheeled carts, buggies, carriages, bobsleds, gun stocks and repaired all kinds of related equipment.

Hirum Murdock made brooms of ironwood. To make a broom he cut slender green ironwood the proper length and sawed a girdle around it sixteen to twenty inches from the bottom end. He shaved the long end down until it was the right diameter for a handle. At the opposite end, he cut down in thin, narrow shavings nearly to the bottom, letting them fall over and hang down from the broomstick. When one layer was finished he would start on another, shaving them all around, each layer falling over the one previously cut until the mass of shavings formed a broom. When it was dried, the broom gave years of service on the puncheon floors.

The first houses were made of logs because of the difficulty in sawing logs into lumber. To saw boards from a log, a hole about six feet deep was dug in the earth. A log was laid across the pit and one man stood underneath the log in the hole while a second man stood on a platform above the log. Working together to pull the long saw, two men could cut about 250 feet of lumber in a day if the logs were frozen. If the logs were green and thawed out, the cutting was more difficult and men did well to saw 170 feet in a day.[110]

During the cold winter months the men's principal activity was providing the fuel for the *next* winter's cooking and heating. The only fuel was wood and a principal source was a tamarack swamp seven miles north of the village. It took a full day to bring in one sled-load of wood. A team would be hitched to a bobsled and if the men left at eight in the morning they would arrive at the stand of tamarack by ten or eleven. The horses would be tied up and given hay to eat while the men took their axes and began cutting the trees. At noon they would build a fire to keep warm while they ate their lunch. By three o'clock the sled was loaded with wood and they would start for home, driving across Battle Lake where strong winds usually kept the ice clear of snow. When they reached the shore, however, they would run into such huge drifts that it often took an hour or more to shovel their way through.

Once the men got the wood home, the logs had to be sawed into lengths to fit into stoves. The cut blocks were tossed into huge piles until they could be split. The splitting was done while there was still frost in the blocks as then they would crack open relatively easily when struck with an axe. The split wood would then be piled in another huge pile to dry out and be ready for the next winter's use.

The guns the Cutlerites brought with them from Iowa were percussion-cap muzzle loaders. Lurett Whiting explained how they worked. "We bought our lead in small bars, melted it in an iron ladle and while hot ran our bullets in a bullet-mould the size to fit our rifles. We carried powder in a powder horn and gun-caps in little tin boxes. To load we poured powder into the barrel, put in a ball, and with a ram-rod drove the bullet tight against the powder, then put a percussion-cap in place and were ready to shoot. After shooting once, it took quite a while to reload and be ready for another shot."[111]

They had lived in Clitherall only a year or two when Francis Lewis Whiting bought a second-hand horse-powered threshing machine from a farmer near what is now Sauk Center. Since the Cutlerites had only a few horses, they hitched two yokes of oxen to the machine and started up. The machine required the oxen to walk in a circle but after two or three laps the oxen became dizzy and lay down. Lurett Whiting remembered that they took the oxen off and "managed to thresh out what little grain we had with the horses by feeding the machine light. After a year or two farmers began to settle all around us and we were then able to get all the horses we needed."

In the fall of 1868 the Cutlerites took their threshing machine to Silver Lake to thresh for George Gould, a homesteading neighbor. While working with Gould, they learned to make shingles. The Cutlerites had used shakes to roof their houses and saw that shingles were a great improvement. Lurett Whiting noted with interest that Gould had made a roof of small poplar poles that had been flattened on one side and nailed to the rafters. Shingles were nailed to the flat side of the poles, which, as Whiting could see, made a serviceable roof. Gould showed Whiting his tool for cutting shingles from 16-inch oak blocks and then thinning down one end with a shaving knife. Shingles were hand-made in this way until Jesse Burdick rigged up his shingle knife in a frame so it could be powered by his horse. He made a steam box of iron, similar to but larger than the maple-sugar boiler, in which he could steam up to 20 blocks of wood which made them easier to cut. As Lurett explained, "All the one operating the block had to do was to shift the block one way and another as the knife went up and down cutting off a shingle at every downward stroke, one shingle thick at one end and the next one thick at the opposite end so as to waste none of the block. After this we used these shingles for our roofs in place of the shakes on them previously."[112]

Hunting was a major source of food and despite the primitive nature of their rifles, Isaac Whiting and his brothers became proficient at bringing deer and bear back to the colony. As Lurett Whiting boasted, "My rifle carried an ounce ball and I could shoot mighty close." On one occasion he and his brothers brought down eleven deer. "We took the cover off the wagon and arranged the deer so that the bucks' heads were all sticking out over the edge of the box and the does were in the center and a nicer load of deer I never saw." Occasionally the brothers found themselves stalking the same bear as parties of Indian hunters. Lurett Whiting had been tracking a bear for several miles only to lose it to Indians a few minutes before he arrived on the scene. "Well, I was mad," he later recalled, "to have had that long tramp only to be disappointed when I had so nearly reached the game, but I knew the Indians had as good a right to the wild game as the white people had."

Not all of the settlers were hunters. Hugh Hunter, who married Cutlerite Rhoda Sherman, frequently saw deer and bears on his homestead, yet never killed one in his life. Instead he traded a calf to a neighbor for a fawn which became a family pet that followed Hunter wherever he went. "It was afraid of dogs," he remembered, "and sometimes ran into the house if a dog came near. It would eat from the table if we would allow it to. One morning the fawn was tied to a tree where it became entangled in the rope and choked to death. We reached it just an instant too late. We thought so much of it that it was mighty hard to see it die. I finally dressed it and my wife cooked a piece of the meat but it was not touched. Neither of us could eat a bite."[113]

Fish were so abundant in the lakes and streams that they could be speared from shore or even caught with bare hands. One Sunday morning some Cutlerite boys slipped out of church and went to the outlet of Clitherall Lake where it empties into Battle Lake. "The sight that met our eyes was enough to stir the blood of older and wiser fishermen than we," one remembered. "The outlet was just jammed full of the largest pickerel we had ever seen. They were actually crowding one another out upon the banks. We spent two hours pounding fish on the head with fence rails before we noticed what an enormous pile we had."

Fish were particularly plentiful in the spring. Using pitchforks for spears, they speared muskies and catfish weighing over 40 pounds. George Hammer had a memorable spear fishing experience with Francis Lewis Whiting. "Uncle Lute was watching close to the boat when I called his attention to a monstrous pickerel about twelve feet away. He made a good stroke at it and struck the fellow close to its head. The fish made a rush directly toward the boat. Uncle Lute stepped backward and in doing so pushed me over the edge into the water—my feet still in the boat but my body all under water except my head and hands that gripped the boat. Uncle Lute was sitting on my knees, hanging on to the fish for dear life."

The other passenger, Odd Albertson, struggled to keep the boat from overturning. "Mr. Whiting," he shouted. "You are drowning Hammer!" "Can't help it," Whiting replied. "This is the biggest fish I ever speared and I've got to get it." Whiting landed his fish, helped Hammer back into the boat and, when they reached shore, weighed the fish. It weighed twenty-seven pounds.[114]

The lake provided recreation winter and summer. It was usually frozen over by the first of November and if it froze when the wind was still the entire surface of the lake would be as smooth as a sheet of glass. The young people skated on the ice and, when the wind was blowing, held their coats open and let the wind carry them at what seemed a tremendous speed for miles down the lake. The ice went out of the lake during the month of April. It would melt first near the shore, opening up twenty to thirty feet of open water around the lake. Then a strong southwest wind would come up. At first there would be no perceptible movement but, after a few hours, the whole mass of ice would begin to move, starting slowly, but picking up speed and moving faster until it crashed into the shore. Trees a foot or more in diameter would be snapped as if they were twigs by three and a half miles of moving ice. Surging onto the shore the ice piles would reach 30 feet in height.

The settlers thought nothing of walking long distances to supply their needs. When Hugh Hunter needed supplies or a plow blade sharpened he let his oxen rest and walked the eighteen miles to Otter Tail, carrying the supplies and equipment home on his back. A few years after his marriage Hunter, who had previously lost the sight in one eye when a nail flew into it, lost the sight in his other eye. Although his family urged him to give up his homestead, Hunter refused and, with the help of neighbors and his children, he managed his farm. As he later explained, "With the help of a cane I could soon find my way around the place and one day started alone to a neighbor's. I felt so nervous and half-frightened that the perspiration rolled down my face, but I counted my steps as I had done when someone led me there and, as the road was straight, I found their gate all right. I went there often and soon found that as I neared the house my footsteps had a different sound. After that it was not necessary to count my steps as I could tell quite easily when to turn in at the gate. There was a different sound as I approached a building, or even a tree or post—a sensation I had never known before I was blind."[115]

Soon Hunter was taking short cuts across the fields, guided by the crowing of roosters, barking of dogs or lowing of cattle. One winter when his children were ill with "lung fever" he started out in the middle of the night to get help from a neighbor over two miles away. The ground was covered with snow and on the return trip Hunter lost his way and turned into a field. "I wandered around in every direction, suffering with the cold and knowing it would be hours before morning when anyone could find me." After stumbling about for over an hour, he heard his dog, Bruno, bark. The bark came from the opposite direction. Hunter immediately turned around and walked towards the barking. He found his dog "standing squarely in the middle of the road. He jumped up on me with little barks of satisfaction and frisked around me all the way home." That was the only time Hugh Hunter was ever lost.

With the aid of his children, Hunter was able to clear his land. He took his little daughter, Bertha (whom he never saw), to the fields with him when he was grubbing out large trees. It was Bertha's job to watch and determine which way the tree would fall. Hunter would chop away at the roots until the tree began to sway. When it started to fall, Bertha would grab her father's hand and shouting, "Run, Papa, run," would guide him out from under the crashing branches. He was able to split logs for posts by having his boys place the wedge in the logs while he struck it with the maul. One year he split 30 loads of firewood, enough to last for two years, in 30 days. He built a granary and chicken-coop with only a little help from his children who, at the time, had no knowledge of carpentry. To build fences his sons would locate the places for the post holes and Hunter would dig them. He harnessed his own teams and plowed his fields with a child to guide his team.

Over the years Hunter's hearing became acute. He could discern by a difference in sound when his wagon was passing houses and he memorized the turns in long stretches of country road. He could recognize hundreds of people by their voices, some of whom he had not met for over twenty years. One man lost a watch in the woods and had given up ever finding it when Hunter located it from the sound of its ticking. A five dollar gold piece, which had accidentally been tossed from a dish on the table into the dishwater and later into the pigs' trough, was found by Hunter who located it by hearing it clinking against a pig's teeth.[116]

In 1877 a plague of grasshoppers descended on Otter Tail County. The grain had headed out and the harvest promised to be a good one when, around noon one day in August, Ella Whiting Gould was startled to see a cloud of grasshoppers settling over the fields. "I went out to see where they were coming from and as I looked up there seemed to be a heavy snowstorm, the air was just full of big flakes. As soon as the grasshoppers touched the ground they began eating everything in sight."

Ella's father-in-law George Gould was fishing on Clitherall Lake when the grasshoppers appeared. He soon stopped because the fish were surfacing to eat the grasshoppers, ignoring his bait. When the insects had eaten everything in the fields, they laid their eggs and flew off in a great cloud. That year Gould harvested only eighteen bushels of grain. For two years the Cutlerites experienced almost total crop loss to insects, leaving the settlers nearly destitute. "One thing spared to us," Ella remembered, "were pig-weeds or red-root, so we usually had red-root greens for dinner. We ate homemade maple sugar in the place of granulated sugar we could not afford to buy. Another way we economized was by using a kind of lamp burner that required no chimney. The lamp did not smoke and saved kerosene, though the light was not good."

The second year of the grasshopper invasion got the attention of the governor of Minnesota, John Pillsbury. He visited Otter Tail County with a Prof. Charles V. Riley, an entomologist who worked for the state of Illinois. Riley had no solution for the problem other than to look over a field and remark that there were "enough grasshoppers in that field to cover the entire state when they begin flying." The governor was equally helpless and was expressing his frustration to A.C. Hatch, a pioneer settler at Battle Lake, when Hatch said that one of Chauncey Whiting's sons, Alonzo, had an idea for how to kill grasshoppers. Eager for a solution, the governor agreed to finance Alonzo Whiting's plan.

With the financial support of Governor Pillsbury, Whiting and Hatch ordered two carloads of kerosene and some sheet iron. From the sheet iron they made "hopper-dozers" in which to scoop up and kill the insects. The two men worked day and night for two weeks and estimated that they incinerated 32,000 bushels of grasshoppers enabling the farmers to eventually harvest about ten bushels of grain to an acre. That ended the massive infestation of grasshoppers in Otter Tail County.

CHAPTER 9

Dissension and
The Works of Evil Spirits

In the early years the only road to Clitherall was a wagon track that ran through the grass of the prairie from Otter Tail City through Clitherall to the village of Chippewa. In the late 1860s this trail became the route of a stagecoach that ran from Chippewa to Otter Tail City one day and back to Chippewa the next. The coming of the stage was a harbinger of change. The Hirum Murdock home was halfway between the two villages so the family was the first to benefit. When the route was laid out the stage company arranged to place a fresh team for the stage in Hirum Murdock's barn and paid him $25 a month to board a man to look after the team. The stage driver would arrive hungry so Rachel provided a meal for him, often of bear meat and venison, for an additional 50 cents. Before long passengers on the stage were also purchasing meals from the Murdocks.

Chauncey Whiting made a sign to post by the side of the road with a picture of a stagecoach on it and the words, "Farmer's House." A bear's claw was nailed to the post. Within a few months the stage was disgorging passengers every day to eat lunch at the Murdocks' home. The income was welcomed but the work of preparing meals was an additional burden for Rachel and the children.

One night the log house caught fire. Lyman and Alva Murdock awoke in the upstairs bedroom to find their mattress blazing. Both boys had to be dragged from their beds. Everyone rushed to carry possessions out of the house. The last item saved was a clock Murdock had purchased the second year after their arrival in Minnesota. His hair was ablaze as he ran from the house with the clock in his arms. The house was a total loss.

During the confusion Rachel Murdock had handed an envelope to Emily saying, "Keep this safe. It is all the money we have." Then she sent the girls to the lake with the burning quilts to be soaked to quench the fire. The walk to the dark shore was frightening because of the unspoken fear that Indians lurking in the woods might have set the fire. When the blaze had been put out and it was daylight, Rachel asked Emily for the envelope but Emily had no memory of receiving it. Later her brother Orison found the envelope, not even scorched, lying on the doorsill. It contained $200. When the clock was picked up, it was found to have stopped at 3 o'clock in the morning.

Following the fire, the family moved into a small wheat granary. An even smaller shed was fixed up for the boys and the stage man to sleep in. Though the granary had a single door, Murdock cut another door in the back, near the girls' room. Emily overheard her father tell the boys that if they ever heard a noise at night at their door, or about the place, to run in the back door and warn the rest of the family. Though he never stated it, Emily knew it was the Indians whom he feared.

The day after the fire a neighbor, Marcus Shaw, and another man arrived on the stage. Shaw went up to Murdock and said, "Mr. Murdock, I am sorry. I am sorry $10.00 worth," and handed him a ten dollar bill. The other man gave him $5. That was all the money Murdock received to help him recover from the loss of his home, but the Cutlerites banded together and helped the Murdocks build another log home. The new house had a small front room that was used as a bedroom for boarders.

A high bluff on the north side of the Murdock house was the site of a structure that played a major role in the lives of the second generation. The object was a swing on which poles approximately twenty-five feet long, instead of ropes, were used to suspend the seat. Built in 1867, the pole swing stood on the bank overlooking the lake. Its location one half mile from the village, made it a desirable site for trysts and picnics away from the center of the community. In the long summer evenings when it was light until well past 10 P.M., the young people gathered at the swing for singing, courting, and conversation. Many young women were proposed to on the pole swing, as Emma Anderson wrote:

> "But my lover sat beside me
> There, and asked would I his bride be,
> While so gently swayed the Old Town swing."

The old town swing, Clitherall, Minnesota.

George Hammer, who taught the Clitherall school for a term, called it a "happy trysting place" but added that "to some of us there is a sting in the memory, for t'was there we saw the other fellow walk off with our best girl, all because we lacked the courage to tell her what our thoughts were until she mistook our silence for indifference." In the society of Clitherall, the simple structure of a tall swing on a lake bluff enriched the lives of the young pioneers.[117]

The Cutlerites continued to be preoccupied with the notion of evil spirits. Emily Murdock wrote, "One terror of our lives was the fear of the Fletcher spirit. Whether their evil power over others was real or only imagined I do not know, but by some it was believed to be real." Emily and her father Hirum Murdock were among the believers.

An incident with a Cutlerite woman, known as "Mother Mack Fletcher," frightened Emily and her parents and reinforced their beliefs in the occult. Mother Mack was an elderly woman, probably senile, who, though she had a place to live in Clitherall, often came to the Hirum

Murdocks' house to eat and spend the night. Because she was old and penniless the Murdocks did not turn her away. One day Emily, who had been working at one of the other Cutlerite houses, came home for some of her clothing and found Mother Mack asleep in her bed. Rachel told Emily that Mother Mack had slept in the bed for a week and if Emily planned to come home on Saturday, she should tell Mother Mack.

Emily went a few steps up the stairs and called up, "I'm coming home on Saturday and I'll want my bed. So you be out of it." Emily's words made the old woman angry and she threw a pillow at Emily. Though Emily was not hurt by the pillow, she began to feel strange as she went downstairs. Going outdoors she sat down on the banking of the house where Hirum and Rachel Murdock found her. To their dismay, Emily was unable to speak. As she explained, "I could not talk or think for some time. I did not know anything. It was not until after Father administered to me that my mind came back and I could talk." The prayerful Mormon rite of "administration" or the "laying on of hands" was used for all kinds of emergencies. Emily and her father were convinced that by throwing the pillow at Emily, Mother Mack had cast an evil spell over her.

Joseph Edmund was another elderly Fletcher who imagined himself to be a prophet or seer. He claimed to receive messages for different persons from heaven and would write them down on scraps of paper and deliver them to the recipients. Many of the messages were directed at Hirum Murdock who intensely disliked and feared Fletcher. On one occasion Murdock refused to take the paper from Fletcher and insisted that his daughter take it for him. The two men argued frequently, despite Rachel's attempt to get her husband to ignore the old man. After a particularly bitter argument, Murdock thought he had got the better of Fletcher and began laughing at him. The old man, angry and with his black eyes flashing, said in a threatening tone, "Brother Hirum, the sectarian spirit don't like to be laughed at."

Fletcher went home, but soon after the encounter Hirum Murdock fell ill, growing rapidly worse until he became delirious. From the onset of his illness he feared Fletcher and begged his family not to let the old man in the house. The Fletchers lived over the hill, out of sight of the Murdock home, but Murdock knew when Fletcher was on the way. "Go lock the door," he told his family. "Father Fletcher is coming." Each time Murdock's family would do as he requested and, sure enough, in a few minutes Fletcher would be seen coming up the hill. When he reached the Murdock house he would pound on the locked door and peer in the windows. After walking around the house a few times, he would return to his own home.

This happened repeatedly until one day Fletcher caught the family off guard and gained entry into the house. Before they could stop him Fletcher was in Murdock's sick room saying in a jeering voice, "Brother Hirum, the sectarian spirit don't like to be laughed at."

From the day of that incident, Murdock grew worse. Friends came and nursed him. One night, when the watchers fell asleep, Murdock got up and in his delirium left the house. Rachel heard the door bang and went out to find him in the barn. During much of the time Murdock thought there were fires around him. He told his children, "Don't say anything but go and get some water and put out this fire around my bed."

Eventually the fever broke and Murdock told his family that during the three weeks of his delirium he was with Father Fletcher, wandering day and night through woods, prairies, swamps and bogs with Fletcher continually setting fires. Though the fever was gone, an abscess began to form in Murdock's chest. The abscess grew until his whole chest became enlarged and inflamed and his suffering was intense. The Cutlerites gathered and, after administration and prayer, resolved on a course of action. Warren Whiting sharpened his jackknife blade as sharp as he could make it and bared Murdock's chest. Aiming for the center of the angry-looking infection and, with nothing to deaden the pain, he stuck his blade into it. Prodding, he plunged the blade in to the hilt and turned it slightly. Instantly a stream of pus and blood shot all the way to the ceiling of the room. Emily, standing at the foot of the bed, was certain that her father was being killed. For weeks the wound drained, so the women brought clean white cloths for Rachel to use.

When Murdock was finally able to be out of bed and on his feet Emily saw him coming out of a closet under the stairs, his head covered with cobwebs and dust, holding a small stout box in his hands. He took it to Rachel. The box contained their savings, several hundred dollars that she had not known existed. During his illness and delirium, Murdock had feared he would die and no one would ever find the money. Emily had mixed feelings about her father's savings. "How," she said, "he could have saved that money with his children going barefooted in the cold I cannot understand."[118]

Murdock's honesty was legendary. George Hammer recalled that Murdock "at one time refused to take more than $1.50 for seed potatoes when we offered him the market price of $2.00 a bushel. He told us that he could not sleep nights if he charged a neighbor that much for potatoes."[119]

Another individual whom some of the Cutlerites thought used witchcraft was Laura Lang, whom they called Aunt Laurie. Though rumored to have once been married, Laura lived alone in Manti, sustaining herself with a flock of sheep. When the Cutlerites moved to Minnesota, Laura went along, driving her flock the entire way. Her possessions (bedding for one bed, a few clothes and dishes, a small stove and cooking utensils, a clock, looking glass, spinning-wheel, broom, mop, washtub and board) were carried in one of the travelers' wagons. Once in Clitherall the men joined together to build her a one-room log cabin with a shake roof, puncheon floor and a chimney of sticks, stones, mud and mortar. Her home had a door and one window with six panes of glass. During the first year, Laura's home was used for church services. One of the men plowed a garden for her and when the wheat fields were sown, a plot of ground was set apart as the "widow's field." With this assistance, and her few chickens, cow and sheep, she was able to survive. Every day, in all kinds of weather, she herded her sheep. When night fell she led them to a low shed and returned to her house where a cat was her only companion.

Laura Lang was a tall, slightly stooped, woman whose gray hair hung about her face and whose piercing eyes looked out from under heavy brows. Dogs were the bane of her life and, to protect her flock, she often carried weak little lambs in her soiled apron. No one ever went to her house and Laura seldom mingled with the other Cutlerites, except at church. People gossiped that Laura Lang might be a witch and everyone avoided the old woman, fearful that she might bring them bad luck.

Everyone, that is, but thirteen-year-old Emma Whiting. Emma watched Laura as she started off in the morning with her sheep and returned each evening, tired and worn. One day Emma told her mother Ann Jeanette that she thought Laura was lonely and she was going to visit her. Taking her quilt blocks along and trying to quell her nervousness, Emma waded through the snow to Laura's house. When she knocked on the door the old woman called out, "Come in," and then stood in the doorway and waited for the girl to state her errand.

"I came over to see if you were well," Emma explained. When Laura had recovered from her surprise, she dropped her austere manner, invited Emma to take off her wraps and sit down. Soon the two were talking and laughing. After Emma's third or fourth visit, Laura made tea for her visitor and talked about her past. She said that her parents had been well off and she had had fine things and did not look as she did now. However, when Laura had joined the Latter Day Saints she had been "cast off" from her family. Laura opened her trunk and showed her treasures to Emma—the remains of a silk dress and a heavily brocaded silk blouse. Emma thought they were wonderful. "She gave me a good many quilt scraps which I pieced on shares," Emma remembered. Though rumors of Laura being a witch persisted until her death in about 1885, the young girl remained the old woman's friend. Sociologist Danny Jorgensen suspects Lang may have been one of Cutler's plural wives whom he had "put aside" in Iowa. If so, Lang cooperated with the church leadership's attempts to expunge polygamy from Cutlerite history. There is no mention of Lang's marital status or of her past history in the Cutlerite letters or records that are public.

The first death in the Clitherall community occurred in February 1867. William Mason was a shoemaker. Needing to earn money he had left his wife in Clitherall and gone to Alexandria where he found customers for his shoes. (The eleven Murdock children needed shoes but their father either had no money or was unwilling to spend it for his children's shoes.) That February Mason decided to leave work and walk home to Clitherall, a distance of about thirty-two miles. The first day he went as far as Millerville, a village on the western side of the Leaf Mountains, and stayed with a settler there. The next morning, though the weather was threatening and the friend in Millerville urged him to wait, Mason set off on foot for Clitherall. A light snow began to fall and by noon it was a raging blizzard. The wind shifted to the northwest and the temperature dropped. Mason made it through the Leaf Mountains and was crossing the ten miles of prairie that separated him from Clitherall when, overcome by the cold, he fell headfirst into a snow bank. He was only a few miles from his house.

Since no one in Clitherall knew that Mason was returning home, no one raised an alarm. Not until several weeks later when the man from Millerville chanced to ask Hirum Murdock if Mason had arrived safely, did the community learn that Mason was missing. Search parties on snowshoes combed the lake and prairie without success. Not until later in the spring, when several of the men loaded their sleighs for the one-week trip to Sauk Center with grain to be ground into flour, was Mason found. They were only a short distance from Clitherall when Marcus Shaw saw what looked like a stove pipe sticking up out of the snow. He jumped down from his load to see what it was and found a boot. William Mason was lying on his face as he had evidently fallen. The sleighs turned back to Clitherall bringing the body with them.

Back at the village they stopped at Francis Lewis Whiting's house on the corner and Mrs. Mason, having heard the news, came from across the road. The body was taken to the log church for services and burial. Isaac Whiting made the coffin. Cowbar Hill overlooking the lake, part of Hirum Murdock's claim, was chosen for the cemetery. The next day the first of what would be many funeral processions wound up the hill. Sadness and gloom over the death of William Mason hung over the little community for many months.

The village by the lakeshore soon faced other problems. It was apparent to the farmers that not enough land had been claimed. The Cutlerite families were large and they could see that the coming generation of boys would need more land. Preoccupied though they were with their own activities, they could see that other settlers were moving rapidly into the area and it would not be long before all the good farmland would be taken. To complicate matters, the ownership of land was intertwined, for the Cutlerites, with issues of religious belief and practice. While the four homesteads had been filed under the names of four Cutlerite leaders, the implicit understanding was that the four were holding the land for the church. The land was to belong to all of the members—it was their "inheritance."

Unfortunately, the Cutlerites had never come to terms with one of their basic church doctrines called the "Order of Enoch" or "The Oneness." Like other utopian communities, the Cutlerites were striving for economic and social equality. Under the principle of The Oneness, all property and land, except for certain personal possessions, was to be turned over to the church and held in common. Each family was to keep enough of the harvest to supply its own needs and to put whatever was left over, especially grains and storable crops, into a common storehouse to be issued to members as needed.

Their attempt to institute a communal system in Manti in the early 1860s had met with only partial success. Some members participated by deeding their property to the church and others did not. In Clitherall they started over and, at least during the first year or two, agreed to hold the land of their four homesteads in common. The question of ownership of houses, tools, livestock and surplus crops was left undecided. While the pioneers willingly shared labor and supplies, they were reluctant to define the precise perimeters of their Oneness participation. Lacking any kind of formal mechanism to put their Oneness philosophy into practice, for the most part they let the matter drift. Because disagreements could be threatening to the survival of such a small group, the Cutlerites avoided controversy and postponed making potentially divisive decisions.

A decision they could not avoid, however, was the question of who should be the leader of the church. The issue had only been resolved temporarily in Manti. Though the problem was framed in terms of religious authority, the unspoken issue was one of land. When the question of authority was brought up in Minnesota, it led to the first major schism of the Minnesota Cutlerites. The issue of who had the authority to lead the church had been always been central to early Mormonism. Following the death of Joseph Smith, Brigham Young claimed authority to lead the Saints by virtue of his position as president of the Quorum of Twelve Apostles. Young's assumption of authority did not prevent other claimants from coming forward with their own legalistic arguments. When Alpheus Cutler died, the question of who had the authority to lead the Cutlerites was equally hard to resolve. Chauncey Whiting, who assumed leadership after Cutler's death, had been Cutler's *second* counselor. The *first* counselor, and technically the one in line for the presidency of the church, was the elderly Charles Sperry.

Despite his secondary ranking, Chauncey Whiting was recognized as the *de facto* leader of the Cutlerites after the trek north. However, the knotty problem of legitimate leadership succession was never satisfactorily resolved in Manti and, in 1866, the question was reopened in Clitherall. The problem was further complicated by the fact that Cutler had been recognized as the President of the *Priesthood,* as well as President of the *Church* and thus the holder of the keys to the heavenly Kingdom of God. The presidency of the priesthood was seen as a role separate from the more secular role as leader of the church on earth. In the Cutlerite view, there should be *two* presidents, one who was President of the Priesthood and the other who was President of the Church. In practice this was not workable and the two roles soon merged into one.

While most of the Cutlerites accepted Chauncey Whiting's leadership, members of the Cutler family did not. The matter was debated for several months before Sperry attempted to resolve the problem by agreeing to recognize Whiting as President of the Church. On June 30, 1867, Chauncey Whiting was officially ordained President of the Church of

Jesus Christ under the hands of Charles Sperry and Almon W. Sherman. Chauncey Whiting selected Isaac Whiting (his eldest son) and Lyman Murdock as his first and second counselors. On February 25, 1873, a corporation known as "Church of Jesus Christ" was incorporated and registered with the Register of Deeds of Otter Tail County.

While Sperry appeared to be reconciled to his loss of the presidential office, his supporters were not. The controversy over the selection of Chauncey Whiting may have given them the opportunity they desired to move away from Clitherall, avoid the problems of The Oneness and acquire their own land. The dissident members, including Lois Cutler, Alpheus' widow; her married daughter Lois Cutler Sherman and her son-in-law Almon Shermon with their children; L.D. Sperry; Henry and Jane (Sherman) Way (Almon's daughter and son-in-law) and Amelia Stillman, the widow of Clark, moved away from Clitherall. Amelia Stillman moved to Deer Creek, a community about eighteen miles from Clitherall where she homesteaded a farm, while the rest of the disaffected Cutlerites moved out of Otter Tail County altogether. They went about sixty miles north to Oak Lake, in Becker County, where they filed on land. Though the ties of kinship and friendship remained intact, the Oak Lake and Deer Creek residents were officially cut off from membership in the Cutlerite Church.

The departure of so many prominent families from the tightly knit Cutlerite society was a major blow to the residents of Clitherall. Though Chauncey Whiting wrote that "in process of time all disagreements in regard to authority were amicably settled," that was clearly not the case. Secretive about their affairs, the Cutlerites were careful not to expose their internal conflicts to outsiders. Years after the first departures, Chauncey Whiting admitted that there were differences among the Cutlerites. In a speech about the community's history given at the Old Settler's reunion at Clitherall on June 24, 1897, he said, "We had our sorrow and disappointments. Soon after our arrival five families more went back to Iowa and subsequently others moved to Deer Creek, which reduced our settlement to sixteen families. Nevertheless we were not disheartened or swayed from our purpose."[120]

CHAPTER 10

Cutlerites and Lamanites

The Cutlerites came to Minnesota to convert the Indians. The mission of the Latter Day Saint church, to bring the Indians to a knowledge of their forefathers, held extraordinary significance to the Cutlerites who believed that Joseph Smith had given Alpheus Cutler special "keys" and authority to take the church's message to the Lamanites. The fact that Lewis Denna, the highest-ranking Indian among the Latter Day Saints, had come with the Cutlerites reinforced their sense of sacred duty.

The Cutlerites should have had few illusions about the difficulty of their task. The disaster of their mission to Kansas with Alpheus Cutler had demonstrated that Native Americans could be mercurial and that Indian concerns often differed sharply from those of the whites. The Cutlerites surely remembered that, despite their best efforts over a period of five years, they had been unable to convert a single one of the Indians in Kansas to Cutler's message. Nevertheless their sense of mission to the Indians remained strong. As soon as cabins were built in Clitherall and crops planted, the Cutlerites began to reach out to their Indian neighbors. They were met more than halfway by the Reverend John Johnson Enmegahbowh.

Enmegahbowh was not like other Indians. He spoke English, had become a Christian minister and was about as close in culture to the Cutlerites as it was possible for an Ojibwe to be at that time. For the Cutlerites to seriously pursue their religious mission to the Indians they would have had to learn Ojibwe and live among the Indians in their villages. Since that was not possible, and the Cutlerites needed a relationship with Indians to satisfy the demands of their religion, they turned to Enmegahbowh who could become, if not a literal convert, at least a symbolic one. By nurturing a relationship with Enmegahbowh the Cutlerites could maintain the fiction that they were "doing something" to carry the gospel to the Indians.

As soon as he was settled in Clitherall, Chauncey Whiting began a correspondence with Enmegahbowh that continued, with few interruptions, for the remainder of their lives. Both men were extensive letter writers. As a result a close friendship developed between Whiting and Enmegahbowh, that also included Lewis Denna. They visited each other's homes in Clitherall and on the White Earth Indian Reservation. Enmegahbowh conducted religious services at Chauncey Whiting's home, where he was well received, and the Cutlerites may have believed he would at some time become a member of their group. That did not happen but Enmegahbowh maintained close contact with the Cutlerites over the years. From the evidence of their correspondence the Cutlerites, given their own straightened circumstances, did as much as they could to carry out their religious mission to the Indians.

In an undated letter addressed to "Messrs. Whiting, Sherman and Denna" that must have been written in late 1865, Enmegahbowh reported that he had been travelling with the Episcopal Bishop Henry Benjamin Whipple and "three or four gentlemen from New York" to visit all the bands of Indians in Minnesota and that he would soon be going to Washington, D.C. He promised to visit Clitherall as soon as he could manage. "My wife has been long anxious to visit and see you people at your new homes. I am truly sorry to say that it may be yet some time to come before I can have my own time so as to visit my friends elsewhere." He went on to write, "The removal of the Indians is not to take place this year but on the next year. Part of the Mississippi bands will be removed without fail. . . . You cannot imagine my thankfulness and prayers for you as a people, who came from a far country to save the Red Man from his present condition. If my countrymen can only see the true language of your hearts, as I see, a general move will take place to embrace and accept the great plan of salvation which you offer to them."[121]

In January 1866, Enmegahbowh acknowledged a letter he had received from Chauncey Whiting and wrote from Mille Lacs that "money-makers" were trying to move the Indians onto timbered land. "I shall do my best to have the unmoved Indians located on the edge of the prairie, or if we can have the permission from the government, to make a settlement near you people. . . . If the government do really in earnest consent to save the remaining few of my poor country men, I say, give them a good and suitable farming country, where there is no impediment in the way of opening farms extensively for themselves. An Indian, unaccustomed to chop a tree, it would be a great trial to him, to open a farm on heavy timbered land." He added that he expected to leave for Washington, D.C., in the winter with the Chiefs and Bishop Whipple whom he called "a true friend of the Chippewas [who] is working hard for the good of the Indians generally." Enmegahbowh inquired about his son. "If my son George is doing well, and will be contented and study hard, please tell him I hope to come there before sugar time. I will bring him a good double gun."[122]

In another letter to Chauncey Whiting, dated April 30, 1867, Enmegahbowh said he had been in Washington, D.C. and met with the chiefs of fourteen different Indian tribes in the ongoing process of treaty-making with the federal government. He wrote, "In our treaty we have succeeded this much, that a portion of them [the Indians] will move to other homes north of Otter Tail. Another portion of them will go toward Leech Lake Country. . . . After the crop is fairly set in under ground then we expect to go and select the locations. . . . We have made ample provision for school purposes and other improvements.

"Among the Indians I saw Mr. Denna's friends and was inquiring of him," he wrote. "I told them where to find his address and I think he will soon hear from them." On his return home Enmegahbowh found that his oldest daughter had died four days before he arrived. "My sorrow is deep and keen. I have buried four children underground and have never felt so deep affections upon me as it is at the present. My heart would almost break because of my sorrow and crying as I walked to and from where lies my daughter that I have just buried."

This letter from Enmegahbowh gives the first indication that his son, George, had problems with school. Enmegahbowh wrote, "With regard to my George, I feel not quite right about him. I don't blame your people. I blame him personally of leaving without my permission. He says he left the school on account of his home-sickness and lonesomeness; nothing else but that. He says he likes you and your people generally. He was kindly treated and well taken care of. I shall again send him away to some school. About George's books and charges; the money I will send to you just as soon as the agent arrives home. What little greenbacks I have I gave to him to take charge of it before I left Washington and I hope I may be able to see you all soon. I expect to be able to own a horse and when that is accomplished, I shall then go where I please. My love to Mr. Denna and all your good company. I have often think [sic] much of you all. Excuse my short letter. Your truly friend. J. Johnson."

John Johnson Enmegahbowh believed in education for all his children. In the same letter in which he lamented George's leaving the Clitherall school, he wrote that his two daughters were "learning very fast. I heard them the other day reciting in the first lesson of geography, to my great satisfaction."

In a letter to "Dear Friends" at Clitherall dated November 25, 1867, Enmegahbowh noted receipt of a letter from Chauncey Whiting and then went on to give an account of how Indian agents were cheating the Indians. According to his letter, the Mille Lacs Indians were to have received $10 each from the Indian Agency, and were only given $6.75. "I have never seen such a bold act of rascality carried out on the poor Indians. I have written and talked with the most prominent men in the state, including the governor. . . . The people of the state are awake to the importance of doing justice to the Red Man and the governor has particularly requested me and six of the principal chiefs also to be present when the legislature is in session," he wrote. "It seems the agents are determined to set the feelings of the Indians in motion. I only feel sorry for your company not being near enough to reach the Indians, and as you are looking for an interpreter to go on with your work of mercy. And I believe you can do a vast deal of good amongst us, both spiritually and temporally." He closed writing, "Please remember me kindly to Mr. Denna and family and all the good brethren. I hope to see you all some day."[123]

On April 23, 1869, Enmegahbowh wrote asking the Cutlerites to contract with the Indian agent to provide hundreds of bushels of seed potatoes for the Indians on the White Earth Reservation. Payment was to come from the agent who, at the time Enmegahbowh wrote his letter, had failed to put in an appearance. "[He] is expected every day, when we shall immediately make provision to buy potatoes," he wrote. Enmegahbowh was realistic in his assessment of the Indian Agent. Having little confidence in the government, Enmegahbowh contacted Episcopal Bishop Henry Whipple for money to purchase one to two hundred bushels of seed potatoes and also asked Chauncey if the Cutlerites could sell the Indians several loads of potatoes on credit "until we get the money. Now, Mr. Whiting, if we should call on you for potatoes without money, can you let us have them now, until we get the money? It would pay you, sir, to haul two or three loads of potatoes to here immediately, but at this time you cannot get the money now. . . . Please let us know what you can do for us, by the bearer."

Chauncey Whiting must have replied that the Cutlerites could not supply seed potatoes in the quantity needed by the Indians, for on May

6, 1869, Enmegahbowh wrote again that "I have read your letter to the
Chiefs in regard to the seed potatoes and they are very sorry indeed that
you cannot furnish potatoes to the amount they are required and they
are at [a loss] what to do in the way of getting them seed potatoes. . . .
They tell you, by all means, to bring all the potatoes you can spare to
White Earth. . . . They have no teams to use to come after the seed potatoes. Most of the oxen are useless and nearly starving. The only way
they can stand and eat grass now is by leaning on or against the tree or
stumps, the oxen are so poor."

Enmegahbowh had become deeply concerned that the Indians might
not survive the winter on the reservation. In the same letter, he wrote
Whiting, "I feel for them, if they do not well prepare for seeds now. How
in the world are they going to live in the winter? I shall wait and see how
much seed potatoes each person shall be given for planting and shall act
accordingly. If enough seed is given to each family, I shall remain here,
and if not, I shall certainly leave for help for I do not want to see starvation. We cannot depend on hunting as we always have at our old homes.
Now is the time to prepare against the hard winter and, poor fellows, they
are all willing and are working hard. Truly yours, J. Johnson."[124]

By May 11, 1869, when Enmegahbowh wrote again to "Rev. and Mrs.
C. Whiting, Dear Friend and Brother," the situation on the reservation
had improved slightly. A new Indian agent had arrived who authorized
the purchase of 600 to 700 bushels of seed potatoes. The Indians' oxen
were too weak to transport the potatoes so Enmegahbowh asked the Cutlerites to haul the potatoes for them. "We expect to pay you within a
month's time and can you furnish me one or two pounds of rutabaga
seed? What are the prospects to have you furnish flour and other eatable
articles in the winter?"

Enmegahbowh continued to be seriously concerned that the Indians would go hungry during the coming winter. He wrote, "I have just
received a letter from the Bishop with the means to buy seed potatoes
for my own Christian Brothers here and now I want at least 200 bushels
besides the government's. Planting time is advancing towards the close
of seed time and this is so important. We put all the seeds under ground
now. How long we may have to wait for the potatoes, we know not. We
hope not very long. What are the prospects of getting potatoes from
you or where can they be bought? We must have potatoes from somewhere or starve in the winter and this is the reason I urge the matter so
earnestly" Enmegahbowh also asked Chauncey to send along "one
dozen more of your chairs."

The Cutlerites must not have sent the potatoes ordered by Enmegahbowh for on May 20, 1869, he sent another letter addressed more formally to "Reverend Mr. Whiting" saying that he was feeling "discouraged, having no seed of any kind to go on with my planting. Having not heard from you since my last letter was written, I feel quite discouraged. Having a continual communication between Otter Tail and here, I have had two mails since my last letter to you. Thinking my last letter must have become lost to you, I gave Mr. Ruffee $100 to bring me 100 bushels [of potatoes] wherever they can be found. If I don't get them in time, I must leave. The planting time now is already advancing too far. I should have been most glad to have received potatoes from you, but my letter must have been lost. Truly yours, J. Johnson."[125]

Enmegahbowh did not write another letter to the Cutlerites until 1871, a silence of almost two years. Chauncey Whiting must have tried to contact Enmegahbowh because Whiting received a letter dated January 15, 1871, from William W. McArthur, postmaster at White Earth, stating, "Yours received. I am happy when my old friends write to me. . . . I will have Mr. Johnson write to you. I will show him your kind letter. . . . I would like to go down and see you all but I can't leave, being postmaster. Respects to all old friends at Clitherall."[126]

McArthur must have shown the letter from Chauncey Whiting to Enmegahbowh because on March 25, 1871, Enmegahbowh wrote Whiting. Addressing his letter to "Esteemed Friends and Brothers" he acknowledged that "for a long time I had kept silence" and stated that "frequent visits between us would, I think, strengthen a friendship and become more acquainted. A strong attachment would exist between us. . . . My dear friends, we have not forgotten you and we hope we never shall while life shall last. But we are very sorry that we cannot make frequent visits to your settlement and interchange with brotherly greetings." He explained that he had fallen ill in St. Paul and for a more than a month had been bedridden. Enmegahbowh lamented that he did not have a team and thus could only visit places to which he could walk. He signed the letter "White Fishes Chief," a name he had been given on the White Earth Reservation.[127]

Chauncey Whiting must have continued the correspondence with Enmegahbowh for on February 25, 1886, Enmegahbowh acknowledged receipt of a letter from Whiting. "Your good and welcome letter came to hand and its contents taken notice. The Head Chief was with me when I received my mail and when I read your letter I turned to the chief and read the letter to him. He said to me, "I do remember these dear friends and I know where they are living. I believe their hearts are all right toward the Red Man. If there are any white men in these United States living who have a loving and right heart toward the Red Man, these white men are to be found at Clitherall or near Battle Lake." Enmegahbowh added, "I believe the White Earth Indians all recognized you and your people as you all are the true friends to them."

Whiting must have written about the death of Lewis Denna for Enmegahbowh wrote, "I am truly sorry for Mr. Denna's death. It was through him, in great measure, that you have been acquainted with my people here and yet how true that in the midst of life we are in death."

Enmegahbowh continued to be involved in treaty negotiations with the federal government. "A great destitution are [*sic*] now prevailing among my brethren," he wrote. "There are millions of dollars now in the hands of this great government belonging to this people. My downtrodden poor people are crying and groaning for it but their groanings are not heeded. . . . Shall the righteous and the judge of all the earth notice when the whole Indian tribes call for it? I have been away from home during the last summer. Four of the principal chiefs came to see me in June and asked me to visit their country, Turtle Mountain region, in Dakota. . . . I did partially consent but my people and the government said I cannot go, that I have a greater work to do here. . . . We have just learned that a commission to negotiate with my people are expected to be here soon. So I do not expect to leave home, at least until the sugar season is over."

The year had been a difficult and sad one for Enmegahbowh. "I have lost all my children, except the oldest son, Gaines. Dear George died on last April, a great loss to my people. He was beloved by all. . . . Now we are alone. I am, my friends and brethren, very hard up at the present time. Nearly the whole fields of wheat of White Earth were destroyed by the heavy frost in the first part of last August. I had 40 acres in wheat and 20 acres in oats. A very heavy frost came on two successive days. My wheat and oats have all been destroyed now and it is very hard on us, with scanty food this past winter. I have no prospect of getting seed wheat or oats for this spring's seeding. . . . If I find seed to plant this coming spring, I shall remain. But if not, I shall be preferring to leaving for Canada if I do not starve out before that time. I was intending to visit you and your people before making my final decision to leave. Even now, I shall be most glad to come and see you. . . . Ever your true friend, J. Johnson."[128]

On June 21, 1886, Enmegahbowh wrote to Chauncey Whiting expressing gratitude for his letters. Enmegahbowh wrote, "It is always our greatest pleasure to hear from you and read your letters; to know there are Pale Faces living in this wide world who feel and sympathize with the Red Man. . . . If my people throughout the Indian Country can see and understand the true sentiments of your people and the desires of your hearts toward them it would give them a new impulse, yes a new impulse to grasp your hands with hearts of gratitude and love. A deep friendship would be written with ink, ink which would never be effaced by time or years. . . . We are not (as the Pale Faces have expressed) destitute of feelings and emotions."[129]

Enmegahbowh went on to explain to Whiting, "The agent tells me I cannot go until the big council is over. Three commissioners are expected to visit our reservation in the last part of this month to make a final treaty with my people. This will be to us, life or death. . . . If we can make a good treaty for our people and our children and our grandchildren, we shall be satisfied. I think it is very important for me to be with my people and give advice. It is not yet fully ascertained at what month or day we may expect the distinguished visitors to arrive. So here I am, and will remain until the big council is over."

The correspondence between Chauncey Whiting and John Johnson Enmegahbowh continued until the end of their lives. The two men died just five days apart, in 1902, Enmegahbowh on June 12th and Chauncey Whiting on June 7th. A few days before his death the last letter Whiting wrote but never finished was addressed to his friend, "Reverend John Johnson, Dear Friend and Brother."

The council referred to by Enmegahbowh was the Northwest Indian Commission of 1886 which was called in an attempt to convince all of the Indians of Minnesota, except those at Red Lake, to move onto the White Earth Reservation. Commission members were Bishop Henry B. Whipple, Charles F. Larrabee, an official from the Indian office and John V. Wright, a judge and former congressman from Tennessee. Though the council meeting lasted for six days, the problems attendant to the attempt to consolidate the Indians on a single reservation were not resolved.

John Johnson Enmegahbowh had been ordained a deacon in the Protestant Episcopal Church in 1859 by Bishop Jackson Kemper and a priest in 1867 by Bishop Henry B. Whipple. In the mid-1990s the Diocese of Minnesota began the process to place Enmegahbowh on the "Calendar of Remembrances"—the Episcopal version of sainthood.

The day of his death, June 12th, is recorded in the book *Lesser Feasts and Fasts* and is celebrated in the church. The process of recognizing a person to be remembered is a lengthy one. The Minnesota application on behalf of John Johnson Enmegahbowh was accepted by the national body of the Episcopal church in 2000 and the final vote recognizing him as a saint—one whose life has inspired and instructed others—will take place in 2003. The final vote is anticipated to be but a formality.[130]

An early Ojibwe name for Battle Lake was "ish-quon-e-de-win-nig" meaning "where but few survived." The French called it "Lac du Bataille" which was translated later from Nicollet's map of the Missis-

This portrait of Reverend John Johnson Enmegahbowh was painted by Reverend Johnson Loud, Jr., in 1996. It hangs near the altar of the Episcopal Cathedral of Our Merciful Saviour in Faribault, Minnesota.

sippi Valley as Battle Lake. That the area was the scene of a major Indian battle was all the Cutlerites knew of the history of the region until the summer of 1917 when Birch Whiting, a son of Warren and Zeruah Sherman Whiting, and Ben Kimber, a farmer from near Battle Lake who had married Birch's sister Grace, were visiting the village of Beaulieu on the White Earth Reservation. The two men were spending the night at a small hotel when the landlady, an Ojibwe woman, told them that an old chief named Hole-in-the-Day lived nearby and enjoyed having visitors, especially white men. Curious, Whiting and Kimber resolved to call on the old man and the next day they drove to the home for the aged where he was living. The Ojibwe matron at the home assured them the old chief would appreciate their visit, but as he did not speak English, they would have to find an interpreter to translate for them. Fortunately a young Sioux from South Dakota was also visiting the home and agreed to interpret.

When Kimber and Whiting entered the room which was furnished with a bed, table and two chairs, they encountered a 97-year-old man, large and powerfully built, who, though dressed in western clothes, wore his black hair long in the style of an Indian. The man was almost certainly Ignacius Hole-in-the-Day, son of the warrior Hole-in-the-Day the Younger, and a distant relative of Enmegahbowh's wife, Biwabikogijigokwe. Either as a result of an accident or old age, the chief was totally blind. When Hole-in-the-Day learned the two visitors were from the Clitherall-Battle Lake area, he began to tell them of the time the Ojibwe drove the Sioux from that region of Minnesota and of their decisive victory at Battle Lake.

The old chief told them that, though the Chippewa and Sioux considered themselves traditional enemies, they had lived in relative peace in the Otter Tail area for long periods of time, sharing the bounty of the region. The area was rich in fish and game; it offered fur for clothing, fuel for winter campfires and building material for wigwams and canoes. Wild strawberries, raspberries, chokecherries and currants grew in abundance from June until late in the fall. Maple and box elder trees yielded sugar and there were roots and herbs for food and medicine.

Buffalo could be found a day's journey to the west and the Indians dried and cured the meat. Wild rice was plentiful and was gathered by bending the cane-like stalks of rice over the side of a canoe and beating the heads so that the rice fell into the canoe. After the rice had been flailed to remove the chaff and winnowed in the wind, it was pounded with stones into dried buffalo meat to make pemmican, a nourishing food. The pemmican was packed tightly into skin bags, covered with hot tallow to seal it and buried in the ground for future use. The Indian women also planted corn and pumpkins in small gardens near their camps.

In early May 1845, during one of the periods of truce between the two groups of Indians, a band of Sioux arrived at an encampment of Ojibwe near the east end of West Battle Lake. The two groups feasted together until supplies began to run low. A hunting party of thirteen braves drawn from both tribes left on a two-day journey west to shoot game for the camp. While on this trip the men somehow got their hands on some whiskey, a drunken brawl followed, during which all but one Ojibwe was killed. When the lone survivor returned to the encampment with his story, both the Sioux and the Ojibwe forgot about their friendship and went to war.

At first the Sioux were successful. They drove the Ojibwe across the winding creek connecting West and East Battle Lakes. The Ojibwe retreated northward into the tall grass and woods, which gained them time to rally their forces and counterattack the Sioux, who were in possession of a range of hills beyond the creek. The north side of the hills was heavily wooded which provided cover for the Ojibwe as they approached. The first part of the battle was fought in the hills, ending with the Sioux retreating westward and around the west end of the lake, where the town of Battle Lake now stands, to a point of land called Stony Point. On the eastern point of this peninsula the Sioux made their stand and were routed in a desperate engagement. Many were forced into the lake and were killed. Those who escaped continued their retreat through the woods near the shore, making their way along the narrow ridge separating Battle Lake from Beauty Shore Lake. The few survivors eventually fled into a large swamp covered with a dense growth of spruce and tamarack. Here the pursuit ended. The victory, although undoubtedly one of many in the bloody history of the two tribes, was a decisive one and was commemorated in the name of the lake.

As a fiery young brave, Chief Hole-in-the-Day said he had taken part in the battle which had ended near what was now Ben Kimber's farm. When the two men rose to leave, the old chief expressed regret that he had only one token of friendship that he could give to his visitors, but he wanted to give them that. Going to his bed, he turned back the mattress and brought out a stone pipe that he presented to the two men. The bowl, of pipestone, was of excellent workmanship and the chief told them he had made it himself before he had lost his eyesight. The stem, about two feet long, had been made of alder wood by another person, he said apologetically, and was somewhat inferior.[131]

At the time of the Cutlerite arrival in 1865, a few years after the epic battle between the Sioux and Ojibwe, a band of Ojibwe maintained their permanent camp of about a score of wigwams on Hirum Murdock's land, which was separated from the village of Clitherall by the marsh. The walls and floors of the Indians' homes were covered with reed mats, made by the women; cooking was done over an open fire with the smoke escaping from a hole at the top of the wigwam. Food was prepared in a kettle hung over the fire and everything that was to be eaten—beans, squirrels, fish, vegetables, went into the same pot as Clitherall's one-time school teacher George Hammer discovered to his distaste when he was invited to an Indian home in the region for supper.

Hammer was following a deer. When night came he was twenty miles from home, exhausted and hungry. He came to an Indian camp and asked to stay the night. The Indians invited him into a wigwam to eat and sleep. Hammer removed his moccasins and lay down with his feet toward the fire as the young woman prepared the evening meal. Hammer was hungry and watched the dinner preparations with anticipation. The woman put two quarts of flour into a pail, poured water over it, stirred the mixture and placed it on the coals to bake. "Good," thought Hammer, "unleavened bread but good so far." The woman next poured water over a pail of cranberries and hung that over the fire. Hammer thought he was about to have a supper of cranberries and bread when the woman picked up half a dozen pickerel and, without scaling the fish or removing the heads or internal organs, dropped them into the kettle with the berries and began stirring it all with a stick. Hammer felt his appetite departing and he spent the night without eating.[132]

When the Indian women near the Clitherall settlement wanted to do laundry they borrowed tubs and washboards from the Cutlerite women to wash and iron the brightly colored cotton dresses they wore in summer. In the winter the women wore heavy flannel dresses, leggings, hoods and shawls. Babies were carried in slings on the mothers' backs, wrapped in the down from marsh cattails. If an infant died, as many did, the mother often made a rag doll and carried it in the baby's sling. The Cutlerites offered their help but their own medical resources were meager and, in most cases, there was not much they could do. On one occasion, when they went to assist with a sick child, they found a dog nailed to a post with the explanation that the dog's spirit would take the disease away from the baby. Both the infant and the dog died. Often, when an Indian baby died, one of the Whiting brothers would make a coffin for the child and give it to the bereaved Indian family. When the Cutlerites first came to the county they found that the Indians had a designated burying ground for their dead, but later, when it was rumored that a building would be built near the burial site, the Indians took up their dead and reburied them near Otter Tail.

It did not take the Indians long to discover that the Cutlerite women and girls were a little afraid of them and so did not hesitate to open the door of a house and walk in without knocking. They came in search of a gift of food, to trade for butter (an item they especially liked) or, in the winter, simply to get warm. Indian dances were held both around their campfires and in the settlers' yards. A group of Indian women and children would suddenly appear, carrying tomahawks, clubs and tin kettle-drums. Seating themselves on the ground, the ones designated to drum would begin while the others danced around them, waving hatchets, and shrieking "Hi-ah, hi-ah, hiii-ah" over and over again. At the end of the performance the Indians would come to the door and ask for bread, flour, butter, beans, potatoes or sugar that they usually got from the nervous housewives.

On other occasions Indian hunters would bring their muskrat hides into the houses to sort and count, sometimes spending long evenings in the process. The Cutlerites put up with the odor, reluctant to order the Indians out. When the Indians were finished with their muskrats, they would lie down on the floor and sleep until morning. The Cutlerites often awoke in the morning to find that Indians had crept into their unlocked houses during the night and were sleeping peacefully on the floor.

An Indian walked into Hirum Murdock's home one day when the children were there alone and asked for food. Though frightened, the eldest girl put food on the table for him. After he finished eating the Indian explained in broken English that he had been working for a white man and had not been paid. "No cow meat, no hog meat," he explained. "Damn poor eat." The man then put 40 cents on the table and departed.

Another day an Indian woman with a baby stopped at Francis Lewis Whiting's house and seeing a large rutabaga in the kitchen asked to have it. Ann Jeanette Whiting asked the woman what she had to trade for it. When the Indian woman shook her head, Ann Jeanette mischievously asked if she would trade her baby for it. The woman refused, but after some time had passed she suddenly handed over her baby, took the vegetable and departed. The Whiting children were excited to have an Indian infant and looked on delightedly while their mother bathed and fed the baby and dressed it in some of the children's baby clothes. The infant had been put to sleep in a big rocking chair when the Indian mother came back to the house and, saying nothing, sat down on the floor. When Ann Jeanette left to get a pail of water, the mother picked up her baby and silently disappeared into the woods.

On another occasion a dozen Indians came into Francis Lewis Whiting's home and were sitting around the stove when they observed a string of red peppers hanging on the wall. Never having seen red peppers before they were curious and finally one old woman reached up and, jerking a pepper from the string, took a big bite. Slowly the woman's face flushed and in a few minutes big tears began running down her face. The other Indians watched her in silence but no one else was tempted to take a bite out of a pepper.

Not all the Indian visits were so benign. At the same home where the Indian had taken a bite of the pepper, Ella and Lou Whiting and their grandmother Burdick were alone when the elderly Ta-todge, a usually friendly Indian, stumbled into the house. Ta-todge had a horrible expression on his face and his eyes were glazed, perhaps from drink. Ta-todge raised his tomahawk and advanced on the girl's elderly grandmother sitting helpless in her rocking chair. Ella was paralyzed with terror but Lou grabbed a chair and lifting it over her head, charged Ta-todge, shouting "march on," an expression used by the Indians. Ta-todge dodged the girl with the chair, Ella recovered her wits and the two girls succeeded in getting the crazed Indian out of the house.

For years after the Sioux Uprising of 1862 rumors of imminent Indian attacks flew about the frontier. About a year after the Cutlerite arrival in Otter Tail County word came from travelers that the Sioux from North Dakota were coming to incite the Ojibwe to attack the whites. The rumors were half-way believed and caused concern. One day a war-whoop was heard and, at the top of the hill above Clitherall, a band of Sioux warriors appeared on spotted ponies. Women grabbed their children and rushed indoors and men went for their guns. The Indians, about eight in number, charged down the hill and wheeled in at Sylvester Whiting's house, one room of which had been turned into a makeshift store. After a fearful few minutes, the Indians began to laugh and let the Cutlerites know they were just a bunch of young Sioux out frightening the white people for the fun of it.

The Cutlerites also inadvertently frightened the Indians. One of the early weddings was the double wedding of Freeman Anderson to May Whiting and Arthur Whiting to Lois Murdock. The first night of their marriage the two couples stayed at the home of Lois's parents, Hirum and Rachel Murdock. At midnight the two couples were roused by the popular and noisy charivari, when friends banged tinware, rang cowbells, shot off their guns and shouted. It never occurred to the revelers that the Indians living a few rods away on the point would not understand a charivari. To the Ojibwe, these were the sounds of war. Convinced that the Sioux from North Dakota had arrived, the Ojibwe scattered into the woods, rifles in hand.

Chauncey Whiting, Jr., who for some reason was not participating in the charivari, also heard the racket and came to the same conclusion as the Ojibwe—that an Indian war had broken out. He rushed out of his house, gun in hand, to encounter an Indian crawling up over the lake bank. Whiting took aim at the man but the Indian shouted "Don't shoot!" and convinced him that he was a friend. As they stood trying to figure out what was going on another Indian ran past them into Whiting's house gasping out, "What for so damn much shoot?" It was morning before many of the Indians came back to their camp and the Cutlerites claimed it was several days before all of the Indian women had returned.[133]

On other occasions, the Indians came to the settlers' rescue. A group of women and children took a flat-bottomed boat across the lake to an island to go berry picking. On the way one of the oarlocks broke, but the group managed to reach the island and spent the morning picking grapes, hazelnuts and cranberries. They were not alone in the berry patch. A group of Indian women and children were also there and one of the Cutlerite women remembered feeling resentful that the Indians were picking so many of the berries—though at the same time she reminded herself that the Indians had as much right to the berries as anyone. When the Cutlerite women started for home, after having made a makeshift repair of the oarlock, they discovered that the wind had come up on the lake. The waves grew higher in the middle of the lake, the repaired oarlock suddenly gave way and they lost an oar. With one oar gone, the boat immediately swung broadside to the waves and began to take on water.

The women in the boat shouted frantically for help and their calls were heard by the Indian children playing on the beach by the berry patch. Within a few minutes two Indian women ran down to the shore, launched a birch bark canoe and paddled out to the foundering boat. Though the two groups of women could not understand each other's speech, by gestures the Indians explained how the women should leave the sinking boat and get into the canoe.

"They knew just what to do and took us aboard in short order, but we had to be very careful in seating ourselves—the six of us—in that frail craft of birch bark," one of those rescued explained. The Indians took the cold and wet but thankful women to shore. The sun was setting and the women went to where the Indians' tents were pitched and, through signs and motions, asked the Indians to take them back to Clitherall. The Indians made the women understand that they would have to wait, that the boat with which they had been rescued was too small to take them on the lake again. For several hours the women and children stood around the campfire, warming themselves and drying out their clothes. As one of them later said, "Night settled down around us but we never dreamed of being afraid of those Indians."

Eventually two tall Indian men strode out of the dark bearing a larger bark canoe on their shoulders. They loaded up the women and children and, without saying a word, paddled them across the lake to Clitherall. It was after 10 o'clock at night. The Cutlerites, who had been frantic with fear for the members of their families, loaded the Indians down with melons, potatoes and whatever they could find in their gratitude for the rescue.[134]

Both the Indians and the white settlers often saw humor in their situations. Once, in about 1870, George Hammer poisoned a dozen wolves and, after stripping them of their pelts, hung the carcasses in a tree. A band of twenty-five Ojibwe on a hunting trip had stopped in a grove near Hammer's cabin to cook their meal. When Hammer came out of his cabin to greet the Indians he discovered that the poisoned carcasses of the wolves were gone from the tree. Horrified, he immediately pictured twenty-five dead Indians, poisoned from eating the wolves he had evidently given them.

Hammer rushed to the Indian camp making frantic gestures and tried to take the meat, which they were eating with relish, out of their hands. He pretended to eat something from their kettle and then threw himself on the ground, clutching his stomach and grimacing to simulate poisoning. He acted as if he had died to show them what would happen to them if they ate the tainted meat. Instead of grasping Hammer's meaning, the Indians began to laugh. Hammer intensified his efforts to communicate the danger they were in while the Indians continued their meal. When they were finished eating, one of the men stopped laughing long enough to say, in English, "Poisoned wolf no kill Indian." Hammer was indignant and embarrassed. "You redskin! Why didn't you tell me that?" The Indian chuckled, "It was heap fun to see white man have big scare."

As a boy George Hammer, who lived a short distance from Clitherall in the Norwegian community of St. Olaf, attended the first Fourth of July celebration in the county. Although the date of the celebration is given in the *Old Clitherall Story Book* as 1870, other sources give the more likely date of 1867. To observe the Fourth, the residents of Clitherall had invited the settlers from St. Olaf, Silver Lake and Oak Lake to come to Clitherall as their guests. Several wagonloads of revelers from St. Olaf accepted the invitation and, with some trepidation, began the trip to Clitherall. As Hammer later wrote, "We were most anxious for the day to come as many strange stories concerning the Mormons had come to us. Some said the men had horns on their heads like yearling calves. Others said the women had noses like fish-hooks."

The ride across the unbroken, roadless prairie was uneventful until the wagons were just west of the outlet of Lake Clitherall. There they encountered the woman known as Mother Mack Fletcher. "Someone said, 'There's a Mormon woman.' I looked at her nose. My! But my very hair stood on end. I now fully believed all the stories I had heard about the men. Then at the top of the hill ahead of us we saw a flag waving in the breeze. My! What a flag! We had a flag with us, made years before in Fillmore County. We were proud of that flag. We brought it along to show the Mormons that we had a flag. It was sadly faded and weatherbeaten but it was a flag.

"Well, when theirs came in sight we would have hidden ours if we could. Theirs was borne aloft in a bandwagon. The band, with a gay crowd of young people, had driven out to meet us. . . . In the wagon was. . . George Gould making his fife fairly burst with melody while his foot kept time to the martial music. Clayton Gould, looking as sober as a judge, made his drum-sticks fly over his snare drum, while "Cy" Albertson kept time on the large bass drum. We removed our hats and cheered loudly when the welcoming music ceased."

The wagons continued along the lakeshore toward Clitherall, past Mother Mack's home, to a house on the left side of the road. The man standing in the doorway reminded Hammer of the biblical Jacob who had wrestled with the angel. "He was standing on one foot, his left hand holding his hat, his right hand holding his cane, while he voiced a happy welcome, with his waving black locks and beard, his happy face and whole attitude making such a pleasing picture that my heart then and there went out to 'Uncle Vet.'" [Sylvester Whiting]

A program was held in a grove of trees behind the church. The oldest man present, Jacob Sherman, father-in-law of George Gould of Silver Lake, read the Declaration of Independence and Chauncey Whiting gave the address, recounting God's providence in guiding them to the beautiful shore of Clitherall Lake. Then it was time for the noon meal. Hammer remembered:

> "A long table in the grove had been prepared. It was covered with snow-white table cloths and fairly groaned under its load of good things—green peas, new potatoes, chicken pie, gooseberry pie, maple syrup, maple sugar, sweet cake, great loaves of pure white flour bread and pounds and pounds of yellow butter. Oh, those gooseberry pies. I remember that I called for 'more pies.' A rosy-cheeked waitress, Ellen Murdock, came to me with a glorious combination of flour, shortening, gooseberries and sugar and said, 'Here, try this, I made it.'
>
> "Mother Mack [Fletcher] was at the dinner. Before mealtime she marched over the ground with a buffalo-chip on her head, tied there with a strip of red calico. As she passed the table she picked up a bread knife and scooped out the center of a gooseberry pie as deftly as any Sioux warrior ever scalped a white man. I was frightened and went up a tree like a squirrel. Uncle Francis Lewis Whiting came to my rescue and said kindly, 'Come down, boy. The old woman is crazy but she is harmless. She won't hurt you at all, so don't be afraid.'"

Before leaving Clitherall at the end of the celebration Hammer visited the shops of the village, calling the owners by the honorific of "Uncle." "There was Uncle Vet's store, Uncle Chan's tin shop, Uncle Ed's blacksmith shop, Uncle Al's chair shop and his mules, Rett and Lon's wagon shop, Warren's clothespin factory, the saw-mill run by horse-power and the queer little schoolhouse on the lake shore." A few years later Hammer would teach a winter term in that "queer little schoolhouse."[135]

For a few short years the Cutlerites lived the life they had imagined when leaving Manti, a life in peace with their Indian neighbors and free from the fears that had insinuated themselves into their lives in Iowa.

Their early experiences of persecution had persuaded them to see intolerance and prejudice where often none existed. Their past had become transformed into a founding story, an ancestral myth, a gospel of persecution that altered their perception of the world. In the isolation of their first years in Minnesota the Cutlerites began to relax. It may have been the simple passage of time, rather than the absence of persecution (people in Iowa had not persecuted the Cutlerites) that changed their attitude. While they became less wary for a time, their mental perspective continued to be inward, absorbed in the daily struggle to establish their homes and preoccupied with the minutiae of their religious obligations. As a result they missed the implication of what was happening in the larger community around them in Minnesota.

A flood of immigration from northern Europe was rapidly moving into what the Cutlerites still thought of as an isolated area. When they arrived in 1865 there had been fewer than a dozen white settlers in the county, mainly trappers married to Indian women. Within five years, the population grew to just under two thousand. Though the Cutlerites were certainly aware of the arriving newcomers, they remained largely unsuspecting of the significance of such an event. They failed to grasp the fact that they would soon be overtaken by a wave of immigration that would crest and break on the rolling hills and sandy shores of Otter Tail County and bring both prosperity and heartbreak to the original settlers.

CHAPTER 11

Wolves in the Sheepfold—The Second Josephite Invasion

By 1875 the Cutlerites were surrounded by Scandinavian farmers homesteading on the rich Minnesota land. In the ten years after the Cutlerites came to Otter Tail County thousands of new arrivals filed claims, platted villages, organized schools and constructed Lutheran churches. The population of the county, which had been near zero when they arrived and grew to only 1,371 in 1870, now stood at over fifteen thousand and was increasing daily. While the Cutlerites were generous with their assistance and insistent on performing their share and more of neighborly obligations, they essentially kept to themselves. As a result, the Cutlerites did not feel threatened by the newcomers nor did they see them as candidates for conversion. The immigrants brought their own religions with them and the Cutlerites were steadfast believers in their own creed. They had every reason to believe that the tranquility of their lives as conservative religious pilgrims on the frontier would continue indefinitely. They learned differently in July 1875.

Apostle T.W. Smith was a Josephite missionary. In the summer of 1875 he and his wife Helen came to Oak Lake in Becker County, Minnesota, to proselytize among the group of disfellowshipped Cutlerites, including members of Alpheus Cutler's immediate family who had moved out of Clitherall in the dispute over church authority. Smith was a charismatic preacher who claimed Joseph Smith III (Young Joseph) was the legitimate heir to his father's prophetic role as leader of the Latter Day Saints. Soon Smith began baptizing converts. The Josephite message was an attractive one. Instead of rejecting modern society as did the Cutlerites, the Josephites adjusted to it while retaining many of the unique characteristics of the Latter Day Saints.

T.W. Smith brought an appealing message of participation in the world, of becoming a moral force in society much as the Bible had enjoined Christ's followers to become the salt of the earth or the yeast that would leaven the dough. By disavowing polygamy and the whole panoply of secret temple rituals, sealings, and anointings that had so enthralled the residents of Nauvoo they were able to partially disassociate themselves from the Nauvoo disaster. While the development of utopian societies was still important to the Josephites, it was not as central to their mission as it was to the Cutlerites. The Josephites entertained the possibility that God's kingdom could be an inner, spiritual condition. Where early Mormons and the Cutlerites were intent on removing themselves from the world, the Josephites allowed their converts to rejoin it. Where the Cutlerites looked inward and to the past, T.W. Smith focused his message outward to the future of the ever-changing world. His listeners were intrigued. Before many weeks had passed, the entire Oak Lake settlement had been converted to the Josephites including Lois Cutler, her two married daughters and their families.

It was the Manti experience all over again. To the Cutlerites in Clitherall it looked as if the wolves had again come into the sheepfold. The conversion of Lois Cutler was a particularly painful blow. She was almost 88 years old and the widow of the revered leader, Alpheus. Though Smith explained to the elderly woman that she could be accepted into the Josephite church without another baptism (the Latter Day Saints believe in baptism by immersion) she refused his offer saying that she had withstood the Josephites for so long that she desired the ordinance performed. Within a brief time so many had joined the Josephites that Smith was able to organize a congregation of the church in Minnesota.[136]

The excitement of organizing a congregation of the Josephite church in Minnesota kindled the missionary spirit among the Oak Lake converts and they resolved to carry the message to their friends and family members in Clitherall. The trip from Oak Lake to Clitherall took two days over roads that were little more than trails. It was July when they made the trip, a time when horse flies and mosquitoes tortured both the animals and the passengers in the wagons, one of whom was the erect, sun-bonneted grandmother, Lois Cutler. When they arrived in Clitherall they were welcomed by the hospitable Cutlerites. As they had done a decade before in Manti when the first Josephite elders had come, the Cutlerites made the visitors welcome and housed them in their homes. Apostle Smith and his wife stayed at the home of Francis Lewis and Ann Jeanette Whiting and Smith was offered the use of the Cutlerite pulpit. Smith's preaching of traditional Christian themes was popular and he soon filled the log church with settlers who came from miles away to hear him.

While staying with their hosts in Clitherall, the Smiths made themselves useful. Smith worked in the fields with the men and Helen helped with the housework and washing. Helen had been advised before coming to Clitherall to leave her fancy clothes behind as the Cutlerites disapproved of any ornamentation in dress. She did as was suggested, making herself a simple brown dress and a brown cloth sun-hat with a starched brim. Despite her efforts, Helen quickly gained a reputation as the best-dressed woman in Clitherall. Her sun-hat, in particular, drew notice as the standard headgear of the Clitherall women was the slat sunbonnet. Despite her efforts to blend in, Helen's sun-hat introduced a note of modernity into Clitherall.

The atmosphere between the Josephites and Cutlerites in Clitherall remained cordial, regardless of their religious differences and rivalry, until Lois Cutler became ill. As the days passed the revered, elderly woman grew worse and when the Cutlerites began to fear for her life the old beliefs in witchcraft surfaced. Rumors flew about the community that Lois had been bewitched into joining the Josephites and if she died the responsibility for her death would lie with those responsible for her conversion and rebaptism. Both sides offered fervent prayers for Lois's recovery.

Few events could have better illustrated the stark difference that existed between the Cutlerites and the Josephites. In a crisis, the Cutlerites reverted to their beliefs in the existence of good and evil spirits and in an individual's ability to practice witchcraft. Explanations for events were not to be found in reason, but in the mysterious workings of the underworld. A fearsome belief in the occult and the powers of darkness continually lurked below the surface of Cutlerite life. It took the merest crisis, such as the illness of a woman in her 80s, to bring a witches' brew of old folk beliefs surging to the surface. Little in the Cutlerite experience had occurred to shift their thinking beyond the magical view of the world they had inherited from their ancestors. The cloistered life of Clitherall, based as it was on a determined rejection of society, kept the Cutlerites stranded in their mystical, irrational perception of the world.

Fortunately Lois Cutler recovered and returned to Oak Lake where she lived for two more years before dying a few months short of the age of 90. To the Cutlerites (and perhaps the Josephites as well) Lois's healing was considered miraculous. However, the Oak Lake Josephites did not quickly forget or forgive the accusations of witchcraft the Cutlerites had made against them. The incident of Lois Cutler's illness and recovery engendered feelings of distrust and hostility that continued between the two religious organizations for many years.[137]

Smith's visit to the former Cutlerites at Oak Lake started a movement that could not be stopped. Soon a second branch of the Josephites was established at Silver Lake and settlers who had no previous knowledge of the Mormons were converted. Before Smith left Otter Tail County, more than fifty people had been baptized and organized into thriving new churches. Though the only former Cutlerites to join were those from Oak Lake, and these were individuals whom the Cutlerite church had already cut-off from membership, the Cutlerites felt deeply threatened. They were aware that members of the younger generation of Cutlerites found themselves powerfully attracted to the more liberal religion. Families became divided, with feelings of guilt and sorrow on both sides.

Though the Cutlerites were never able to convert a single Indian to their beliefs, they did convert a few settlers to Cutlerism and established close relationships with other pioneer neighbors. On May 1, 1868, two strangers walked into the Clitherall settlement, each carrying a knapsack, an axe and a gun. They were George Gould and his seventeen-year-old son Winfield. Gould had taken a homestead at Silver Lake, about nine miles west of Clitherall, and he and his son were on their way to build a cabin on their land. The two men were welcomed into the home of Cutlerite Henry Way, where they spent the night, and when they left the next morning Way lent them his mule and a light wagon. He also told the Goulds where they could find a sugar bush on their way, complete with a trough full of sap and a sap pan with which they could boil down the liquid. The Goulds did as Way advised, found the sap and pan and spent the night making maple syrup. "All this Mr. Way did for us without a cent of pay," an impressed Winfield later recalled. When the Goulds were ready to plant their first crop, the Cutlerites again came to their assistance. "They let us take two yoke of oxen and a plow and harrow and we got several acres plowed and planted. And how it did grow!"

During the winter of 1869–70 Winfield Gould attended the Clitherall school, and one day he found himself looking into the eyes of twelve-year-old Ella Whiting, the third daughter of Francis Lewis and Ann Jeanette. As Gould recalled, "I happened to look across the schoolroom and noticed Ella Whiting with her arm on her desk, her head lying on her arm and found she was looking at me steadily. I looked straight into her eyes for some time and a strange feeling came over me as though there was a power drawing us toward each other."

Ella turned thirteen that December and Winfield Gould began walking her home from the log church and parties. One winter night he found the courage to tell Ella that he was going to kiss her goodnight. When they reached the door to her house she raised her face to him and he bent to kiss her. At that instant Gould's wool scarf blew between them and he kissed one side of the scarf and she the other. Both were too excited to try again. The next year, when Ella was fourteen and Gould nineteen, he proposed. She accepted and three years later, on July 7, 1875, they were married in the bride's home. Forty guests crowded into Francis Lewis and Ann Jeanette Whiting's log house to watch Calvin Fletcher perform the wedding ceremony. There was to have been one wedding gift, a young heifer given to the bride from her father, but since she was marrying a "Gentile" (non-Mormon) the Cut-lerite church ruled against giving her the gift. Gould filed on a home-stead next to his father's on Silver Lake.

When the Josephite Apostle T.W. Smith visited Oak Lake, he called on and conducted services in Winfield and Ella Gould's home at Silver Lake. After one evening prayer service, Gould, regardless of the fact that his wife was a staunch Cutlerite, asked to be baptized into the Jo-sephite church. Though the ice was a foot thick on the lake, Gould asked that the ordinance be performed that very night. Warmed by their reli-gious fervor, the attendees at the prayer meeting (except for the heart-broken Ella) trooped down to the lakeshore in the dark and chopped a hole in the ice. Smith walked into the icy water up to his waist. Gould followed. After a brief prayer, Smith lowered Gould into the frigid depths, baptizing him into the Josephite church.[138]

Winfield Gould's conversion was complete. As he later wrote, "As we walked up through the woods to the house, the Saints sang a hymn as we went. As the words of that hymn rang out through the woods there was such a feeling of joy and peace and happiness [that] filled my whole body as I had never known before and it seemed to me that could I have walked into the presence of the Savior that I would have been as sure of a welcome as I would from the dearest friend on earth." Gould's Cutlerite wife, however, felt differently. "I found Ella still grieving and it seemed impossible for me to say anything to comfort her."[139]

To the Cutlerites and Josephites of Otter Tail and Becker Counties, religion was not a compartmentalized aspect of life to be observed on a Sunday and largely forgotten throughout the rest of the week. Instead, religion, to both groups, defined their philosophy of life, revealed who they were, identified them as significant actors in history, formed the boundaries of their social lives, and blazed at the core of their souls. The rituals of the church signified their solemn contract with the divine.

Belonging to the "True Church" had a practical value as well. There were few medical doctors in Otter Tail County and healings through "administration" and prayers by the church elders were relied on by both groups. A major function of their religion was the curing of illnesses and the speeding of recovery from accidents. Hallie Gould, a daughter of Winfield and Ella Whiting Gould, wrote, "I think our early assurances of our church being the true church of God came largely through testimonies of healing under the hands of Grandpa (George Gould) and those associated with him. In arguing church beliefs with schoolmates of other churches, we recognized this as one great advantage of our church. I can almost feel yet," she wrote, "the agony of earache I suffered one evening until I was relieved through administration."[140] George Gould was noted, among the Josephites, for his healing abilities. Bertha Hunter Murdock credited him with curing her of scarlet fever and goiter.

There was rivalry and competition in the claims for healings. When Hallie cut her foot on a scythe her grandfather Gould was called to "administer" to her. Hallie reported, "I've forgotten all but the pain, the flow of blood and the fright. But Aunt Cordie (Cordelia Whiting) remembers that to her amazement the bleeding stopped immediately and that the wound healed with such rapidity that, though she was a Cutlerite with prevailing prejudices, she admitted I received an instant and powerful blessing under Grandpa's hands." Gould's reputation as a religious healer was so great that when his granddaughter Iva was warned that eating some green fruit would make her sick, she replied, "I don't care. Grandpa will pray for me and make me well."[141]

When the Cutlerite pioneers saw their children defecting to the hated Josephites they were distraught and sick at heart over the defection. They were certain that their children, for whom two generations had sacrificed and whom they dearly loved, were being led astray by silver-tongued deceivers. One by one the children of Francis Lewis and Ann Jeanette Whiting joined the Josephites. The defection of their eldest daughter Emma to the Josephites was particularly painful because, as Emma Whiting explained, "My parents felt it was worse for me than for my sisters Ella or May because upon me, as well as my husband, the high priesthood had been bestowed. It was true that in the early part of 1871 we had been taken into the (Cutlerite) high priests' quorum and received our endowment. This was regarded as the most sacred and secret part of the work of God—too sacred and secret to be talked about to those who did not belong. Only those who attained to the priesthood became the Kingdom and Elect of God."[142]

When Emma's younger brother Arthur Whiting and his wife Lois, a daughter of Hirum and Rachel Murdock, decided to leave the Cutlerites and join the Josephites, it was in the middle of a Minnesota winter. Not to be deterred, the minister chopped a hole in the ice in the lake and plunged the baptismal candidates over their heads into the freezing water. The next day when they told their parents what they had done, the parents were heartbroken. "We've suffered and come up here to

Francis Lewis Whiting (1830–1909) and Ann Jeanette Burdick Whiting (1831–1917). Photograph by C. A. Johnson.

Clitherall and now you've left the church," Ann Jeanette wept. Whiting could not stand to see his mother crying so the next week another hole was chopped in the ice of Clitherall Lake and Arthur and Lois Whiting were rebaptized into the Cutlerite church, again by a cold immersion in the lake. As Whiting explained, "If it will make Ma feel better about it, I'll get rebaptized." The change of heart did not last. Arthur and Lois Whiting waited until the summer when Whiting declared he was "ready to fight any of them" over his religious beliefs and once again he and Lois were immersed in the lake for the sake of their faith.

Every one of the founding Cutlerite families lost some or all of their children to the Josephites. In one of his letters to his sister Emeline in Utah, Chauncey Whiting wrote of the "terrible foolish move" his children had made "in joining the Josephites, as they are called." In another letter to Emeline he wrote that he was "sorrowful to say some of our children have turned a listening ear to the flattering tongue and been drawn away to the so-called Josephite faith or church, and which people, as we have been informed by a prophet of God, are led by a spirit of deception."[143] He added, "It is most sorrowful to think that a people raised up and schooled directly under the prophet's watch care, and having a right in the order of the Holy Priesthood to hold converse with heaven, and learn of things past, present and future, should have overlooked the importance of obeying the last command, seemingly which the Lord gave for the salvation of the whole church; and knowing meantime that such careless neglect would result in the downfall or rejection of the church, is indeed astonishing and sorrowful in the extreme." The "last command" referred to by Whiting undoubtedly referred to "The Oneness."

The Cutlerite response to the Josephite threat was to turn ever more inward and carry their rejection of the world to even greater lengths. As Daisy Whiting Fletcher wrote, "Failure to achieve the desired perfection led to a search among the membership for the reason, with the result that each was observed for signs of evildoing, negligence, infractions of strict rules that governed dress and daily living habits, lack of the Holy Spirit, etc."[144]

In 1872 Chauncey Whiting once again tried to institute "The Oneness." Everyone was to be equal in what they possessed and each was to comply with all church requirements. The church council attempted to regulate all the affairs of individuals, the community, the school and the church. Francis Lewis Whiting's daughter Emma wrote, "We undertook to go into what they called 'a oneness' or an organization of equality where we were to be equal in temporal things. . . . We always had dressed plainly, but now we were counseled to lay aside all unnecessary adornment, so for several years no trimming was allowed to adorn our apparel, neither collar nor jewels nor ribbon bows were worn. Sunbonnets for women and girls in summer and warm hoods for winter were the only style." She added, "[This was] a very good style for poor folks in a new country but a little on the extreme."[145]

To satisfy the demands of "oneness," Emma and her husband Edwin B. Anderson, though they were desperately poor, "settled up with the bishop Warren Whiting and turned in our buildings to the society of equality. . . . We had been holding the land we were on as a preemption for the church, but let them have it back to hold it for themselves if they wished."[146] Edwin and Emma Anderson thus walked away from eight years of hard labor on land they had homesteaded and, after giving it to the Cutlerite church, filed on another claim near East Battle Lake.

In the winter of 1884 the Josephites sent another missionary, Thomas Nutt, to Otter Tail County. Emma and Edwin Anderson invited him to preach in their home in Girard Township with the result that eleven people, including the Andersons, asked to be baptized into the Josephite faction they were beginning to call the Reorganization. It was March 4, 1883, and the lake was still covered with two feet of ice. Not to be put off, the men spent most of the day clearing snow and cutting a large hole in the ice so that the candidates could be immersed in the icy water. The coldness of the water in which a candidate chose to be immersed almost became a measure of religious devotion. One of the converts was Ella Whiting Gould, Winfield's wife, who after debating for eight years, also asked to be baptized into the Josephite organization. One by one, the children of the Cutlerite pioneers abandoned the faith of their fathers.[147]

In an August 10, 1885, letter to his "Dear Sister Emeline," Sylvester Whiting wrote:

> "Chauncey, Almon, Lewis and families are all well and all are believers in Joseph the Seer. [They are] also as firm in the belief that Father Cutler was ordained to all the keys, power and authority that was put on Joseph, as we are that Joseph was called of God. We have not taken a course to get very rich as to the things of this world, but have been seeking for another

object. . . . We all have looked and prayed for the redemption of Zion and have all failed to see it for some cause and now it is time we should find out the cause and remove it and realize the blessings that we have so long expected and desired. The Josephites are all around us and have got the most of Father Cutler's church to join them—some out of all our families which makes it hard for us to visit together with the same feelings of union as if we all believed alike."[148]

Despite the strains of the religious division between them, within the closed society of the Clitherall community the Cutlerites and Josephites maintained their ties of family and kinship. For the most part, they did not allow their personal relationships to be torn apart by religious warfare. Nina, one of the six daughters of Winfield and Ella Whiting Gould, devout Josephites all, wrote of the delight and excitement she and her sisters felt when they went to visit their Cutlerite grandparents, Francis Lewis and Ann Jeanette Whiting, who had moved from Clitherall to Girard Township near East Battle Lake. If tensions existed between the adults over their religious differences, the children were unaware of them.

"'We are going to Grandma Whiting's tomorrow!' No more exciting words ever fell on my ears during all the days of my childhood than those," Nina wrote. She added:

"It was the one big event of the year. It meant rising early, having our pigtails neatly braided and our Sunday dresses put on. It meant that Ma would pack the old black satchel with clean print dresses and our nightgowns. And when the chores were done, Pa would drive up the hill from the barn with the two-seated buggy. Ma would climb in beside him. Gladys, Iva and I in the back seat, a happy little row with our wreathed straw hats held on by tight rubber bands under our chins.

"Over the familiar road to school, enchanted now, past the deserted schoolhouse to the winding, woodsy road near Camp Corless where we could reach out on either side and gather big basswood leaves or the round shining poplars and sort them in our laps. Then came the breathtaking moment when, just past John Murdock's, Pa would get out, let down the checkreins and drive the buggy out into the shallow water of Clitherall Lake and hot, tired old Pat and John would drink and drink and drink. When they had finished and turned to go, out the water would splash, the wheels cut deep in the sand, the buggy would tip and lurch and I would hang to the seat and say my prayers until we were safely back up in the road.

"We were scarcely settled on our seats when we found ourselves at Old Clitherall, pointing out Grandpa's little house on the corner where Pa and Ma were married, Uncle Ike's house, the old log church, the school house, Uncle Chauncey's house—all standing in place of the rows of log houses our parents remembered. We took the road past the old pole swing, beautiful Lake Clitherall, Cowbar Hill with its grassy winding road over which so many many sad hearts have gone up to where the white marble sentinels forever stand.

"We ride up the long slow hill onto the Girard prairies. Up here we can look far over the fields of grain. We see the Fletcher fields, Uncle Orison's fields and come to the little road that winds over the hill to Uncle Art's (Arthur Whiting) little hidden house. Just a little ways and we are in sight of big Battle Lake with its miles of whitecaps rolling toward us to break with a splash on the yellow sand. We cross the outlet bridge up to Uncle Vet's home. We were getting nearer and nearer now and our excitement grew. Our road became shady. The last stretch, jack oaks and chokecherries on one side, yellow wheat on the other, till we came to the short, magic turn in the little grove that hid Grandma's house from our view.

"If Grandma could have known the happiness that filled the hearts of those three little girls on the back seat at sight of her home, her dear old heart would have been glad. But we never told her. We did not say much to anyone but we felt a lot. Pa's 'Whoa' brought the horses to a standstill beside the brimming water trough, a great hollow log under the two tall pines in front of Grandma's house. Grandpa, hearing the sound of wheels, would come from the barn across the way, a welcoming smile crinkling around his eyes, his heavy beard as white as snow. We loved him but feared him a little. I don't know why. He was never anything but kind to us and we dearly loved his tales. Then the screen door under the porch would open and Grandma would come out just as we knew she would, little and trim and neat and spry, in a dark print dress and clean checked apron, her snow white hair held smoothly in place by its black silk net. Never did a stray hair escape and her face, to me, was beautiful. After what seemed like a long journey, really only twelve miles, we climbed out and were made welcome by their kindness.

"How those old rooms live in my memory—the clean swept porch with its splint-bottom chairs and seed corn hanging from the rafters; the cool, dark kitchen, its old oak floor darkened by so many sudsy scrubbings, the drop-leaf table against the wall where we would soon gather for the evening meal—warm chicken gravy and strawberry sauce with a little pieplant in it which nobody minded but Pa, the tall cupboard with its blue glass dishes, blue flowered china and tall heavy goblets, wooden sink and hard black chairs with leaves painted on the backs. But the thing that drew us like a magnet was the corner where the little room jutted out that hid the stairway. How we loved, after a while, to lift the latch and climb those steep stairs to the chamber where Lester, Grandma and Grandpa's boy, slept and where our beds awaited us and to peep into the low, clean attic where the spinning wheel stood.

"Lester gave us crabapples and hazel nuts and smiled at us but we didn't dare talk to him much. In the evening in Grandma's front room with its rag carpet, braided rugs, soft cushioned chairs and red sofa, we loved to listen to him and Ed and Harry make music on their fiddles. The high-back wood box in the corner with the old bootjack underneath is part of the picture. So also was the silent little old lady [Mary Denna] with bobbed white hair who sat eternally knitting by the window. We watched her in awe for had she not once been the wife of an Indian?

"Before we went to our beds at night we all knelt together in the sitting room and Grandpa prayed. One sentence I always remember, 'Bless our children and our grandchildren. Keep them from the power of evil and designing men.'"

There was no question in any of the listeners' minds whom Francis Lewis Whiting considered to be the "evil and designing men."[149] It was the wily Josephites.

Hallie Gould, another daughter of Winfield and Ella Gould, recorded the second generation's curiosity about the secret upper room of the Cutlerite church. In an article for a Josephite youth publication, Hallie wrote:

> "At the right side of the door as one entered [the Cutlerite church] was the enclosed staircase with two low steps outside. The story of what was beyond those steps and locked door is one that has not been handed down to the younger generations, much as we have curiously or seriously desired to know. We know merely that only those holding the priesthood (either men or women) were allowed to enter that secret chamber, and we have heard rumors of strange ceremonies, covenants and endowments, the alter [sic], the tree of life, the ordinance of feet washing, and the peculiar though necessary and significant grave clothes which no one will explain. Even those of the priesthood who later forsook the church organization have been sufficiently true to the binding covenant made there to prevent their satisfying our demand for knowledge."[150]

Despite the religious division between them, Josephites and Cutlerites fell in love with each other. Nina and Ethel Gould married Orison and Frank Tucker, sons of one of the few Minnesota pioneers to convert to the Cutlerite faith. Abner Tucker had come west from New Jersey to settle in Otter Tail County and found himself among the Cutlerites at Clitherall. When he met Emily Murdock, eldest daughter of Hirum and Rachel Murdock, he fell in love. When the two were married, Tucker wholeheartedly adopted her Cutlerite faith. Their sons, Orison and Frank, grew up amid the bitterness and heartache of the religious strife that divided the community. When young Orison Tucker went to Winfield Gould to ask for Nina's hand in marriage, the older man remembered the eight years he and his wife had been divided over the subject of religion. "Your religion is the only thing I have against you," he told the younger man, "but if you can both agree to attend church together—you go with her one Sunday and she with you the next—I believe it will turn out all right." The young couple agreed and were married in 1909. In 1911 Orison Tucker, over the objections of his parents, joined the Josephites.

Regardless of the happy childhood memories of family visits, life

Warren Whiting (1847–1889), the photographer.

on the Minnesota frontier was never easy for anyone. Every settler struggled, but women who were widowed and had children to care for had an especially difficult life. Zeruah Sherman's experience was not untypical. In September 1868, Zeruah married Warren Whiting, Chauncey's son and one of the boys who had been her pupil in the Cutlerite one-room school. Warren Whiting first had a clothespin factory in Old Clitherall and later became a photographer who loaded up his equipment, including glass plates for negatives, in a covered wagon and traveled from village to village taking glass plate pictures. His children remember having to get dressed up in their best clothes to act as models for their father as he worked to perfect his photograph technique. For a time Whiting set up his equipment in a hotel room in Peas Prairie (now Henning) where he took pictures of the Indians and the Scandinavian immigrants. While still a young man he became ill and, after a long illness, died at age 42 in 1889, leaving Zeruah with five children ranging in age from ten months to eighteen years.

In the last years of his life Whiting had purchased a seven acre farm with a small pasture and a few acres of field which Zeruah and her eldest son planted and cultivated to produce feed for their animals. Their livestock consisted of one cow, a pig and a few chickens. From the cream her cow gave, Zeruah churned butter and took it, and a few eggs, a mile and a half into town to exchange for calico to clothe her children—walking all the way. She took in washing and ironing, worked as a nurse, boarded teachers and, in the summer, took her children by boat across the lake to pick gooseberries that they sold for five cents a quart, using the money to buy flour. At the age of 56, when her youngest child was twelve, Zeruah, the first schoolteacher in Otter Tail County, died—worn out by her struggle to care for her family. She had liver cancer and the doctor attempted surgery on the kitchen table. Zeruah's daughter Grace assisted with the anesthetic. At the time of Zeruah's death two of her children were sick with typhoid fever and were nursed back to health by Grace. Zeruah's tragedy was not uncommon.

Compared to other residents on the frontier at the time the Cutlerites, while they had to work continuously to survive, were well-to-do. They were literate people with many skilled craftsmen among them. They had a strong social organization through their church and lived on rich land. Every family appeared to be able to supply itself with the basic needs of food, clothing and shelter and could count on the support of the community in times of crisis.

While the Cutlerite society was a patriarchal one, Cutlerite husbands and wives shared equally in the ownership of property. Widows inherited land, fathers left inheritances to their daughters as well as their sons, and, even more unusual, women appeared to hold at least nominal offices in the priesthood. Professor Danny Jorgensen has analyzed the *Pliny Fisher Patriarchal Blessing Book,* one of the earliest and most detailed records left by the early Cutlerites during their residence in Manti. The blessing book records blessings bestowed on individual Cutlerites by the Patriarch, a church official.

The blessings are filled with Biblical imagery reflecting the values of wisdom, intelligence, obedience, peace, joy and prosperity; they admonish the believers to be faithful. One woman is advised that she "will be able to overcome all the evil propensities of your nature," while a man is told that "as you are faithful you shall be blessed with mighty faith, wisdom, intelligence and knowledge, to know the things that concern your peace. . . .You shall be blessed both temporally and spiritually . . . to do good in your day and generation on earth in helping to gather up the honest in heart."

The blessings also contained a dark side in that they warned of evil and vengeful spirits and of the "powers of the adversary." Recipients of the blessings were continually admonished to be watchful lest they be deceived by false spirits. Fisher told Lois Sherman, Cutler's married daughter, that she would "become a terror to false spirits." The possibility of being led astray by evil spirits was a constant threat to the Cutlerites. The world, in their view, was a battleground where unseen but none-the-less real forces continuously contended for their souls. Nothing but the thinnest of veils separated the two worlds from each other.

In most cases the blessings given to women defined them in relation to a man—either a husband or a father. Unlike adult males, what women were called to do was defined by their husband's work. Lois Cutler was told that she was "entitled to all the blessings of the priesthood with him . . ." and "to help thy companion in all his work that he is called to do." While it appears from the *Pliny Fisher Patriarchal Blessing Book* that the Cutlerites envisioned a female priesthood, in actual fact, Fisher promised the priesthood to twice as many men as women. When he did promise the priesthood to women, it was qualified by gender. In Caroline Davis's blessing Fisher refers to "the great work that thou shall be called to do *for thy sex* for the living and the dead." He tells Harriett Richards that ". . . you will have all the gifts that you shall desire by the spirit that belongs *to thy sex*."

Jorgensen has concluded that the priesthood powers spoken of by Fisher for women and his references to women as being queens and priestesses refer to women's role in the celestial world and not in the Kingdom of God on earth as the Cutlerites envisioned it. In Pliny Fisher's book Jorgensen did not find a single case of women being appointed to preach.[151]

Emma Lucine Whiting Anderson, while still a member of the Cutlerite Church, resented the fact that she was denied an active role in performing priestly duties. Although she had been admitted to the most sacred of the Cutlerite secret ordinances, she was confused as to what they meant and what she was permitted to do. As she later wrote, "I never knew what office I held in the high priesthood. I was never called an 'elderess' or 'high priestess' or anything. I had a right to anoint with oil and administer to the sick by laying on my hands and praying to God to heal if no man was present. But if a man was present he never thought of asking a woman to assist but went ahead alone. It only serves to show how they esteemed a man so much superior to a woman. I never knew them to ask a woman to pray or to ask a blessing at the table if a man were present."[152]

Emma Anderson's resentment and confusion over her role in the Cutlerites' religious life was not typical of most Cutlerite women. Almost all of the Cutlerites accepted the fact that their religious and secular life was a patriarchy, which, they believed, was the appropriate and natural order. Men and women worked side by side doing heavy manual labor in true partnerships. Making a success of farms on the frontier took all of the energy a couple could muster. Tragedy and misfortune were regular occurrences, and the best they could do was help each other weather the constant storms of fate.

CHAPTER 12

The Death of Old Clitherall

The residents of Clitherall probably felt most secure in their community between 1868 and 1870, before the defections of members to Oak Lake and the arrival of the Josephite missionaries. In 1881 the Northern Pacific railroad built the Fergus and Black Hills line west from Wadena to Fergus Falls, bypassing the village of Clitherall by the lake and founding a new town, also called Clitherall, a mile and a quarter east of the original settlement.

The establishment of New Clitherall was a major commercial blow to the older community. Trade which once came to the shops and stores of "Old Clitherall" now quickly moved to the new site. The railroad paid Hirum Murdock $10 for an easement across his property. Cutlerite men took jobs building the railroad and found themselves drawn away from the restricted life of Old Clitherall. The coming of the railroad led to the establishment of other towns on the line, spaced four to five miles apart. New Clitherall soon had competition from the towns of Battle Lake on the west and Vining and Henning on the east.

In 1879 two of the original pioneers, Francis Lewis Whiting and his brother Almon Whiting, the chairmaker, moved about six miles from Old Clitherall to take up adjoining homesteads in Girard Township near East Battle Lake. (Almon's wife was Lydia Maria Garfield, a first cousin of President James Garfield.) Lewis Denna and his wife moved into an unused log house on Francis Lewis Whiting's property. Though the Whitings' departure was strongly opposed by the Cutlerites, it was dictated by economic necessity. In ten years Otter Tail County's population had increased from 1,371 in 1870 to 20,310 in 1880. Francis Lewis Whiting needed more land to farm and Almon Whiting needed the oak and maple timber growing in Girard for his chairs. The timber was

rapidly being cut for railroad ties, for which the lumbermen were paid
20 to 30 cents apiece.

Chauncey Whiting complained bitterly to his sister Emeline about
his brothers' decision to move. "If all them that had a name in this
church had come right up and filled their place as God required of them
and made Clitherall a holy place, the Lord would have been pleased . . .
to furnish all our children with work and not one [would have] been
under the necessity of going off to get claims . . . but the majority of the
people would not do as the head and the council advised them, and the
spirit of the Lord grieved and withdrew from the people and a spirit of
deception came in among them and led them off from the chosen place
into a spirit of the world."[153]

All parts of the county were growing. By 1885 the Josephite congregation in Girard grew large enough to justify a church building. The
members built the church, called the "Hope of Zion" branch, spending
$85.71 for the lumber and a total of $201.12 for the finished building
which was complete with wall mounted kerosene lamps and polished re-
flectors. Though Francis Lewis Whiting and Almon Whiting now lived
in Girard, about six miles away from Old Clitherall, and they remained
faithful Cutlerites, their move to Girard which took them away from
daily contact with the Cutlerites, further weakened the organization.

The Cutlerites remaining in Old Clitherall were also becoming
more prosperous. They replaced their log houses with larger frame
buildings erected on the same sites as the originals. Despite these signs
of increased well being, in reality their community was dying. Services
in the log church were held sporadically or not at all. The continued loss
of membership to the Josephites grieved them and after discussing the
problem, they decided not to contest the conversions to the Josephites as
they believed that was the advice they had received from Cutler before
his death in Manti. Their response to change was to continue to retreat
from the world and to refrain from seeking converts. The "Oneness"
was no longer practiced. It had never been legally binding and only a
few of the Cutlerites had actually participated by dedicating their property to the church. Chauncey Whiting's discouragement was apparent in
letters he wrote to his sister Emeline in Salt Lake City. At times he even
seemed to regret having made the trek to Minnesota.

In 1885 or 1886 he wrote: "Well, I must give an outline of my little
shanty erected last summer or fall. It is a frame with three rooms below
and nice chamber above, while adjoining on the north is my tin shop.

This arrangement leaves the kitchen about in the center of the whole structure, fronting to the east, and to the main road. But with this comfortable building I feel no better satisfied, neither any more at home than I did in my old log hut of twenty years standing. . . . I do not feel at rest or that my permanent home should be made in Minnesota. Indeed it is a cold country to live in. Long winters and short cropping seasons. Indeed the ground in some places freezes to the depth of from six to eight feet. To sum the matter up, we have a bleak, cold (and might almost say in truth) barren region to live in." In another letter he wrote that "church matters quite dull at present. Everybody wants to go to heaven but view the path too narrow to walk in at present."[154]

When his wife Editha died, Whiting felt even more sorrowful and alone. He wrote to his sister Emeline, "It appears that when old age creeps upon a person and when he is the least able to endure it, the greatest load and sore trials are heaped upon him . . . thinking that sooner or later I may become a tiresome burden to others, the mind is seized with a feeling of despair and I almost regret that I had an existence. Be all of these things as they may, I must . . . be content to finish up the few remaining days or years allotted me on earth in sorrow, misery and loneliness. I suppose that it is something of a task for you to write, but a line and word of encouragement from my dear sister in the far off country would be very thankfully received. Your sorrowful and lonely brother, C. Whiting."

Chauncey Whiting died in June 1902, followed by his brother, Francis Lewis Whiting, in 1909. The only remaining Elders in the Cutlerite church were the elderly Sylvester Whiting, Chauncey's son Isaac Whiting (who no longer attended church), and the convert Abner Tucker who had been baptized when he married Hirum and Rachel Murdock's daughter Emily. A few meetings of the church were held in 1903 in the Old Clitherall school building (the log church had fallen into disrepair) but after a few sporadic attempts to hold services, meetings were discontinued altogether. Chauncey's First Counselor and president-elect of the church was Isaac Whiting who had no interest in leading the church. Isaac Whiting preferred to go wolf hunting with his sons on Sunday and he was quoted as saying, "They want me to lead the church but I tell them there ain't no church to lead."[155] On summer evenings Isaac and Jennie Whiting would drive around Clitherall in a covered buggy pulled by a white horse and call on the neighbors who found them to be jolly company and made them welcome.

The Cutlerite Church might well have ended at that point if, in 1909, Isaac Whiting had not had an accident that put out one of his eyes. He suffered terribly. When he was well he called the church together and told the members that after three days in hell he was ready to take his place as president of the church. The accident was viewed by Whiting and the church members as God's chastisement of him for his rebelliousness and refusal to accept his religious responsibilities.

For the rest of his life Isaac Whiting attempted to make up for his earlier failure. He immediately began to set the church in order. As his First Counselor and heir to the presidency he chose Emery Fletcher, a son of Joseph Edmund Fletcher, the man the Murdocks believed had an evil eye. Isaac's son Erle was Second Counselor. Since the original incorporation of the church in 1872 had been forgotten, they incorporated again naming Erle Whiting, James Fletcher and Emery Fletcher as trustees. As they had done in the 1870s, they again ignored their corporate structure and for the next 52 years no official minutes were recorded.

Isaac Whiting's leadership led to a brief resurgence of the Cutlerites in Old Clitherall. The dilapidated log church was torn down in 1910 and the logs traded to Abner Tucker for the cemetery land at the top of Cowbar Hill. (The log church building was reassembled as a shed and can still be seen on the Stabnow property 1.4 mile east of the cemetery.) Under Whiting's leadership, weekly church meetings were reinstated and held on alternate Sundays in the homes of Isaac Whiting or James Fletcher (one of Joseph Edmund Fletcher's sons). A new two-story white frame church was built on the site of the old log church, paid for by contributions from the newly energized and more prosperous Cutlerites. The design of the new Cutlerite church recalled, though on an exceedingly modest scale, the first Mormon temple built in Kirtland, Ohio—which itself reflected the design of eighteenth century Puritan churches of New England.

When Isaac Whiting assumed responsibility for the Cutlerite church he reinstated the Nauvoo temple ordinances that had been allowed to lapse. In a letter to her daughter Bonnie, Jennie Whiting told of her own participation in the rites. "Other places are prepared for those who have not accepted the teaching of Christ but they still have a chance through the baptism for the dead to gain a place in the Terrestrial or Celestial Kingdoms. Everyone will receive a just reward for the deeds done in the body, good or bad. You know Daisy was never baptized while she was alive but before her death she asked us to send for the elders to adminis-

The new Cutlerite church, built in 1912. Photograph by the author, 2001.

ter to her, saying she knew this was the true church." (Daisy Whiting, Jennie and Isaac Whiting's youngest daughter, died in 1906 at age 23 from what may have been a burst appendix.) "We sent for Uncle Lute [Francis Lewis Whiting] and Uncle Vet [Sylvester Whiting] who came and prayed for her and anointed her and thus gained the promise given those who do this . . . that their sins shall be forgiven. After her death I was baptized for her and she is now resting in Paradise until the resurrection." In her letter Jennie added that during Whiting's tenure as church president they "were permitted to work for the dead. I was the first one to be baptized by your father for Daisy. Aunt Nett [Ann Jeanette Whiting] came next and was baptized for her daughter May. We had several of these baptismal meetings." Jennie went on to list five additional individuals who were baptized into the church in this way and adds that there were "many others."[156]

In 1911 Isaac Whiting's son Julian and his wife Amy visited Clitherall from their home in Wolf Creek, Montana. The couple was so impressed by the renewed activity in the Cutlerite Church that Julian Whiting resigned his railroad job and moved his family back to Old Clitherall where they joined with Isaac Whiting and the other Cutlerites in the task of reviving the church. Amy, in particular, added an element of optimism and cheer to the group. She was a calm, serene woman who was musical and played the zither. As Ronald Stabnow, who grew up in Clitherall and was the long-time mayor of Battle Lake, observed, "[By temperament] she did not quite belong with the Cutlerites."

Stabnow remembers that when he and his sisters walked the mile from their home to the school in Old Clitherall they followed a straight path over the swamp (frozen in winter), crossed a pasture and trudged past Amy Whiting's back door on the way to the door of the school. In the winter when it was cold or a blizzard was brewing Amy would watch until she saw the children pass her back door. Then she would pick up the party-line telephone and crank two longs and two shorts, which was the Stabnow number. Mable Stabnow would pick up her phone to hear Amy report, "The children just went by." In the afternoon when school was out Amy would again watch for the children to pass before calling Mable to report, "The children are on their way home now." Mable Stabnow would know when to expect her children home from school, an important consideration during a Minnesota winter when the temperature often stayed below zero for weeks and the snow was deep on the ground.

In 1912 Isaac Whiting, encouraged by the return to Old Clitherall of his son and daughter-in-law, the renewed commitment of members, and believing that the "law of consecration" was an essential requirement of the church, put "the Oneness" plan back into operation yet again. As they had tried to do in Manti and earlier in Clitherall, all property owned by church members was to be held in common with each member being allotted enough to provide for his needs. Profits beyond what was needed for an individual or a family went to the church for what was called the "Bishop's Storehouse." On September 25, 1913, Isaac Whiting and his wife deeded the lot (lot "E") on which their house and the church stood to the Cutlerite church. Abner Tucker formally deeded the cemetery land to the church. This attempt at operating the "Oneness" was partially successful. Several farms and homesteads were turned over to the church. James and Emery Fletcher gave their property to the church as did Isaac's sons Erle and Charles Whiting.[157]

Though the group had more success than it had had before in getting members to participate in their communal society, there were still some who resisted. Among those who were slow to sign their property over to the Cutlerite church was Frank Tucker, one of Abner Tucker's sons. Though Tucker, a station agent for the railroad, was married to Ethel Gould, a fervent Josephite, he had retained his membership in the Cutlerite church and knew well his wife's feelings on the matter of contributing their property to the church. Despite many reminders, Frank Tucker had never gotten around to signing the necessary papers. Finally the exasperated Cutlerites gave him a deadline. "Come to a church meeting prepared to sign the documents by a certain date," they said, "or be expelled from the church." The evening Frank was to appear at the church the train was late and he could not leave his post at the railroad depot in time to get to Old Clitherall. To his wife's vast relief, his failure to appear caused a rift with the Cutlerites and within a few months Frank Tucker, too, had joined the Josephites. Ethel was sure her prayers were what had caused the train to be late on that fateful day.[158]

In the wave of optimism that engulfed the Cutlerites at Old Clitherall over the reestablishment of the "Oneness" and the construction of the new church, they failed to foresee that their settlement by the lake was doomed as a viable town. By 1900 the town of New Clitherall had 167 residents, Battle Lake had 420 and Old Clitherall had but a score. New Clitherall and Battle Lake were attracting more and more business from the farmers in the area. Residents were looking to the future. A clerk in the bank at New Clitherall even had a crystal radio set with a cat hair resting on the crystal. By moving the cat hair around on the surface of the crystal the clerk could pick up a radio station and listen to it on earphones.

Blinded by their belief that divine providence had guided the location of Old Clitherall the Cutlerites could not grasp the fact that their village had no economic future. In 1916, using church funds, the Cutlerites built a two-story brick grocery store they called Justice Store #2 in Old Clitherall and stocked it with merchandise they were able to buy by trading a church-owned farm. Charles Whiting and later Julian Whiting operated the business as trustees for the church, serving the immigrants who had moved into the county.

The decision to build the store hearkened back to the tenets of early Mormonism. The Cutlerites could see that the new arrivals in the county offered an economic opportunity but they took advantage of it in a strictly Cutlerite way. The Cutlerites believed that their financial well-being would come about, not through individual effort, but through cooperation, working together, pooling ownership of resources and taking for oneself only one's "needs and just wants." The Bishop was the chief financial officer of the church who maintained the "storehouse" for the "surplus." While such a process served to keep everyone on the same economic level, regardless of their contribution, the Cutlerites' expectation was that, over time, such a system would raise the group's economic status. The Cutlerites were not opposed to making money; they just insisted on doing it in their own way.

Since there was no electricity in Old Clitherall, the first task for Julian's sons every morning was to fill the store's refrigerator with ice cakes from the icehouse. The ice blocks were packed in layers insulated with six inches of sawdust. A tool called an ice chipper was used to pack sawdust between the blocks and if they were kept well covered, the ice would last the store and houses of Old Clitherall until the end of the summer.

The ice for the icehouse was cut in January when the lake was frozen to a depth of several feet. Blocks about a foot and a half square were cut with an ice saw and pulled out onto the surface where they were loaded onto a sled towed by a team of horses to the ice house. Pulling the floating blocks from the icy water was a dangerous procedure. The men would cut heel notches into the surface ice on which to brace themselves as they hauled the slippery blocks of ice onto the lake surface. With water flowing over the blocks of ice and onto the surface making it incredibly slippery, a man would occasionally find himself sliding into the water. The others would immediately pull him out of the lake but with the temperature below zero, the wet clothes would freeze instantly. The drenched man, his teeth chattering, would be rushed to the house, wrapped in blankets, and his feet placed in a pail of hot water.

On one occasion a worker who had stayed behind to pull some final blocks out of the water while the others went to the house for dinner found himself unexpectedly in the lake. In desperation, realizing he would die in minutes, he thought of something that saved his life. He was wearing heavy mittens which had gotten soaked when he fell in the water. Reaching out he planted his wet mittens on the surface of the ice. Almost instantly they froze solid enabling him to pull himself out of the water. Though he still had to run to the house in his freezing clothes, he lived to tell his story.

The store often took farm produce in trade for merchandise. Julian Whiting, Jr., remembers the Scandinavian customers coming in from the Leaf Mountains. "They would hold their eggs and butter for up to a month before bringing them in to exchange for groceries," he recalled. Whiting would have to candle each egg to make certain it was not housing a chicken and the butter was so strong he could not sell it to the store's customers. The Scandinavian customers bought coffee beans, twenty pounds at a time. The coffee would have to be ground for the customers in a hand grinder, a task Whiting assigned to his sons. To avoid having to spend an hour grinding coffee, the boys soon learned to escape out the back door when they saw Scandinavian customers driving a team of horses up to the front door.

Julian Whiting soon discovered that his Swedish and Norwegian customers were not interested in the cost of a piece of merchandise so long as they could haggle over the price. He learned not to write the selling price on an item such as shoes, but to use a code word that would remind him what he had paid for it. He would quote a price 50 cents higher than his usual retail price and then, showing proper reluctance, allow his customers to argue him down.

Goods for the store arrived at the railroad station in Clitherall twice each week. Julian Whiting and his boys would take Roy Whiting's team of horses to Clitherall to pick up the merchandise which usually included large gunny sacks of peanuts in the shell. On the way back to Old Clitherall a hole would mysteriously appear in the back of the gunny sacks and the road behind would be littered with peanut shells.[159]

In 1930 the Minnesota Highway Department constructed a new highway, number 210, between Fergus Falls and Wadena, paralleling the railroad. The new road passed one half mile north of Old Clitherall, bypassing the village and shortening the distance between Clitherall and Battle Lake. A ribbon of gray concrete ran in a straight line past the cemetery hill, over the outlet (now confined in a culvert), on to the county seat at Fergus Falls, and North Dakota. Soon grass and weeds began to crowd the margins of the sandy road, pock-marked with deer tracks, which led to Old Clitherall. The isolation of Old Clitherall that had begun with the building of the railroad in 1881 was now complete. Business at Justice Store #2 quickly dropped and before the year ended the store closed.

The same year that Justice Store #2 opened in Old Clitherall, the Cutlerites opened a second grocery store, called Justice Store #1, in the village of New Clitherall, trading a second farm for goods. This store was operated for the church by James Fletcher and his son Lee and lasted until 1951. Ronald Stabnow remembers Lee Fletcher. "He was large and fat. I can still see him slicing bologna and eating a slice or two after an order was filled—although not while Jim was looking. Everyone liked Lee. There was always a little sack of candy in the box of groceries when it left the store if Lee knew there were children at the home."

Around 1892 Lucy Erwin, the youngest daughter of Chauncey and Editha Whiting, began acquiring large parcels of the land her father had homesteaded for the church. In 1909 she purchased lots G and F, which fronted on the lakeshore, for $300. The abstract of title indicates that as early as 1892 various groups of Cutlerites were giving Lucy quit claim deeds to portions of her father's homestead property for the token sum of $1. Altogether five groups of Cutlerites gave Lucy quit claim deeds—all for the same piece of land! There was obviously some confusion over who had ultimate rights to the property. Lucy solved the problem and insured her claim by getting quit claim deeds from everyone who could have a potential interest; she paid three of the groups $1 each and two groups $12 each for the property. In 1913 Lucy and her husband Alfred Erwin deeded lot H, on which the school stood, to School District 1.[160]

After Lucy's husband died in 1914, she lived alone in her father Chauncey's house in Old Clitherall for a year before marrying Julius William Rosenkrans. Little is known about Rosenkrans. Lucy's nephew, Julian Whiting, Jr., described him as "a floater. He would come once in a while, stay a week or so and then disappear until the next time. No one knew how or why." In 1920 Rosenkrans, too, died and Lucy moved away to live with her sister. Then on October 25, 1923, a Robert Rosenkrans, writing from Carrol, Iowa, sent several threatening letter to Roy Whiting, Lucy's nephew in Old Clitherall, accusing him of trespassing on Lucy's property, presumably on the lots F and G she had acquired near the church.[161]

There is no record of a response to the letters from Roy Whiting, who was a quiet farmer who loved horses and appeared to share his father Isaac Whiting's sense of responsibility for the community. Roy Whiting lived in his father's house. During the winter he plowed the road and paths to the school, store and church with a home-made plow constructed of two 12 inch-wide lengths of lumber fastened into a long V. By towing this rig behind his team of horses he was able to clear the snow so that children and vehicles could move about the village.

It is doubtful that Lucy ever knew of the threatening letters. Whatever problems may (or may not) have existed between Lucy Rosenkrans, her nephew Roy Whiting, and the members of the Cutlerite church, they were resolved on September 28, 1927, when Lucy sold her land in Old Clitherall, including lots F and G on the lakeshore, to non-Cutlerites Harry and Clara E. Lord from Wahpeton, North Dakota, who paid $2,000 for the land on which they planned to build a summer fishing camp.

The sale of Chauncey Whiting's homestead forever ended the Cutlerite dream of a utopian community, a Kingdom of God by the Minnesota lake that would foreshadow the Zion they hoped to build in Independence. The hallowed spot where the men had knelt in prayer for guidance, the land between two lakes seen in Cutler's vision, was about to become a fishing camp for Gentiles. The only land now owned by members of the Cutlerite church in Old Clitherall were lots C and E, the property on which the church, store, and Isaac Whiting's home still stood and the cemetery on the top of the hill. In 1950, the Battle Lake School District sold lot H, the land where the school had once stood, back to the Cutlerites for $600.

Though they could not know it at the time, the end was also approaching for the Cutlerites in Minnesota. A new generation was taking control. An innocent act by Sam Lykken, a Gentile from Battle Lake, would awaken old controversies over who had the authority to lead the church. Before the struggle ended, the Cutlerites would be permanently divided.

CHAPTER 13

Return to Zion

The sale of the Old Clitherall village land awakened the newly formed Otter Tail County Historical Society to the fact that one of its prime historic sites was disappearing to development. The Society resolved to put up the first historical marker in the county at Old Clitherall. On July 5, 1928, the largest gathering (estimated at 2,000 people) in the history of Old Clitherall gathered for the dedication of the marker near the place where Sylvester Whiting had kept his store. John Murdock, son of first-settler Lyman Murdock, with the help of Whitings and Fletchers, built the monument—a circular base of concrete on which were cemented round lake boulders in the shape of an inverted cone. A bronze plaque reading "Site of the First Permanent Settlement in Otter Tail County, Minnesota. Members of the Church of Jesus Christ came here from Iowa, May 5, 1865" was provided by the Historical Society and cemented near the top of the monument.

The occasion was auspicious. The Battle Lake Men's Chorus sang "The Star Spangled Banner;" A.C. Krey, a history professor from the University of Minnesota, gave an address; and at the climactic moment Mae Whiting, a great granddaughter of Chauncey Whiting, lifted the flag that unveiled the monument. In the background of pictures taken that day stands one lone remnant of the original village by the lake—the Oakes log cabin, once used as the first schoolhouse in the settlement, now tumbledown and abandoned.[162]

Isaac Whiting died in 1922. With Whiting's death Emery Fletcher, Isaac's First Counselor, became President of the High Priesthood and of the Cutlerite church. Emery named Erle Whiting as his First Counselor. He did not choose a Second Counselor until 1950 when he named his nephew, Clyde Fletcher, a grandson of Joseph Edmund Fletcher, to that position.

Historic marker, 1928. Photographed 2001.

By the 1920s Otter Tail County had a population in excess of 46,000 while New Clitherall had only 187 residents. The only residents of Old Clitherall were the aging Cutlerite families. To President Emery Fletcher it must have been clear that there was no longer a future for the Cutlerite church in Minnesota and the time had come for a return to Independence to reclaim the city of Zion. The Missourians were no longer a threat. The rival Josephites, as well as other factions of Joseph Smith's movement, had moved back to Independence. An eventual move to Missouri had always been a central tenet of Cutlerite belief and, in a church council meeting held in 1924, the Cutlerites decided to begin their return to the land of Zion.

In October 1924, driving a Ford Model T car purchased by the Cutlerite church, two of the church elders drove to Independence, Missouri. After a brief search they found two lots, 807 and 812 South Cottage in a residential neighborhood, suitable for a church building. There was a small house on lot 812. For the next three years the Cutlerites made plans to build their Independence church at 807 South Cottage, and when another house next door, at 819, came on the market, they purchased it to use as a parsonage.[163]

In the spring of 1928 Emery Fletcher and his wife, and Rupert Fletcher moved to Independence and into the house at 819 Cottage. With funds supplied by the Minnesota Cutlerites, they hired a building contractor and supervised the building of the Independence church. The building is almost identical to the two-story white church in Old Clither-all. On May 30, 1929, the church council in Clitherall decided to send First Counselor Erle and Gertrude Whiting to Independence to live in the house at 812 and help with the work of the church. In a conference of the Cutlerite church held in Old Clitherall on April 12, 1931, the members named Emery Fletcher, Erle Whiting and Charles L. Whiting as trustees of the Cutlerite church properties in Independence. The re-turn to the land of Zion was underway.

To provide a means of support for the members living in Independence, the Cutlerites went into the trucking business. Rupert Fletcher began hauling freight and, as the business grew, he wrote to the church in Clitherall asking it to send others to Independence who could help him. At first the Church, not understanding the need, sent elderly members who did not know how to drive. Eventually Julian Whiting, Jr., joined Rupert Fletcher in the church trucking business which maintained two vehicles, a flatbed truck and a van-type vehicle. After eight years, the enterprise came to an end. When the business closed, the Independence members decided to stay in Missouri and take salaried positions. None of them moved back to their former homes at Clitherall.

In her section of the book *Alpheus Cutler and the Church of Jesus Christ,* Daisy Fletcher wrote about this period:

> "The separation into two branches has often caused misunder-standings due, in a large measure, to the lack of communication and a wide difference in environment. The Minnesota congregation are [sic] primarily members of a rural society, engaged in agrarian pursuits, while the Missouri membership live and work in an urban environment. The problems and needs of each have little in common with the other which has often caused disunity."[164]

The discord referred to by Daisy Fletcher broke out into the open in 1952. On October 7th, four Cutlerite elders—Clyde Fletcher, Lee Fletcher, Emery Fletcher and Julian Whiting, Sr., all living in Minnesota—voted to expel the four leaders living in Independence from the church. They wrote:

> "In General Council assembled at Clitherall, Minnesota, acting pursuant to its own rules and regulations for the government of its spiritual life as published in the Doctrine and Covenants of

said church unanimously, and pursuant to the rules and regula-
tions aforesaid, excommunicated Erle Whiting, Rupert Fletcher,
Richard Whiting and Julian E. Whiting, Jr., for cause, inasmuch as said members had not prior thereto repented of the
transgressions committed by them, and of which transgressions
they had been convicted at said General Council. Said former
members have ever since been, and now are of record, excommunicated, and have no membership in the said Church of
Jesus Christ."[165]

By this action, two of the Minnesota elders, Emery Fletcher and
Julian Whiting, Sr., excommunicated their own sons (Rupert and Julian,
Jr.) and threw four of their fellow religionists in Missouri, all of whom
were relatives and one of whom was a First Counselor, out of the
church! The transgressions that warranted such drastic action were not
named. In his sworn statement Clyde Fletcher said, "Here those who
were cast out from our church were led by Rupert Fletcher who sought
to exalt himself by seeking to undermine the authority of the presidency
led the few in that divisive movement in disregard of his and their excommunication."[166]

Emery Fletcher continued to serve as president of the Cutlerites,
both those in Minnesota and those in Missouri, until his death in 1953.
Emery's death once again threw the church into confusion, much as it
had been a hundred years before when Alpheus Cutler had died.
Emery's legal successor was First Counselor Erle Whiting who had
been excommunicated by the Clitherall Cutlerites. The members in
Missouri, believing that the Minnesota members did not have the authority to excommunicate anyone, went ahead and ordained Erle Whiting as the new President of the Cutlerite church. Officiating at the
ceremony was Rupert Fletcher, Emery's son, another of those who had
been excommunicated. Erle Whiting named Rupert Fletcher his First
Counselor and successor.

The Cutlerites in Minnesota were outraged by the actions of the
Cutlerites in Missouri. They could not accept a man they had excommunicated as their president and spiritual leader so, in October 1954, they
held their own church conference and ordained former president Emery
Fletcher's *second* counselor, Clyde Fletcher, who was living in Minnesota, as *their* church president. Each group claimed that its president was
the lawful leader of the Church of Jesus Christ (Cutlerite).

The two groups' religious disagreement over church authority and the dual presidencies would have gone unnoticed by their neighbors in Otter Tail County if, in 1960, Clyde Fletcher had not offered to sell a farm owned by the Cutlerite church to Sam Lykken, a farm implement dealer in Battle Lake who had grown up on a farm in North Dakota and wanted to raise cattle. "One day I was visiting with Clyde Fletcher, who was a very good customer of mine," he explained, "and I told him that I was looking for some pasture land to rent." Fletcher replied that he did not have any pasture land for rent but he did have a 144 acre farm for sale. The farm in question was part of the old Hirum Murdock homestead that Murdock had sold in 1903 to Winfield Gould for $2,000. Winfield and Ella Gould, in turn, had sold that piece of land to the Cutlerite church in 1919 for $12,000.

Lykken was interested in buying the farm but he was a young man and had invested most of his money in his implement business. Clyde Fletcher told him not to be concerned. "You have been very good to me," he said, "and I respect you and I would be willing to sell you the farm on a contract for deed." The papers were drawn up and Lykken began making payments on his farm. By 1964 he was ready to pay off the remainder of the contract. When Lykken inquired about the title to the land Clyde Fletcher told him that he was "having a problem with the people in Independence." The president of the Independence branch of the Cutlerite Church was now Rupert Fletcher (Erle Whiting had died) and Rupert Fletcher was contesting Clyde Fletcher's authority to sell the farm.

"Clyde was very upfront about it," Lykken remembers. "He told me, 'I am the president of the church and I have the authority to sell this farm and they can't contest this. I will go to my deathbed to make sure you have the farm.' Working with Clyde I really grew to love and respect him. He was a good customer for farm machinery and did a good job on his own farm. I got to know him well and was out on his land quite a few times. Being born and raised on a farm in North Dakota, I recognized good farming practices. Organic farming was his specialty and he put a lot of manure down and fertilized properly. Clyde was extremely conscientious and wanted to make his word good. I could not help but like him. He was eccentric, in the ways of the old, a staunch churchman. He would tell me how much his church meant to him. I respected him for that. Clyde was not a big man—was quite small, in fact. His wife Edna and son Harvey were always with him. Edna did all the writing for him. She had beautiful handwriting."[167]

When Rupert Fletcher came up to Minnesota from Independence to meet with his cousin Clyde Fletcher and attempt to resolve the problem,

relations between the two cousins grew more strained. Lykken remembers that Clyde Fletcher was upset with the church members in Independence for not recognizing his authority. "He said they had no authority to question him whatsoever. He was vehement about it and he got
emotional. When Rupert came up they got into it right away and I
thought they were going to come to blows. Clyde was almost insane.
Rupert was smart enough to back away and leave. He saw they were getting nowhere."

With both church presidents, Rupert Fletcher from Independence
and Clyde Fletcher in Clitherall, claiming to hold the authority to sell
the farm, the matter went to court on July 12, 1966, at Fergus Falls, Minnesota, where it was heard by Judge Norman H. Nelson. Rupert
Fletcher's son, Russell Fletcher, remembers the difficulty:

> "When the news reached Independence [about the sale of the
> farm] my father and other members decided that the sale
> would be contested because they felt that Clyde did not have
> the right to sell the property. An attorney was procured. Inter-
> estingly it was Carol Olson, who was then attorney for the Re-
> organized Latter Day Saint (Josephite) Church. Mr. Olson
> flew up, or perhaps took a train, and I drove my dad up to meet
> him. Olson stayed at the hotel in Fergus Falls right next to the
> Otter Tail River. I recall that we drove him to Clitherall to
> look at the disputed land. A trial date was set and Olson pre-
> pared the case for the Independence group. I attended the trial
> although I was not called upon to testify. My father testified as
> did Clyde and others."[168]

In his hearing of the case the judge established several findings of
fact. One was that the entire religious society known as the Cutlerite
church consisted, in 1966, of 23 members, seventeen in Independence,
Missouri and six in Clitherall; that the legislative body and supreme
authority of the Church was the "General Conference" composed of all
the members of the religious society; and that the administrative and judicial decisions of the Church were made by the "Church Council"
composed of all of the male elders of the church. Before a legitimate
meeting of either the General Conference or the Church Council could
be held, legal notice had to have been given to all of the members. The
requirement to give notice before holding a meeting is what had tripped
Clyde Fletcher up.

The judge noted that the October 7, 1952, meeting of the Church Council held in Clitherall was attended by Clyde Fletcher, Lee Fletcher, Emery Fletcher and Julian E. Whiting, Sr. (who died in 1956). No notice of the meeting had been given to Cutlerite elders Richard Whiting, who was living in Clitherall about a mile from where the meeting was held, or to Rupert Fletcher, Erle Whiting or Julian Whiting, Jr. This was the meeting where the Cutlerites excommunicated Richard Whiting, Rupert Fletcher, Erle Whiting and Julian Whiting, Jr.,—two of whom were sons of the men attending the meeting and doing the excommunicating.

As if holding one meeting without giving notice and excommunicating members were not enough, on April 6, 1959, Clyde Fletcher called another meeting at Clitherall attended only by himself, his brother Edmund Lee Fletcher, his wife Edna Fletcher, his son Harvey Ray Fletcher, and Amy Whiting. No notice was given to any other members of the meeting. At this session Clyde and his family members voted to excommunicate from the church *all* of the members living in Independence. None of the Independence members even knew Clyde had removed them from the church rolls in Minnesota until 1966 when the lawsuit began.

Besides holding meetings without notice for the purpose of casting people out of the church, Clyde Fletcher also called illegal meetings to elect trustees. On August 6, 1958, at a meeting attended by Clyde Fletcher, Edna Fletcher, Lee Fletcher, Harvey Ray Fletcher and Amy Whiting, Edna Fletcher and Amy Whiting were elected trustees of the church corporation. A similar meeting, called without notice and attended by the same family members, was held on April 6, 1962, to elect Clyde Fletcher a trustee of the church corporation.

Unknowingly Clyde had dug himself into a deep hole. The judge ruled all of his meetings, called without notice, to be illegal. Amy Whiting and Clyde Fletcher and Edna Fletcher were not trustees of the church corporation and therefore had no legal authority to engage in a sale of church-owned land to Sam Lykken. Furthermore, Clyde Fletcher and his friends had not given notice of the proposed sale to other church members as required by Minnesota Statutes, Section 315.12, nor had they received any authorization from the Church Council for the sale.

On October 24, 1964, the Independence Cutlerites called a Church Council meeting of the Cutlerite church to be held in Fergus Falls, Minnesota. Notices announcing this meeting were sent out fifteen days in advance, were posted in the church in Independence, sent to the church in Clitherall and, in Independence at least, read aloud to the congregation. When the meeting was held, the first legally selected trustees of the

Cutlerite church to be elected since the incorporation of the church in 1912, were chosen. Clyde Fletcher was not among them. Instead the trustees were Richard Whiting, Julian E. Whiting, Jr., and Rupert Fletcher—all individuals Clyde Fletcher had deemed unfit to be church members, let alone trustees of the church corporation. Following their election the three trustees adopted written by-laws of the corporation and elected officers.

Clyde Fletcher, testifying before the judge in his first-ever encounter with the legal system, struggled to make his case. He had never heard of such basic procedures as giving notice for meetings. A lifetime spent on his organic farm and his Cutlerite 19th century values left him utterly unprepared to cope with his more sophisticated city cousins or the American legal system. Russell Fletcher reported that, "There was no jury and after several days of testimony the decision by the judge was in favor of the Independence group. The terms of the sale were not changed and the buyer was allowed to keep the land but Clyde Fletcher and the Minnesota group were forced to recognize the Independence group as having the right to determine property matters."[169]

Clyde Fletcher, old and frail, was ordered by the court to deliver the three $1,500 certificates of deposit issued by the First National Bank of Battle Lake to the Plaintiff corporation (the Independence Cutlerites) as well as "all of the remaining assets and funds of said corporation, all documents and evidences of debt, insurance policies, abstracts of title and all other records and documents of whatsoever nature belonging to said corporation." Lykken was told to make his final principal payment of $8,000 plus interest to the Independence Cutlerites.[170]

The judge's order to turn over all of the church records to the Independence group was a sorrowful task for the Minnesota Cutlerites. Clyde Fletcher's wife Edna had been the devoted custodian of the church records—minute books going all the way back to their years in Manti—and though she dared not disobey the judge's order, she decided she would interpret it in her own fashion. In her beautiful handwriting, Edna, assisted by Amy Whiting, set about the task of copying all the Cutlerite church records, every letter, account of a blessing, ordination, baptism, sealing and special ordinance for the past 100 years. They decided they would be the ones to preserve the records. So far as is known, no one outside the fellowship of the Cutlerite church was ever allowed to examine the records they copied which stayed with Edna until her death. Edna complied with the judge's order and handed over the original records to the Independence Cutlerites but she kept the copies in her home. Both Danny Jorgensen and Ronald Stabnow saw the record books she filled out while the original records were still in her possession. With the judge's decision on March 17, 1967, the Minnesota Cutlerite Church of Christ ceased to exist. The Cutlerite church had indeed returned to Independence but not in the manner the church founders had envisioned.

The property dispute was not about church doctrine. As Russell Fletcher noted, "It was simply about who 'had the say' in running the church. It was an embarrassment to both sides that it had to be taken to court. If it had not been for the property it never would have turned into a legal case. The estrangement between the two groups went right back to the fact that they were physically separated when a sizeable part of the church came to Independence. Communications were poor. Phone calls were only for very occasional emergencies. Letters often conveyed little. The Minnesota church felt that the folks in Independence were out of their [Minnesota's] control, which was to a large extent true. I'm sure that the intent of the church in 1928 was that everyone would move to Independence for, after all, the Temple would be built on the appointed spot by 1930.[171] Certainly no one would want to stay in Minnesota when Zion was about to be redeemed."[172]

At the time of the land dispute, there were only five Cutlerites left in Minnesota: Clyde Fletcher, his wife Edna, their son Harvey Ray Fletcher, Edmund Lee Fletcher and the only one living in Old Clitherall itself, Amy Whiting. In reference to their small numbers, Amy Whiting professed not to be discouraged. Alpheus Cutler had told them long ago, she said, that "the work would go down to seven, maybe five and possibly as low as three, but that a stem would yet hold and it would rise again. We are indeed low in numbers," she conceded, "and we realize we are laughed at, to think we could do anything of value, but if we can truly learn just what the Celestial Law consists of and seek with all our hearts to build to that, perhaps we can gain the Lord's favor. That is what will really count."[173]

In 1961 the five remaining Minnesota Cutlerites journeyed together to Manti, Iowa. The town was gone but the old cemetery was still there. The stone from Cutler's grave had been moved and it grieved them to find the cemetery neglected, stones knocked over and a portion of the cemetery plowed under as part of a farmer's field. From Manti they went to Carthage, Illinois, where they viewed the jail in which Joseph Smith and his brother Hyrum Smith were killed. From there it was but a few miles to Nauvoo where they saw items that were owned by Alpheus

The last Cutlerites posed for a picture published in the *Battle Lake Review* on July 22, 1965. They are Edmund Lee Fletcher, Amy Whiting, Harvey Ray Fletcher, Edna and Clyde Fletcher.

Cutler. They saw the tools he had used as a stonemason on the Nauvoo temple, the weapon he carried in the War of 1812 and the sword he had flourished as a Colonel in the Nauvoo Legion and as Captain of Smith's bodyguard. Then they returned to Clitherall.

On November 15, 1969, Clyde Fletcher was the first to die. Edmund Lee Fletcher followed on August 18, 1970. Amy Whiting died January 22, 1977, and Edna Fletcher on June 5, 1994. All are buried in the Old Clitherall cemetery on the hill. After Edna's death, Ronald Stabnow suggested to Harvey Ray Fletcher that he give his mother's papers, including the copied Cutlerite records, to the Otter Tail County Historical Society. Influenced by his mother's penchant for secrecy, he declined. Instead the Independence Cutlerites came to Minnesota, collected the church documents, closed the house where Fletcher and his mother had lived together and moved him to Independence, Missouri. Harvey Ray Fletcher was the last Cutlerite in Minnesota. The organization that had once presented a serious challenge to Brigham Young was now merely a footnote to Mormon history.

CHAPTER 14

Ghosts of Nauvoo
Haunt Old Clitherall

The Cutlerite version of Mormonism, with the exception of the practice of polygamy, was to a great extent a continuation of what had developed at Nauvoo and was the only schism of the Latter Day Saint Church that continued to perform temple work and work for the dead.[174] Cutler was one of only 24 men to whom Joseph Smith had secretly given the priesthood power to perform Mormon temple rites.[175] These included baptism (by proxy) for the dead, washings, anointings and related ceremonies, celestial marriage, the sealing of people to each other for eternity, the wearing of sacred garments, and the giving of the "fullness of the priesthood," also known as the "second anointing." Of all the religious organizations growing out of Joseph Smith's teachings at Nauvoo, with the exception of the Latter Day Saint Church in Utah, only the Cutlerites retained the panoply of temple practices. It was the practice of polygamy, which they rejected, that nevertheless continued to haunt them.

In her book *Alpheus Cutler and the Church of Jesus Christ,* Daisy Fletcher wrote that the first task of the founding Cutlerites was to "eradicate any taint of plural marriage." Chauncey Whiting and Sylvester J. Whiting undertook that task by creating a new myth and a new origin story for the Cutlerites. In an undated statement Sylvester Whiting wrote, "After Father Cutler reorganized the church in 1853 he, by the authority of the holy priesthood, vetoed polygamy till the coming of Christ. Anyone who says Father Cutler ever sanctioned, upheld, or practiced polygamy are [*sic*] ignorant, unlearned, dishonest, or deceived, for they took false reports for facts, not knowing the truth."[176]

Chauncey Whiting insisted that the early Cutlerites did not know that polygamy had become a part of Mormon doctrine. According to his new story, when the Cutlerites in Iowa heard rumors in 1849 about the

practice of plural marriage they sent emissaries to Winter Quarters to investigate. Upon learning that the rumors were indeed true, Chauncey
Whiting said that the Cutlerites, in shock, rejected Brigham Young's leadership and accepted Alpheus Cutler's. In Whiting's version, repugnance
over the practice of polygamy was the principal reason for the break with
BrighamYoung, the founding of the Cutlerite Church of Jesus Christ and
a contributing factor in the group's decision to move to Minnesota.

While it was true that polygamy was a secretive practice and may
not have been known to many Gentiles, among Mormons who lived at
Nauvoo plural marriage was not a secret. Cutler maintained his six plural wives (one had died in Kansas) until 1851 when F. Walter Cox was
arrested (and Cutler threatened with arrest) by Iowa authorities for
practicing plural marriage. Cox solved the problem by moving two of
his three wives to other jurisdictions until he could take them all to Utah
in 1852. Cutler "put aside" his remaining plural wives though what "putting aside" consisted of is unclear. One of his plural wives, Luana Hart
Beebe Rockwell Cutler, continued to live among the Cutlerites—even
moving to Battle Lake where she lived for a time under the name "Mrs.
Boyd" to be near her son Jacob.

In the creation of his new story, Chauncey Whiting ignored the fact
that two of Alpheus Cutler's daughters had become plural wives of Heber
C. Kimball in Nauvoo and that their sons Isaac and Abraham had lived
with Cutler and his son Thaddeus in Manti. Chauncey Whiting somehow
put out of his mind the fact that his sister Emeline was a plural wife of F.
Walter Cox as was the sister of his wife, Editha; that his sister Jane and
his widowed sister-in-law Martha were both plural wives of the Mormon scout Return Jackson Redding; that his father-in-law, Isaac Morley,
had multiple wives as did Chauncey's own brother Edwin Whiting.
Other leading Cutlerites had also participated in plural marriages, either
as principals or as the officials performing the ordinances. Calvin Beebe,
a brother of Cutler's plural wife Luana, had performed plural marriages
in the Nauvoo Temple. Cutlerite Silas Richards and one of Calvin's
brothers also took plural wives before leaving Nauvoo. Since Chauncey
Whiting himself had participated in the ceremony of sealing of himself
to Isaac Morley in the Nauvoo Temple he had undoubtedly taken part in
and personally witnessed many of the plural marriages.[177]

Chauncey Whiting was aided in promulgating his new origin story
by the fact that the Cutlerites wanted to believe it. They were a deeply
monogamous people. Polygamy was as naturally abhorrent to the Cut-

lerites as was incest. Rejection of plural marriage became a way to justify their breaking away from the leadership of Brigham Young. Like the
Josephites, who desperately wanted to believe Young Joseph's denials
that his father had ever been involved in plural marriage, the Cutlerites
readily joined in the conspiracy. Both the Cutlerite and the Josephite
survival as religious institutions depended on this revision of history.
The removal to Minnesota took the Cutlerites safely away from any reminders of their past, from any individual who would question or let
drop an indiscreet comment to challenge Chauncey Whiting's recon-
struction of their past.

Very few of the founding generation of Cutlerites who went to
Minnesota ever became members of the Josephite Church. The converts
came from the second and third generations who, believing that plural
marriage began with Brigham Young in the West, were not concerned
over the issue. For these later generations it was an easy matter for them
to accept the Josephite and Cutlerite positions as the truth.

While there was nothing in Cutlerite literature to question Chauncey Whiting's version of events, doubts remained. In an undated letter
in the RLDS Church archives Iva Gould, granddaughter of Francis
Lewis Whiting, wrote:

"I asked my folks some of the questions about the Cutlerites
that you asked yesterday. They said it was common belief in the
early days that Alpheus Cutler had been a polygamist, though
the present generation of Cutlerites deny it. My father [Win-
field Gould] said that at one time on a short journey he stopped
at the home of a Mrs. Boyd who told him she was one of the
wives of Alpheus Cutler, that she had been a poor girl without
relatives to care for her and Cutler told her if she would be
sealed to him he would support her.

"On reaching home my father asked my grandfather, Francis Lewis Whiting, a brother of Chauncey Whiting, if it was
true that Father Cutler had more that one wife. He answered re-
luctantly, 'I suppose it is true that he had three wives.' And
when I asked if Mrs. Boyd was one of them, he said, 'Yes, I suppose she was.' He was a staunch Cutlerite and did not like to
admit it but was too honest to deny it. My grandmother [Ann
Jeanette Whiting] then said that Father Cutler got rid of his
wives before he started the church, that he took one of them on

a mission to the Indians and she died there. Another he gave
away to a man who wanted to marry her."

Despite these statements, the official position of the Cutlerite
church remains that there is no "taint of polygamy" in the background
of its founders.[178] This kind of falseness in what are otherwise truthful
people has been described by psychologists as a kind of psychological
blindness in which subscribers to a belief system accept as true the magic
beliefs of their own charmed inner circle.

There was no place in the Cutlerite philosophy for religious innovation or differing interpretations of their philosophy. Hypotheses that
appeared to contradict the story that had been "passed down" were rejected. The Cutlerites had convinced themselves that American society
was secular and profane and, like Sodom and Gomorrah, would be destroyed by God for its wickedness. Their explanation for the trek to
Minnesota was that they went to escape the coming turmoil in the world,
convert the Indians, preserve their understanding of Nauvoo Mormonism and keep themselves faithful and apart until God called them back to
build the holy city of Zion, God's Kingdom in Independence, and there
witness the glory of His second coming.

In many ways the first generation Cutlerites were indistinguishable
from other Americans on the frontier. They believed in the sanctity of
faith and family, in honesty, loyalty, cooperation, agriculture and industry—the accepted values of nineteenth century society. Other than
their Mormon peculiarities such as sectarian exclusivity (not unknown
to other religious organizations), the Cutlerites were remarkably similar to other mainstream Americans. Yet, instead of living contentedly in
their Iowa communities, the Cutlerites departed for the wilds of Minnesota, insisting that they were in flight from persecution and from the
evils of the world.

Some of the reasons for their actions may lie in Mormon beliefs
and history. Early Mormons believed that their church burst upon the
religious scene perfectly conceived. Through the true prophet Joseph
Smith, God had given Mormons (and the world) the divine plan of salvation. The plan encompassed not only a life after death, but a precise
method for organizing society on earth. Every time the Mormons had
attempted to put that plan into operation—in Independence, Far West
and at Nauvoo—they had been driven off their land and their communities had been destroyed by hostile neighbors. Even the Cutlerites' di-

vinely sanctioned mission to the Indians of Kansas had ended in a debacle. The Cutlerites, who believed themselves to be God's chosen people, ran headlong into the forces of history and were turned aside. In their minds, it was not the unfolding saga of America that had prevented their success, but "the evil of the world." While the mob violence directed against the Mormons in Missouri and Illinois certainly had been "evil," their lives in Iowa had been comparatively tranquil. If they earnestly imagined the "evil of the world" hard enough, it was not difficult to believe it was true.

Historian Robert Flanders has observed that flight is a common response to troubles that groups or individuals can not ultimately overcome or face. The Cutlerites had to have been haunted by the disasters of Far West, Nauvoo and Kansas and may even have been wracked with uncertainties about the whole Restoration experience.[179] Flanders notes that on the Missouri and Arkansas frontiers there was a saying to describe either physical or psychological flight. It was called "going to Texas" which desperadoes did for generations to evade the law. He suggests that the Cutlerites "went to Texas," except that in their case the destination was Minnesota. For the Mormons of that generation, most of whom had been forced out of their homes on at least three occasions, taking flight yet again was the repetition of a pattern that had become habitual.

The Cutlerites attempted to do what the eleven-million-member Utah Mormon Church accomplished with much more success—which was to isolate themselves from the modern world until they could institutionalize their mode of living. The Rocky Mountains proved to be a far more effective barrier in protecting the Mormons of Utah from modernity than did the lakes of Minnesota for the Cutlerites.

As Daisy Whiting Fletcher observed about the Cutlerites, "From the days of Alpheus Cutler, the Church of Jesus Christ has been plagued by apostasy, inability to retain the natural increase, failure to achieve unity and a variety of other mistakes. . . ."[180] The Josephites confronted the modern world by attempting to adapt to it. By rejecting Nauvoo Mormonism with its esoteric practices and reinterpreting Joseph Smith's religious visions in a modern context, the Josephites tried to adapt their organization to contemporary society.

The founding of Clitherall by a group of pioneers with modest resources was an extraordinary achievement. They moved a utopian community more than seven hundred miles by covered wagon, traveling in winter with infants and the elderly without the loss of a single life. They gained the friendship and cooperation of Indians some of whom, only three years before, had been at war with white settlers. They developed a unique religious identity, a story of a divinely sanctioned journey, and a sacred mythology that ennobled their efforts and captured the imagination of their descendants.

The Cutlerites were pioneers who suffered all things, risked all things for an improbable vision. Their descendants (many of them) wince at their ancestors' naïveté, their innocence, their dogmatism, their rejection of the modern world, knowing in their hearts they could not have gotten along with a single one of them. Yet there remains a grudging admiration and an emotional connection. They admire the doggedness and mutual concern that helped the Cutlerites survive the trek to Minnesota without a serious injury, the boldness of their conviction that, weak and poor as they were, they were vessels of God—directed by the divine will to create a better world in this place. In their imaginations they can still see these builders of a new society striding in homemade boots over the peaceful ground of Otter Tail County, sunbonnets firmly in place, sharing their gardens with the Indians, singing the Lord's song in a strange land, holding fast to a belief as old as the Pilgrims, as Moses, as Abraham himself, that the Lord will lead His people through the wilderness to a new land.

Old Clitherall does not exist on any map of the United States or of Minnesota. It is known only to those descendants of the Cutlerites who grew up enthralled by their stories and to the fishermen who come every year to the fishing camp that stands on the site of the original village. The brick store, built during Isaac Whiting's brief revival of the Church in 1912, is still there, but the rear of the building has collapsed, and trees grow out of the foundation. Next door stands the two story white frame church, the doors locked, the windows of the upper story still covered as if to keep modern-day visitors from learning the Cutlerites' ritual secrets. Visitors who peer in the downstairs windows see the chairs lined up as if in readiness for a service, the pulpit is in place on a low platform at one end, and in a corner on a stand by the steps to the second story sits a pewter water pitcher. A photograph of the interior of the old log church, taken more than a century ago by Warren Whiting, contains this same pitcher.

Isaac Whiting's home stands empty, the only Cutlerite residence in Old Town still owned by the church. Like the church, it is padlocked and the building is slowly collapsing. Asbestos siding covers the original wood, the porch roof sags, and sills are honeycombed with rot. Except for Amy Whiting's house and one other, the homes that lined the road are gone and cattle graze where the buildings once stood. The schoolhouse, built in 1867, was sold to the camp, moved to the lake shore and converted into cottage number seven where it is occupied during the summer by fishermen. A careful observer, looking closely at exposed rafters, can still see portions of the original building under the modern paneling.

The owner of the Old Town Camp understands that for descendants of the Cutlerites the area is full of ghosts. While it is the Independence Cutlerites who contract to keep the grass around the aging buildings mowed, the owner of the camp keeps an eye on the properties and welcomes the strangers who drive onto the site, walk around the church and Isaac's home, peer in the windows, test the locks on the doors, and trespass among the camp cottages in an attempt to trace the original route of the road and locate the sites of their ancestors' log houses.

Each summer descendants of the Cutlerites find their way to Old Clitherall to look for signs of that peculiar community their progenitors founded. They stand on the shore of the lake to gaze into the clear water sparkling in the sun, the benign landscape of distant hills. They take pictures of their children standing before the monument, now restored and moved from its 1928 location to a spot near the shuttered Cutlerite church. If they think of it, they visit the logs of the first church, now reassembled on the Stabnows' property that was once the home of Joseph and Sarah Fletcher and later Nina and Orison Tucker. They trespass on Hirum and Rachel Murdock's homestead to visit the site of the Indian village on the point. Before leaving, they drive up the rutted road to the Mt. Pleasant cemetery on the hill to place flowers before weathered markers bearing ancestral names. From the top of the hill they can look down on Clitherall and Battle Lakes and the narrow strip of land between them that so fired the religious imaginations of their ancestors. The excitement and promise of those days has long since drained away and birds nest in the grass where homes once stood. Like the Indians they came to convert, the Cutlerites have departed, leaving only the faintest trace on the land of their passing.

EPILOGUE

On a now forgotten date in a summer near the end of the 1950s or early 1960s I chanced to be in Clitherall at the same time that Nina Gould Tucker also came to visit. Nina was then an elderly widow, living with her sisters in Independence. I had spent the previous afternoon in Clitherall wandering about the Mt. Pleasant cemetery trying to recognize names and create some order out of the ragged lines of tombstones. I could identify only a handful of the names, yet I knew that the family interrelationships were as tangled as the roots of the oak trees growing amid the graves.

When I heard that Nina was in town it occurred to me that hers was one of the last living memories of the first generation of Cutlerites. Nina was a daughter of Winfield and Ella Whiting Gould. She had known her grandparents Francis Lewis and Ann Jeanette Whiting, could remember Hirum and Rachel Murdock and was the sister of the wife who had prayed for a train to be late so her husband would not sign over their property to the Cutlerite church. Suddenly it became very important that, before she returned to Independence, Nina be asked to recall what memories she could of the people lying in the Old Clitherall Cemetery.

The problem was how to record them. This was before the days of electronic recording. I did not know shorthand. When I discussed the problem with Nina's family a young relative, who was also visiting, offered to follow her aunt about the cemetery and take down her remarks in shorthand. She promised to write a transcription and mail it to me. I agreed to type the result and distribute it to anyone who was interested.

A few weeks after I returned home, a shorthand notebook arrived in the mail. It contained both the shorthand notes and the transcription. I immediately sat down at my Smith-Corona portable to record Nina's recollections of people who, though long gone, seemed to come to life through her words. Her remarks unraveled some of the complicated family relationships and laid bare the day-to-day sorrows of the Cutlerites and their neighbors in Otter Tail County. They died from accidents,

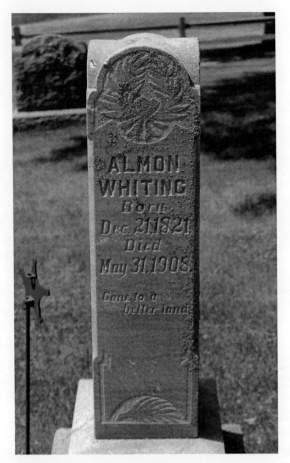

Gravemarker for Almon Whiting, the chairmaker, in
Mt. Pleasant cemetery. Photographed 2001.

exhaustion, exposure to the brutal Minnesota winters and from a tragic
ignorance of the causes of disease. Many died of typhoid and tuberculosis. Nina said:

Winfield Gould, Jr.
My second brother, died of typhoid fever, age 24. I helped him
fan out his seed wheat the day before he got sick. He loved to
hunt and fish and trap, used to sell lots of muskrat skins and
ship boxes of frozen ducks to Minneapolis. He took a claim in
Bemidji and was to marry Bertha Hunter at Christmas, but he
died in October. I was 13.

Lovell Kidder

Lovell was a tall old man with snow-white hair and beard. He was a Strangite [another splinter group of Mormons] but always came to our meetings to argue with our preachers. Aunt Eleanor came for my wedding decorations to use for his funeral and the first day in my new home his procession passed by.

Birdie Murdock

Birdie was a little baby that Ollie and her husband, Albert Edingfield, found in their barn manger one morning out near Henning. Lucy helped care for it. Its eyes were sore and one night Lucy got up to doctor it. She got the wrong bottle and put carbolic acid in its eyes and made it blind. The baby died soon after.

Hulda Fletcher

Hulda was the wife of Albert Fletcher and mother to Inez and Enez and seven others. Inez Emogene was a twin of Enez Imogene. I heard that Edna Whiting kicked Inez on the knee when playing in a swing which caused her death. Enez went to school to me. One day she brought the baby Charles to school with a bag of diapers. Charles died when just a baby. Hulda was a very frail, kind, overburdened woman. Enez and Inez were pretty little things, big blue eyes, yellow curls.

Winfield Falkman

Winfield was a farmer who lived in the grove straight across the lake. His home was named Shady Nook. I boarded with them three terms. He was very deaf but seemed to be a nice husband and father to his children June and David. Later June died when her baby was born. David and his mother went to Texas. Winfield stayed on the farm alone until John Anderson cheated him out of it. Then he lost his mind. He said a big dog kept following him. Finally he shot himself down by his mailbox.

Eva Whiting

Daughter of Dean and Jennie. Their third child. Very pretty with black eyes and black hair. She married and went to St. Paul. She was found one morning in a hotel room sitting at a desk shot to death. Her head was resting on a religious book and she had a revolver in her hand.

Al Whiting

Orison's uncle, Uncle Vet's son. He lived and died in Minneapolis with some strange disease of the hip and leg. They brought him to Clitherall for the funeral. When the family went up to see him in his coffin the brothers all declared it wasn't him. They got quite loud about it right in the church. Orison helped move him some years later and the coffin fell all to pieces.

Joseph Fletcher, Sr.

He was called Father Fletcher and was the father of Ed [Joseph Edmund], Calvin, Seth and John. The Murdocks thought he had the power to curse people. There were some queer things happened to Hirum, Emily and Lois's baby. His house was where Orison and my home was.

Seth Fletcher

A son of Father Fletcher. He was in the Civil War and was called a deserter but he really wasn't. The war was over and he waited for his discharge papers. They didn't come. He grew tired of waiting. Then a dead man's name was called and Seth answered, got the discharge and went home. Later his papers came. He wasn't there and was put down as a deserter.

Joseph Edmund Fletcher

Father of Jim and Emery. [He was] a little man with black, beady eyes. Some thought he had an evil power. Aunt Lou thought he put a curse on her little baby Della Mae who died.

Joseph McIntyre

He came to Clitherall from Manti and died of TB.

Child of Joseph McIntyre

This was Joe's baby who lay beside his sick bed in a trundle bed. They kept a catalog lying on her little bed for him to spit in and kept turning the leaves over. The baby died of TB.

Lionel Kelly

He is buried here somewhere but his marker is gone. He was the baby of Mable Whiting Kelly. She married a good-for-nothing man, Charles Kelly, brought her baby back home to Lon Whiting's to die of the whooping cough.

Laura Lang

She came from Manti with the church. She was all alone except for a little herd of sheep. She walked all the way and drove her sheep. The church men built her a little house. She lived there lonely and alone. She was tall and gaunt and gray. There was a rumor that she was a witch.

William Oakes

Nicest looking one of the Oakes boys. Dark hair and eyes. Married a pretty little fat girl from Leaf Mountains. Her father tried to shoot him so they ran away and hid at Jim Anderson's south of Battle Lake. He was sick there about two weeks and died later from TB.

Francis Lewis Whiting

My grandpa, Ma's father. A good, kind, gruff old man with a white beard from ear to ear. He was tall, stooped a little at the last. He came with the first colony and helped decide on Old Clitherall as a home. He made the prayer of thanksgiving and dedication at the place of the monument in Old Town. We always used to love to have them visit us. They always brought candy and peanuts. When I grew up I taught their school and boarded four terms with them. He kept the first Old Town store and died two weeks before I was married.

Ann Jeanette Whiting

My mother's mother, Grandma Whiting. She was a trim, quiet little woman with a black silk hairnet over her white hair. She wore a black straw sunbonnet to church in Old Town on Sundays. Everyone loved her and called her Aunt Net. After Grandpa died she lived with Aunt Lee in Clitherall. Till she died of old age she wasn't even sick. She saw all of her children join the Reorganization [Josephites] but she remained a Cutlerite. She said even if her children were right she wanted to go where Lewis was and she was sure he would come for her when she died. She was good and gentle and sweet.

Mary Denna

Lewis Denna's wife. After his death she made her home with
Grandpa and Grandma Whiting. I remember her as a little old
lady with straight white bobbed hair. She always sat knitting by
the window and died there of pneumonia.

Alfred Erwin

He was the husband of Uncle Chauncey's youngest daughter
Lucy. He was a witty red-faced Irishman. He was quite a drinker
but when he was sober he was a good friend and worker. He had
a stroke on the way home from Battle Lake one day, fell over
against Lucy and she had to drive home. He lived for a day or
two and died in Old Clitherall.

Effie Sherman

Effie was Plinne's oldest sister. She used to work for Ma when
her babies were born and was in our house quite a lot. She died
when a young woman of typhoid fever. Her funeral was in our
Silver Lake schoolhouse—the first funeral I ever attended. Her
dead face haunted me for years. They sang "Hail to the Bright-
ness of Zion's Glad Morning." To this day that song brings
back her face and funeral.

Charlie Sherman

Pa's cousin. He was the youngest son of widowed Aunt Sarah
Sherman. He was her favorite and the only one who was good
to her. He was odd—talked so loud, always wore a stocking
cap. He never married but lived in Battle Lake with his mother.
He thought a lot of his team of horses. One day a bonfire built
by Calhouns in Battle Lake set his barn on fire. He tried to save
his horses but failed. He was burned so badly he died in a day
or two. I was about ten years old. I climbed on top of Uncle
Will's house at Silver Lake and watched the fire and smoke.
Aunt Sarah never got over it.

Tillie Sherman

She was Cash Sherman's wife, a Norwegian girl but a lovely
woman. Everyone liked her. Cash's folks loved her and were
good to her but Cash wasn't. Their first son was such a sweet

little boy. Aunt Sarah loved him and named him Charlie but when he grew up he went to the state prison for murder.

Almon Sherman
He was loading a boxcar with wood in New Clitherall when the west-bound freight train came in, scared his team which jumped, catching Sherman between his load of wood and the boxcar. He survived about five minutes

Frederick Sherman
Sherman, a trapper, was found frozen to death in his shanty with a match in his hand. He had been attempting to light a fire. It appeared that, while visiting his traps, he broke into a slough. His clothes immediately froze to his body and he died before he could light a fire.

Cassius Sherman
He was Pa's uncle who froze to death on the Everts' prairie in a big three-day blizzard. He wasn't found until spring by Alex and Andrew Tweeten.

Mary Burdick
She was my great-grandmother. She came from Manti to live with Francis Lewis and Ann Jeanette, my grandparents. She is the one the old Indian raised his tomahawk over and Aunt Lou drove him away. Mrs. P.A. Sherman said she broke a chair over his head. I was born on her birthday.

Cora Belle Whiting
Baby of Uncle Ret and Aunt Eleanor. They had had three babies born dead. This one lived two years, then died of pneumonia one night in Old Town during a dreadful electric storm.

Warren Whiting
The first photographer in Otter Tail County. He made all the old tintypes. Married Zeruah, granddaughter of Father Cutler. Warren died quite young of pneumonia and Zeruah years later of cancer.

Euphremia Chapman
Grandpa Tucker's sister. She made me a coat I never liked. She had a big family and her husband was untrue. We took Grandpa over [to her house] when we heard she was very sick and she died just as he went in.

Arlo Clayton Gould
He was the son of Uncle Clayton and Aunt Dea. He ran out to meet Uncle Clayton as he came home from Battle Lake. Uncle Clayton didn't see him. The wagon wheel ran over his head and killed him. They were about all packed to go to Independence.

George Gould
Pa's father. He was an elder and many blessings came to us under his hands. He taught Maud, Hallie, Leon and Winnie to sing. He was the president of the Union Branch [the Josephite Church] for years.

Eleanor Gould
Pa's mother. She lived about five years after Grandpa died. Her heart got bad and Pa and Ma left us to care for ourselves and went and lived with her. She lay down for a nap with her palm leaf fan over her face. When Ma lifted it she was dead.

William Mason
His was the first grave. He was a shoemaker who lived in Old Town. He left his family to do shoe making in Alexandria one winter. He was caught in a big blizzard and froze to death. He was not found until spring when a company of men set out to Alexandria after flour. Down in the Leaf Mountains they saw his boot sticking out of the snow.

Clark Stillman
Stillman was the second burial. While living at Clitherall he made a fateful trip to Sauk Center, late in the fall of 1867. He had taken some sheep along and, after disposing of the sheep and some produce, he bought a load of supplies, including a heating stove and clothes for his family. The weather turned cold, Stillman was unable to find a place to stay in Sauk Center

so started back to Clitherall. Being a humane man, he put all his extra covers on his horses. Stillman suffered so intensely from exposure that he got pneumonia and died a week after reaching his home, leaving a wife and eight children.

Leland Whiting
Leland was the little son of Charles and Clara Whiting. Charles and Clara were both grandchildren of Uncle Chauncey Whiting. When Leland was twelve he lived in Old Town where he was going to school. A few weeks after I was married he was skating home from school with his cousins and skated into an ice hole out from John Murdock's and was drowned. John received a Carnegie medal[181] for swimming down under the ice and finding the body.

Herbert Whiting
Herbert was Charles and Clara Whiting's only child after Leland drowned. When he was about eighteen he dropped dead in the barn where he was pitching hay with his father.

Rebecca Murdock
Lyman's wife, John's mother. A little short woman with one stiff knee. Raised her family alone in poverty. They all finally left her but John. They lived together for years. He brought her to church every Sunday. She never was a Cutlerite. She died on her old homestead after John married Bertha Hunter.

Cora Murdock
John's youngest sister. She was a hunchback. Something broke in her throat one day and she choked to death on John's lap when she was about fifteen.

Charles Taylor
An old bachelor brother of Rebecca Murdock, uncle of John. He lived alone over by Charlie Taylor's hill so long his mind became affected. He buried some money once for safety and hunted for it the rest of his life. He had had a bad canker sore that ate out part of his lip so his teeth showed through. He was harmless but as children we were afraid of him.

Rachel Murdock

She was Hirum's wife and the mother of twelve children. She spun, wove and made clothes for them all and kept a hotel for travelers. She sat down in her rocker one afternoon to rest and died at age sixty-four.

Lyman Murdock

Lyman was the fourteen-year-old son of Hirum and Rachel Murdock. He tried to climb on a load of hay and accidentally shot himself.

Della Mae Whiting

Baby of Uncle Art and Aunt Lois. We stayed there all night the day she died. Pa and Ma sat up with her. Della Mae is the baby Aunt Lois thought Ed Fletcher cursed.

Hugh Hunter

He was Bertha Murdock's father. He came here from Wisconsin and married Rhoda Sherman. Shortly after he was married he lost his eyesight when a piece of nail flew into his eye. She had seven children whom he never saw. He worked hard on his farm with the help of his boys; hoed, built fence, built a barn and many other things. He died one evening while Bertha was reading to him.

Charles Whiting

Charles was Isaac's oldest son, grandson of Chauncey, who lived in Old Clitherall most of his life. He went to Independence for a year or two. Disagreed with the Fletchers and was 'cut off and cast out' homeless and penniless.

Ethel Cook

She was young and very pretty, about eighteen, frail and fair with red spots in her cheeks. We girls thought she was wonderful and that it was terrible when she died so young of TB.

Orison Murdock

My favorite uncle, Cordelia's husband, father of Ellis and Jeanette and brother of Grandpa Tucker. Orison [Tucker] and

I used to like to go there to spend the evening before we were married. That is where we went on our first date. Orison died unexpectedly in the night. Ellis came to tell us; he threw pebbles against our upstairs window to wake us. It was terrible news.

Matie Murdock
Baby of Uncle Orison and Aunt Cordelia Murdock. She was a sweet little thing. She and Ellis had the whooping cough. They brought her to church in the winter and she caught cold, got lung fever and was very sick for quite awhile. I used to work there and hold her, she would cough and choke so I was scared to death.

ENDNOTES

1. Robert Flanders, E-mail dated September 1, 2001, to the author.
2. Lori Taylor, "Telling Stories About Mormons and Indians," (Ph.D. diss., State University of New York, Buffalo, 1999), 73.
3. Frank and Norma Tucker, eds., "Gladys Gould Papers," 1975, 18.
4. Hallie Gould, ed. *Old Clitherall's Story Book, A History of the First Settlement in Otter Tail County, Minnesota, 1865–1919.* Reprinted by the Otter Tail County Historical Society, Fergus Falls, Minnesota, 1975. (Hallie Gould published her collection of articles in the *Battle Lake Review* where they appeared weekly on the front page. The last installment of "First Settlement of Otter Tail County" was published on June 12, 1919. It was followed by a booklet which was then reprinted in 1975.)
5. Alpheus Cutler was a member of the first generation following the Revolutionary War. Revolutionary War veterans were greatly revered and by the 1830s those few survivors were given the honorific titles of "Father" or "Uncle." The term "Founding Fathers" was coined during this period. When no more Revolutionary War veterans remained, the titles were passed on to the next generation of veterans—those of the War of 1812, in which Cutler had participated.
6. Sara Jane Talcott Whiting, Booklet written for her granddaughter Daisy Evangeline Whiting, 1919.
7. Karen Armstrong, *The Battle for God*, (New York: Alfred Knopf, 2000) 83.
8. Taylor, "Telling Stories About Mormons and Indians," 73.
9. Frank and Norma Tucker, eds., "Family Supplement 1," December, 1975.
10. *Doctrine and Covenants*, (Herald Publishing House, Independence, Missouri, 1970 ed.) Section 57. 141–142.
11. Gladys Gould, "Aunt Lu."
12. Frank and Norma Tucker, *op. cit.*
13. *Ibid.*
14. It is hard to know what area Lester Whiting meant by his reference to "Far West." The town of Far West, itself, was never attacked, though it was surrounded on October 30 by about two thousand men, led by General Samuel D. Lucas. It is likely the term "Far West," as used by later generations, referred to the town of that name as well as the surrounding region.
15. Emma Lucine Anderson, "Autobiography of Emma Lucine Anderson," February 24, 1915. (Reorganized Latter Day Saint Church Archives, Independence, Missouri.)

16. Roger D. Launius and John E. Hallwas, eds. *Kingdom on The Mississippi Revisited, Nauvoo In Mormon History*, (University of Illinois Press, Urbana and Chicago, 1996) 57.

17. *Ibid.*

18. "Cordelia Morley Cox, Woman of Wilderness."

19. Not everyone in the United States at that time was a Jacksonian. The period also saw the establishment of numerous Utopian societies such as the Amana Society (1842 to the present), Bronson Alcott's Fruitlands (1843–1844), the Oneida colony of John Humphrey Noyes, (1848–1881) and Adin Ballou's Hopedale, (1841–1856).

20. John D. Lee, *A Mormon Chronicle: The Diaries of John D. Lee, 1848–1876*, 2 vols. Edited by Robert Glass Cleland and Juanita Brooks (Arthur H. Clark, San Marino, CA., 1955) Vol.1, 80.

21. Gustavus Hills, "Map of the City of Nauvoo," Nauvoo Restoration, Inc., 1971.

22. Lawrence Foster, *Religion and Sexuality, Three American Communal Experiments of the Nineteenth Century*, (Oxford University Press, New York/Oxford, 1981) 135.

23. Launius and Hallwas, *op. cit.* 135.

24. *Ibid.* 139.

25. Foster, *op. cit.* 131.

26. Todd Compton, *In Sacred Loneliness—The Plural Wives of Joseph Smith*, (Signature Books, Salt Lake City, UT., 1997). Compton has identified thirty-five women, aged 14–54, who may have been married to Joseph Smith, Jr.

27. "Cordelia Morley Cox," *op. cit.* 22

28. *Ibid.*

29. Danny Jorgensen, Letter to the author, dated April 27, 1988.

30. *Ibid.*

31. Launius and Hallwas, *op. cit.* 2.

32. George D. Smith, "A Preliminary Study of the Incidence of Plural Marriage in Nauvoo, Illinois, from 1841 to 1846," (Mormon History Association Conference, Lamoni, IA., 1993).

33. Taylor, *op. cit.* 188.

34. *Ibid*, 191–192.

35. *Ibid*, 188.

36. Alta Kimber, in "The Coming of Latter Day Saints to Otter Tail County," *Minnesota History* 13 (1932) gives the name of Denna's wife as Pearl Dowd.

37. Alta Kimber and Hallie M. Gould, "Reminiscences for the Scrap Book," *Battle Lake Review* (July 24, 1919).

38. Taylor, *op. cit.* 287.

39. *Ibid*, 289.

40. Sworn statement of William P. McIntire, (Salt Lake City, Latter Day Saint archives, March 21, 1849).

41. It was widely rumored at the time that Cutler had returned to Independence to lay the cornerstone of the temple. Cutlerite tradition is silent on this.

42. Danny L. Jorgensen, "The Second Mormon Mission to the Indians: The Cutlerites' Lamanite Ministries, 1847–1853" (Mormon History Association Con-

ference, San Bernadino, CA., May 1991) 24.

43. Taylor, *op. cit.* 294.

44. *Ibid*, 290.

45. Danny Jorgensen, Letter to the author, March 7, 1995.

46. Cox, *op. cit.* 18.

47. Danny L.Jorgensen, "The Old Fox: Alpheus Cutler, Priestly Keys to the Kingdom and the Early Church of Jesus Christ," in Roger D. Launius and Linda Thatcher, eds. *Differing Visions: Dissenters in Mormon History* (University of Illinois Press, Champaign, IL., 1991). Cutler was the seventh man of the quorum. Joseph Smith was the first. The sixth was John Smith, Joseph's uncle, who Cutler considered to have gone into apostasy since he went to Utah with Brigham Young. The remaining four are not known.

48. Amy Whiting, undated letter to the author.

49. Rupert J. Fletcher, and Daisy Whiting Fletcher, *Alpheus Cutler and The Church of Jesus Christ*, (Church of Jesus Christ, Independence, MO., 1974), 273.

50. The church name was changed in 2001 to "Community of Christ."

51. Mary Audentia Smith Anderson and Bertha Audentia Anderson Hulmes, *Joseph Smith III and the Restoration*, (Herald Publishing House, Independence, MO., 1952), 207.

52. Frank and Norma Tucker, Letter to the author, February 2, 1999.

53. Barbara Bernauer, Letter to the author, January 25, 2001.

54. The picture purported to be of Alpheus Cutler has been handed down in his family through five generations. At Lois Cutler's death the picture went to her daughter, Lois Huntington Cutler Sherman. Lois Sherman gave the picture to her son Cutler Alma Sherman, who, in turn, passed it on to his son Plinne Alfred Sherman. Plinne's daughter Joy Sherman Harris next acquired the picture and left it to her son and daughter-in-law, David Sherman Harris and Iris Harris. The photo is a silvery Daguerreotype picture mounted in a small case that opens like a book, measuring about three by four inches.

55. Russell Rogers Rich, "Those Who Would Be Leaders," (Brigham Young University Extension Publications, Provo, UT., 1958), 50.

56. Michael S. Riggs, "Thou Shalt become a Terror to False Spirits: from New Englander Mormons to Esoteric Cutlerite/RLDS, a Case Study in Early Mormon Folk Magic Beliefs," Master's thesis, Park College, 1999.

57. *Ibid*. It is likely that many of the taunts about Mormons came from non-Mormon settlers in Manti and the surrounding area.

58. Emma Lucine Anderson, *op. cit.* 10.

59. Danny Jorgensen, Letter to the author, March 7, 1995. Jorgensen believes the June date may be in error and that Cutler may have died August 10, 1864.

60. S.J.Whiting, undated memoir in the author's collection.

61. Fletcher and Fletcher, *op. cit.* 69.

62. S.J. Whiting, "Some proofs and testimonies in regard to our move to this country being directed by the Lord," (Otter Tail County Historical Society, Fergus Falls, MN., undated), 1.

63. Anderson and Hulmes, *op. cit.* 208.

64. Emma Anderson, *op. cit.* 6.

65. Hallie Gould, "Like Sheep Who Have Gone Astray," *Autumn Leaves*,

(February, 1921), 3.

66. Chauncey Whiting, undated letter in author's collection.

67. Fletcher and Fletcher, *op. cit.* 64.

68. Danny L. Jorgensen, "North From Zion: The Minnesota Cutlerites, 1864–1964," (Mormon History Association Conference, St. George, UT., 1992), 13.

69. Chauncey Whiting, *Fergus Falls Weekly Journal* (October 13, 1876).

70. Andrew F. Ehat, "It Seems Like Heaven Began On Earth: Joseph Smith and the Constitution of the Kingdom of God," *BYU Studies,* 209 (Spring, 1980), 269.

71. Rebecca Kugel, *To Be the Main Leaders of Our People: A History of Minnesota Ojibwe Politics 1825–1898,* (Michigan State University Press, East Lansing, MI., 1998), 4–6.

72. John Johnson Enmegahbowh, *En-me-gah-bowh's Story: an Account of the Disturbances of the Chippewa Indians at Gull Lake in 1857 and 1862 and Their Removal in 1868* (Women's Auxiliary of St. Barnabas Hospital, Minneapolis, MN., 1904).

73. Kugel, *op. cit.* 27.

74. *Ibid.* 107.

75. Enmegahbowh, *op. cit.* 2–3.

76. Emma Lucine Anderson, *op. cit.* 6.

77. Hallie Gould, *Old Clitherall's Story Book, op. cit.* 8.

78. Emma Lucine Anderson, *op. cit.* 8.

79. Jennie Whiting, *Diary.*

80. Cutlerite documents in the author's collection.

81. Alta Kimber, "Early History of Otter Tail County Reviewed at Winter Pageant," *Battle Lake Review* (February 14, 1935).

82. Gladys Gould, "Aunt Lu."

83. Hallie Gould, *Old Clitherall's Story Book, Ibid.* 8.

84. Enmegahbowh, *op. cit.* 4.

85. *Ibid.*

86. Jennie Whiting, *op. cit.*

87. Richard L. Hahn, "George Bush Burgwin Clitherall—Clitherall's Biography including Clitherall's Service as Federal Land Agent in Otter Tail County & Clitherall's Gift of the 'Mount Vernon Chair,'" (Forest Lake, MN., 1994), 12–14.

88. *Ibid.* 24–34.

89. *Ibid.* 45. There is no record of Major Clitherall having fought for the Confederacy. However, his brother Alexander Clitherall was a member of the Alabama General Assembly before the outbreak of the Civil War and later served as private secretary to Jefferson Davis, President of the Confederate States. Alexander wrote the original constitution of the Confederacy and served as the Register of the Confederate Treasury Department.

90. Hallie Gould, *Old Clitherall's Story Book, op. cit.* 9.

91. Sylvester Whiting, 4.

92. *Ibid.*

93. Jennie Whiting, *Diary.*

94. *Ibid.*

95. Richard L. Hahn, *op. cit.* 49–51. According to Major George Clitherall, the chair came into his family's possession through General Benjamin Smith, a close

friend to George Washington and his family. Following Washington's death many of his personal belongings, including the chair, were given to Smith. General Smith was also a friend and business associate of Dr. George C. Clitherall, Major Clitherall's father. Dr. Clitherall attended Smith and at Smith's death, acquired the chair. He then passed it on to his son, Major George Clitherall. The chair was in George Clitherall's possession for almost 60 years before he gave it to the Minnesota Historical Society.

The chair was received by the society with an effusion of thanks. In his letter accompanying the gift, Clitherall wrote, "This gift I make as evidence of my admiration of, and attachment to, that great state, of which I was a citizen in her territorial days and subsequently. I treasure the memories of my association in the past with some of them, and for the love I bear these, coupled with the hope of the good your society will accomplish, I present this, 'The Library Chair of the Immortal Washington'. May its possession ever remind and keep ever present in the Minnesota Historical Society the sturdy virtues of the Father of his County, and incite them to a love of country paramount to devotion to party."

In receiving the gift from Clitherall and presenting it to the Historical Society, Charles Flandrau and Henry Rice described Clitherall saying, "During his residence among us, his exalted recognition of everything honorable, together with his charming social and genial characteristics endeared him to all the old settlers who were fortunate enough to enjoy his acquaintance: and while he was loved by us all, he, on his part, formed the warmest attachment for the country and the people. . . . In the name and on the behalf of the venerable octogenarian, patriot and lover of the whole country, we present to the Minnesota Historical Society this sacred memorial of the age that gave us liberty and the man to whom more than all others we are indebted for its inestimable blessings."

Flandrau and Rice concluded their remarks with pointed criticism of the state's meager support of the Society. "It is with fear and trembling that we entrust this gift to your keeping: not from any lack of confidence in the guardian care with which you will cherish it, but from apprehensions of the dangers it will encounter from the illy-protected home the state has given us as a casket for our invaluable jewels." According to Hahn, the chair has never been positively identified as having been among Washington's possessions at Mt. Vernon.

96. Cutlerite papers in the author's possession.
97. Hallie Gould, *Old Clitherall's Story Book, op. cit.* 9–10.
98. *Ibid.*
99. Cutlerite papers in the author's possession.
100. Gould, *op cit.* 11.
101. Jennie Whiting, *Diary.*
102. John Johnson Enmegahbowh, undated letter to Chauncey Whiting, Almon Sherman and Lewis Denna.
103. Kimber and Gould, *op. cit.*
104. Emma Lucine Anderson, *op. cit.* 10.
105. Chauncey Whiting, letter dated November 18, 1867 (Latter Day Saint church archives, Salt Lake City, UT.).
106. Emily Murdock Tucker, "The Story of Rachel," 2.
107. *Ibid.* 3.

108. Abstract of Title to Government lot 2, Section 12 of Clitherall Township, County of Otter Tail, Minnesota, last extended May 31, 2001, N. F. Field Abstract Company, Fergus Falls, MN.

109. Kimber and Gould, *op. cit.* December 7, 1919.

110. Frank Tucker and Norma Tucker, eds. *Family History, Supplement 1,* 1975, 7.

111. Hallie Gould, *Old Clitherall's Story Book, op. cit.* 32.

112. *Ibid.* 29.

113. Kimber and Gould, *op. cit.* October 23, 1919.

114. Hallie Gould, *Old Clitherall's Story Book, op. cit.* 58.

115. *Ibid.*

116. Kimber and Gould, *op. cit.* December 4, 1919.

117. Hallie Gould, *Old Clitherall's Story Book, op. cit.* 25–26.

118. Emily Murdock Tucker, "The Story of Emily," 4–5.

119. Hallie Gould, *Old Clitherall's Story Book, op. cit.* 16.

120. *Fergus Falls Weekly Journal* (June 24, 1897).

121. John Johnson Enmegahbowh, undated letter to Chauncey Whiting.

122. John Johnson Enmegahbowh, Letter to Chauncey Whiting, January, 1866.

123. John Johnson Enmegahbowh, Letter to Chauncey Whiting, November 25, 1867.

124. John Johnson Enmegahbowh, Letter to Chauncey Whiting. May 6, 1869.

125. John Johnson Enmegahbowh, Letter to Chauncey Whiting, May 20, 1869.

126. Cutlerite papers in the author's possession.

127. John Johnson Enmegahbowh, Letter to Chauncey Whiting, March 25, 1871.

128. John Johnson Enmegahbowh, Letter to Chauncey Whiting, February 25, 1886.

129. John Johnson Enmegahbowh, Letter to Chauncey Whiting, June 21, 1886.

130. The Reverend Margaret Lucie Thomas and the Reverend Johnson Loud, Jr., conversation with the author, November 19, 2001.

131. Frank and Norma Tucker, eds. *op. cit.*

132. Hallie Gould, *Old Clitherall's Story Book, op. cit.* 22.

133. *Ibid.* 21.

134. *Ibid.* 37–38.

135. *Ibid.* 15–17.

136. The Josephite church did not begin to use the word "Reorganized" in the name of "Reorganized Church of Jesus Christ of Latter Day Saints" until after the court case of 1880 with the Utah church over the ownership of disputed property in Kirtland, Ohio. The name of the church has since been changed to "Community of Christ."

137. *Family History, Supplement 1,* 15.

138. Sources differ on whether Winfield was baptized through the ice. One account says that the ice was two inches thick when he was baptized, another does not mention the ice or the month of the year. What is certain is that once a decision was made to be baptized into either faith, the temperature of the water into which the candidate was immersed made little difference to the participants.

139. Gladys Gould, ed., *Gould Family Memoir.*

140. *Ibid.* G19.

141. *Ibid.*

142. Emma Lucine Anderson, *op. cit.* 13.

143. Chauncey Whiting, Letter to "Dear Sister Emeline," 1885 or 1886 (Latter Day Saint church archives, Salt Lake City, UT.).

144. Fletcher and Fletcher, *op. cit.* 73.

145. Emma Lucine Anderson, *op. cit.* 18.

146. Emma Lucine, Anderson, *ibid.* 10.

147. Winfield and Ella Gould had eight children, two sons and six daughters, many of whom made significant contributions to the Reorganized Latter Day Saint Church. One of the daughters, Hallie, taught in the Clitherall School and, in 1919, compiled *Old Clitherall's Story Book,* a major source book of the period. Fulfilling both the Cutlerite and Josephite dreams of a return to Independence, Missouri, the Goulds moved there in 1920 where both Iva and Gladys Gould became personal secretaries to Fredrick Madison Smith, president of the Reorganized Church (Josephite) and grandson of Mormonism's founder, Joseph Smith, Jr.

148. Clare B. Christensen, *Before and After Mt. Pisgah* (Privately printed, Salt Lake City, UT., 1979), 417–418.

149. Nina Gould, "To Grandmother's," undated.

150. Hallie M. Gould, "Like Sheep That Went Astray," *op. cit.* 53.

151. Danny Jorgensen, "The Pliny Fisher Patriarchal Blessing Book: An Analysis and Interpretation of Early Cutlerite Beliefs and Practices" (John Whitmer Historical Association Conference, Graceland College, Lamoni, IA., 1989), 16–18.

152. Emma Lucine Anderson, *op. cit.* 13.

153. Edna Fletcher, "A Brief Sketch of the History of the True Church of Jesus Christ," 1960 (Clitherall, MN.).

154. Chauncey Whiting, undated letter. (Otter Tail County Historical Society, Fergus Falls, MN.).

155. Michael S. Riggs, *op. cit.*

156. Jennie Whiting, undated letter to her daughter Bonnie. (Kathy Castillo collection, St. Paul, MN.).

157. Russell R. Fletcher, *Fletcher Family History* (Privately printed, Independence, MO., 2001).

158. Nina Gould Tucker, notes taken during a tour of the Mt. Pleasant Cemetery in late 1950s or early 1960s.

159. Julian Everson Whiting, Jr., "The Life and Times of Julian Everson Whiting, Jr." (Kathy Castillo collection, St. Paul, MN.).

160. Abstract of Title, *Ibid.*

161. Robert Rosenkrans, letters to Roy Whiting , October 25, 1923 and May 26, 1924, (Kathy Castillo collection, St. Paul, MN.). The first letter reads, " It pains me to have to write this to you. But am going to regardless. I have been told and have seen you drive over the land of Mrs. J.W. Rosenkrans . . . after signs were set up reading No Trespassing do you know what that means? And do you know the law for trespassing on another party's property after said signs are put up Allowing no one on the property. If I hear any about it I will see you personally. So take these words to heart. Do not go too far. Remember that."

222 - OBSCURE BELIEVERS

Other members of the Cutlerite Church, besides Roy Whiting, must have been trespassing on Lucy's property because on May 26, 1924, this time from Minneapolis, Robert Rosenkrans again wrote to Roy. "How many times do you have to be told to keep off the property? I have called your attention once before on account of trespassing and I also told you that wasn't to happen again. Now it seems as if you don't care how often your [sic] told. I've seen a lawyer about it so you can take your choice. Court action or stay off. This is the last time I am going to be troubled by you or any of your Church members. Mrs. Rosenkrans has put that place in my hands. You and your church members have for some time been trying to make trouble. Now if that is what your [sic] looking for you'll mighty soon get it. This is the last time I'll speak about this so bear that in mind. Take it or leave it."

162. *Battle Lake Review,* July 5, 1928.

163. Julian and Ilo Whiting, undated letter (Kathy Castillo collection, St. Paul, MN.).

164. Fletcher and Fletcher, *op. cit.* 75.

165. Clyde Fletcher, Affidavit of Title sworn statement, 5.

166. *Ibid.,* 7.

167. Sam Lykken, Interview with author, November 17, 2000, Battle Lake, MN.

168. Russell Fletcher, Letter to author, May, 2001.

169. *Ibid.*

170. Findings of Fact, Conclusions of Law and Order for Judgment, District Court, Seventh Judicial District, Otter Tail County, Minnesota, March 17, 1967.

171. The year 1930 marked the centennial of the founding of the Mormon Church. Many early Mormons believed that "Zion would be redeemed" and the temple built in Independence within the first one hundred years of the founding of the church.

172. Russell Fletcher, *op. cit.*

173. Amy Whiting, Letter written in her capacity as Secretary of the Cutlerite Church Corporation, July 1, 1962.

174. Russell R. Rich. *op. cit.* 50.

175. Danny Jorgensen, "The Church of Jesus Christ (Cutlerite): A Sociological Interpretation of a Mormon Schism," *AAR/SBL Abstracts* (Scholars Press, Atlanta, GA., 1991), A34, 199.

176. Russell Fletcher, Letter to author, September, 2000.

177. Danny Jorgensen, "The Scattered Saints of Southwestern Iowa: Cutlerite-Josephite Conflict and Rivalry 1855–1865," *The John Whitmer Association Journal* (October 7, 1992).

178. Iva Gould, undated letter (Community of Christ archives, Independence, MO.).

179. Only about half of the Cutlerites living in Iowa in 1865 ever went to Minnesota. Those who stayed behind joined the Josephites or simply disappeared. After a few years the Cutlerite church ceased to exist in Iowa.

180. Fletcher and Fletcher, *op. cit.* 76.

181. For many years the industrialist Andrew Carnegie awarded medals for heroism. John Murdock's medal is on display in the Otter Tail County Historical Society Museum, Fergus Falls, MN.

BIBLIOGRAPHY

BOOKS

Anderson, Mary Audentia Smith and Bertha Audentia Hulmes. *Joseph Smith III and the Restoration*. Independence, MO: Herald Publishing House, 1952.

Armstrong, Karen. *The Battle for God*. New York, NY.: Alfred Knopf, 2000.

Carter, Kate B. *Heart Throbs of the West, IV.* Provo, UT.: Brigham Young University Press, 1958.

Christensen, Clare B. *Before & After Mt. Pisgah*. Salt Lake City, UT.: privately printed, 1979.

Compton, Todd. *In Sacred Loneliness—The Plural Wives of Joseph Smith*. Salt Lake City, UT.: Signature Books, 1997.

Doctrine and Covenants. Independence, MO.: Herald Publishing House, 1970 ed.

Enmegahbowh, John Johnson. *En-me-gah-bowh's Story: an Account of the Disturbances of the Chippewa Indians at Gull Lake in 1857 and 1862 and Their Removal in 1868*. Minneapolis, MN.: Women's Auxiliary, St. Barnabas Hospital, 1904.

Flanders, Robert. *Nauvoo—Kingdom on the Mississippi*. Urbana, IL.: University of Illinois Press, 1965.

Fletcher, Rupert J. and Daisy Whiting Fletcher. *Alpheus Cutler and The Church of Jesus Christ,* Independence, MO.: Church of Jesus Christ, 1974.

Fletcher, Russell R. *Fletcher Family History*. Independence, MO.: privately printed, 2001.

Foster, Lawrence. *Religion and Sexuality, Three American Communal Experiments of the Nineteenth Century*. New York/Oxford: Oxford University Press, 1981.

Gould, Hallie, ed. *Old Clitherall's Story Book, A History of the First Settlement in Otter Tail County, Minnesota, 1865–1919*. Fergus Falls, MN.: Otter Tail County Historical Society, 1975.

Hills, Gustavus. "Map of the City of Nauvoo." Nauvoo, IL.: Nauvoo Restoration, Inc., 1971.

Kugel, Rebecca. *To Be the Main Leaders of Our People: A History of Minnesota Ojibwe Politics 1825–1898*. East Lansing, MI.: Michigan State University Press, 1998.

Launius, Roger D. and John E. Hallwas, eds. *Kingdom On The Mississippi Revisited, Nauvoo In Mormon History*. Urbana and Chicago, IL.: University of Illinois Press, 1996.

Launius, Roger D. and Linda Thatcher, eds. *Differing Visions: Dissenters in Mormon History*, Champaign, IL.: University of Illinois Press, 1991.

Lee, John D. *A Mormon Chronicle: The Diaries of John D. Lee, 1848–1876*. vols. 1 and 2. Robert Glass Cleland and Juanita Brooks, eds. San Marino, CA: Arthur H. Clark, 1955.

Mason, John W., ed. *History of Otter Tail County, Minnesota*. Indianapolis, IN.: B.F. Bowen & Co., 1916.

Masur, Louis. *1831–Year of Eclipse*. New York, NY.: Hill & Wang, 2001.

Quinn, D. Michael. *Early Mormonism and the Magic World View*. Salt Lake City, UT.: Signature Books, 1987.

Smith, Joseph. *Book of Mormon*. Independence, MO.: Herald Publishing House, 1942 ed.

Tyler, Alice Felt. *Freedom's Ferment: Phases of American Social History from the Colonial Period to the Outbreak of the Civil War*. Minneapolis, MN.: University of Minnesota Press, 1944.

Van Wagoner, Richard S. *Mormon Polygamy, A History*. 2d ed. Salt Lake City, UT.: Signature Books, 1989.

Whipple. Henry Benjamin. *Lights and Shadows of a Long Episcopate: Being Reminiscences and Recollections of the Right Reverend Henry Benjamin Whipple, Bishop of Minnesota*. New York, NY.: Macmillan, 1912.

PUBLIC RECORDS

Abstract of Title to Government Lot 2, Section 12 of Clitherall Township, County of Otter Tail, Minnesota [Old Town Camp], last extended May 31, 2001 by the N. F. Field Abstract Company, Fergus Falls, Minnesota.

Church of Jesus Christ v. Clyde Fletcher, Lee Fletcher, Ray Fletcher, Edna Fletcher and Amy Whiting, File No. 27169, Findings of Fact, Conclusions of Law and Order for Judgment, District Court, (Seventh Judicial District, County of Otter Tail, State of Minnesota, Fergus Falls, Minnesota, March 21, 1967).

Minnesota, County of Otter Tail, Affidavit of Title, No. 20. Filed for record, June 3, 1963, Book 50 of Misc. p. 327.

Washington, D.C., *Eighth Census of the United States*. U.S. Government Printing Office.

Washington D.C., *Thirteenth Census of the United States*, U.S. Government Printing Office.

NEWSPAPERS AND PERIODICALS

Brussemann, Gary, "Frontier Rivertown," *Gopher Chapter, Red Wing Collector's Society*, 1986.

Ehat, Andrew F., "It Seems Like Heaven Began On Earth: Joseph Smith and the Constitution of the Kingdom of God," *BYU Studies*, 20 (Spring, 1980): 253–280.

Gould, Hallie, "Like Sheep That Went Astray," *Autumn Leaves* (February 1921).

Jorgensen, Danny L., "Conflict in the Camps of Israel: The 1853 Cutlerite Schism," *Journal of Mormon History* (Spring 1995): 24–62.

Jorgensen, Danny L., "The Cutlerites of Southwestern Iowa: A Latter Day Saint Schism, 1846–1865, and its Contributions to Early Iowa Community Building," *The Annals of Iowa* (January 1999): 131–161.

Jorgensen, Danny L., "The Scattered Saints of Southwestern Iowa: Cutlerite-Josephite Conflict and Rivalry, 1855–1865," *The John Whitmer Historical Association Journal* 13 (1993): 80–97.

Jorgensen, Danny L., "Building the Kingdom of God: Alpheus Cutler and The Second Mormon Mission to the Indians: 1847–1853," *Kansas History* 15:3 (1992): 192–209.

Kimber, Alta, "Early History of Otter Tail County Reviewed at Winter Pageant," *Battle Lake Review* (February 14, 1935).

Kimber, Alta, "The Coming of the Latter Day Saints to Otter Tail County," *Minnesota History* 13:4 (December 1932): 385–394.

Kimber, Alta and Hallie M. Gould, "Reminiscences for the Scrap Book," *Battle Lake Review* (July–November 1919).

Nute, Grace Lee, "The Red River Trails," *Minnesota History* VI (September 1925): 279–282.

Rich, Russell R., "Those Who Would Be Leaders," *Brigham Young University Extension Publications* (May 1967).

Young, Biloine Whiting, "Why the Cutlerites Went to Red Wing," *The John Whitmer Historical Association Newsletter*, Nos. 58 and 59 (2001).

Young, Biloine Whiting, "On the Trail of the Cutlerite Settlers," *Minnesota History* 47:3 (Fall 1980): 111–113.

_____, "The First Colony," *Fergus Falls Weekly Journal* (June 24, 1897).

_____, "Historical Society Unveils Memorial at Clitherall," *Battle Lake Review* (July 5, 1928).

UNPUBLISHED CONFERENCE PAPERS

Jorgensen, Danny L., "Antecedents of the Cutlerite Schism of 1853." Laie, Hawaii: Mormon History Association, Brigham Young University, June, 1990.

Jorgensen, Danny L., "North From Zion: The Minnesota Cutlerites, 1864–1964." St. George, UT: Mormon History Association, May 14–17, 1992.

Jorgensen, Danny L., "The Church of Jesus Christ (Cutlerite): a Sociological Interpretation of a Mormon Schism." Kansas City, MO: New Religious Movements Group, American Academy of Religion, November 1991.

Jorgensen, Danny L., "The Second Mormon Mission to the Indians: The Cutlerites' Lamanite Ministries, 1847–1853." San Bernardino, CA: Mormon History Association, May 1991.

Jorgensen, Danny L., "The Social Backgrounds and Characteristics of the Founders of the Church of Jesus Christ (Cutlerite): a Sociological Description and Analysis of a Mormon Schism." Quincy, IL: Mormon History Association, May 13, 1989.

Jorgensen, Danny L., and Lin Y. Jorgensen, "The Pliny Fisher Patriarchal Blessing Book: An analysis and Interpretation of Early Cutlerite Beliefs and Practices." Lamoni, IA: John Whitmer Historical Association, Graceland College, September 1989.

Riggs, Michael S., "Nauvoo's Kingdom of God on Earth and Back to Back Half Moons in the Iowan Firmament: New Insights into Alpheus Cutler's Claims to Authority." Quincy, IL: Mormon History Association, 1989.

Riggs, Michael S., "The Cutlerites: A Microcosm of Early Mormon Folk Magic Beliefs." Sunstone Theological Symposium West, 1990.

Smith, George D. "A Preliminary Study of the Incidence of Plural Marriage in Nauvoo, Illinois, from 1841 to 1846," Lamoni, IA: Mormon History Association, Graceland College, 1993.

LETTERS, DIARIES, AND MEMOIRS

Anderson, Emma Lucine, "Autobiography of Emma Lucine Anderson, 1915." Independence, MO: Community of Christ church archives.

"Cordelia Morley Cox, Woman of Wilderness."

Enmegahbowh, John Johnson, Letters to Chauncey Whiting, Author's collection.

Fletcher, Edna, "A Brief Sketch of the History of the True Church of Jesus Christ." Clitherall, MN., 1960.

Fletcher, Edna, "Letter to Danny Jorgensen," Fergus Falls, MN., December 18, 1987.

Fletcher, Russell, Letter to author, September, 2000.

Gould, Gladys, "Family History."

Gould, Gladys, "Aunt Lu."

Gould, Hallie, "The Story of Alpheus Cutler."

Gould, Maud, "Maud's Story."

Gould, Nina, "To Grandmother's."

Gould, Winfield, "Gould Family Memoir."

Hahn, Richard L., "George Bush Burgwin Clitherall—Clitherall's Biography including Clitherall's Service as Federal Land Agent in Otter Tail County & Clitherall's Gift of the 'Mount Vernon Chair'." Forest Lake, MN., 1994.

Harris, Iris, Letters to the author, February 3, and May 25, 2001.

Jorgensen, Danny L., Letters to the author, April 27, 1988 and March 7, 1995.

Kelsey, Seth C., "The Stephen Kelsey and Related Families," Salt Lake City, UT., 1962.

Kimball, Stanley B., "Finding a Great-Great-Grandmother, Clarissa Cutler Kimball: 1824–1853."

"Life History of Lester Whiting."

Lykken, Sam, Interview with author, Battle Lake, MN., November 17, 2000.

"Nina and Orison Tucker's Ancestors."

Palmer, Elyce, "The Cutlerite Settlement at Clitherall, Minnesota." Master's thesis, North Dakota State University, Fargo, ND., 1963.

Riggs, Michael S., "Thou Shall Become a Terror to False Spirits': From New Englander Mormons to Esoteric Cutlerite/RLDS, A Case Study in Early Mormon Folk Magic Beliefs." Master's thesis, Park College, Kansas City, MO., 1999.

Sandage, Muriel Whiting, "The Whiting Family," 1979.

Taylor, Lori, "Telling Stories About Mormons and Indians." Ph.D. dissertation, State University of New York, Buffalo, NY., 1999.

Tucker, Nina Gould, "Notes taken in the Old Clitherall (Mt. Pleasant) Cemetery."

Tucker, Emily Murdock, "The Story of Emily."

Tucker, Emily Murdock, "The Story of Rachel."

Tucker, Frank and Norma Tucker, "Family History, and Supplements," December, 1975.

Whiting, Amy, Letter to the author, July 1, 1961.

Whiting, Chauncey, "Letters to Family and Friends." Salt Lake City, UT: Latter Day Saint Church archives.

Whiting, Isaac, "Letters," St. Paul, MN: Kathy Castillo collection.

Whiting, Jennie, "Diary."

Whiting, Julian Everson Jr., "The Life and Times of Julian Everson Whiting, Jr." 1993.

Whiting, Ray, "Interview," St. Paul, MN., August, 1971.

Whiting, S. J., "Some Proofs and Testimonies in Regard to our Move to this Country Being Directed by the Lord." Fergus Falls, MN: Otter Tail County Historical Society.

LIST OF ILLUSTRATIONS AND MAPS

INDEX